REVISE BTEC NATIONAL
Art and Design

REVISION GUIDE

Series Consultant: Harry Smith

Authors: Daniel Freaker and Alan Parsons

A note from the publisher

Introduction

Which units should you revise?

This Revision Guide has been designed to support you in preparing for the externally assessed units of your course. Remember that you won't necessarily be studying all the units included here – it will depend on the qualification you are taking.

BTEC National Qualification	Externally assessed units
Certificate	1 Visual Recording and Communication
For both: Extended Certificate Foundation Diploma	1 Visual Recording and Communication 2 Critical and Contextual Studies in Art and Design
Diploma	1 Visual Recording and Communication 2 Critical and Contextual Studies in Art and Design 7 Developing and Realising Creative Intentions
Diploma: Photography; Graphics; 3D design and crafts; Fashion, design and production	6 Managing a Client Brief 7 Developing and Realising Creative Intentions
Extended Diploma	1 Visual Recording and Communication 2 Critical and Contextual Studies in Art and Design 6 Managing a Client Brief 7 Developing and Realising Creative Intentions

Your Revision Guide

Each unit in this Revision Guide contains two types of pages, shown below.

Content **pages** help you revise the essential content you need to know for each unit.

Skills **pages** help you prepare for your exam or assessed task. Skills pages have a coloured edge and are shaded in the table of contents.

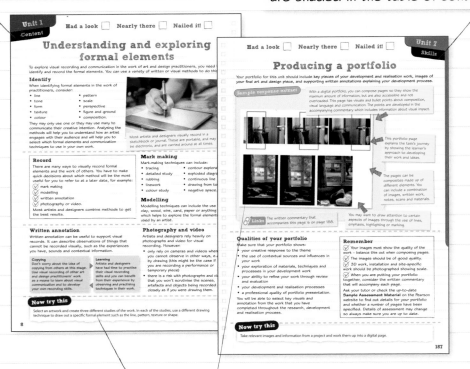

Use the **Now try this** activities on every page to help you test your knowledge and practise the relevant skills.

Look out for the **sample response extracts** to revision questions or tasks on the skills pages. Post-its will explain their strengths and weaknesses.

Contents

Unit 7: Developing and Realising Creative Intentions

. . . .

A small bit of small print
Pearson publishes Sample Assessment Material and the Specification on its website. This is the official content and this book should be used in conjunction with it. The questions in *Now try this* have been written to help you test your knowledge and skills. Remember: the real assessment may not look like this.

Your Unit 1 set task

Unit 1 will be assessed through a task, which will be set by Pearson. In this assessed task you will carry out research, produce a piece of art or design which responds to a particular theme, and produce a written commentary to accompany your research and piece of art or design.

Revising your skills

Understanding how artists record and communicate their ideas visually is important because it will help you to record and communicate your own ideas perceptively and effectively.

The skills pages in this unit are designed to **revise skills** that might be needed in your assessed task and which you will need in order to produce a developed piece in response to a given theme.

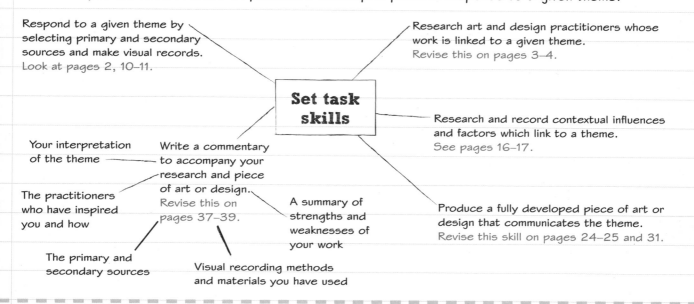

Respond to a given theme by selecting primary and secondary sources and make visual records. Look at pages 2, 10–11.

Research art and design practitioners whose work is linked to a given theme. Revise this on pages 3–4.

Set task skills

Research and record contextual influences and factors which link to a theme. See pages 16–17.

Your interpretation of the theme

Write a commentary to accompany your research and piece of art or design. Revise this on pages 37–39.

The practitioners who have inspired you and how

A summary of strengths and weaknesses of your work

Produce a fully developed piece of art or design that communicates the theme. Revise this skill on pages 24–25 and 31.

The primary and secondary sources

Visual recording methods and materials you have used

Workflow

The process of creating a fully developed piece in response to a given theme might follow these steps:

> Carry out your research, recording the key findings.

> ▼

> Create and present your final piece of work.

> ▼

> Write a commentary about your research, development process and your final piece of work.

Check the Pearson website

The activities and sample response extracts in this section are provided to help you to revise content and skills. Ask your tutor or check the Pearson website for the most up-to-date **Sample Assessment Material** and **Mark Scheme** to get an indication of the structure of your actual assessed task and what this requires of you. The details of the actual assessed task may change so always make sure you are up to date.

Now try this

Visit the Pearson website and find the page containing the course materials for BTEC National Art and Design. Look at the latest Unit 1 Sample Assessment Material for an indication of:

- the structure of your set task, and whether it is divided into parts
- how much time you are allowed for the task, or different parts of the task
- what briefing or stimulus material might be provided to you

- any notes or initial research you might have to make and whether you are allowed to take these into your supervised assessment
- the activities you are required to complete and how to format your responses.

Interpreting a brief

When interpreting a brief and responding to the starting points relating to a given theme for your work, start by reading the information you are given carefully.

Theme

Consider the theme you are given and the starting points provided in the brief to stimulate your thinking. The brief may include a mind map of potential connections to historic and contemporary artefacts, ideas, customs and technology. You can take the theme in any direction if you can justify how it relates logically to the theme and starting points in the brief. Read and explore all the information you are given in the task booklet at the start of your research and preparatory period.

Informed direction

The direction of your response to the brief should be informed by:

- the opportunities available for recording your research from primary and secondary sources
- influence and inspiration gained by exploring practitioners' work related to the theme.

> This extract from a brief gives an example of a page of starting points on the theme of 'Transmission'. Each year the theme will be different.

Set task information

TRANSMISSION

You have been asked to explore and investigate the theme 'TRANSMISSION' to produce creative outcomes. The theme should be seen as a starting point and you should explore appropriate primary and secondary sources and contextual material.

Possible Starting Points. This is not an exhaustive and definitive list and should be seen as possible inspiration start points.

Transmission definitions:
Noun
- the act or process of transmitting
- something that is transmitted
- transference of force between machines or mechanisms
- compact, enclosed unit of gears
- the broadcasting of electromagnetic waves from one location to another

'The great accomplishments of man have resulted from the transmission of ideas and enthusiasm.'
Thomas J Watson

Language   Information

Historic and contemporary TRANSMISSION — Packaging

Giving

Technology

Data

Transmission: broadcast, show, programme, spread, communication, diffusion

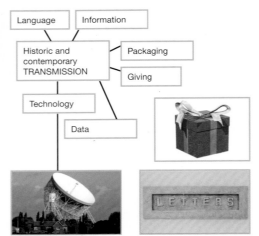

> The task booklet may give you suggestions to help you interpret the theme. Notice that there are different ways of looking at it, e.g. through contemporary artists, historic artists, quotes, dictionary definitions, synonyms, technological relationships and evolution. Try similar approaches in your own initial research.

> Remember that the starting points provided are not exhaustive and definitive. They are provided as possible starting points to inspire you for your own piece of art or design.

Now try this

Create a mind map of initial ideas in response to the theme, showing at least three further modes of transmission.

Researching a theme

Exploring a theme initially might involve contextual research, observational recording from primary sources and visual recording using secondary sources. These provide a wide variety of ideas and inspiration for your own response to a theme.

Theme

In the actual assessment a new theme will be given each year. When exploring the theme, you will need to make decisions early on about:

1 how long to spend undertaking initial research
2 how to collect research
3 how to avoid getting side-tracked
4 how to find your own personal direction
5 what you want to learn.

To show the skills you need when responding to a theme, this Revision Guide uses a theme of 'Transmission' as an example.

Continual research

Most artists and designers continue to research as their project progresses. However, don't expect to develop a perfect idea through research alone. You will need to practise, test, explore and try out visual recording and communication techniques. You will find that specific research needs arise as your ideas become more refined.

Use your time wisely. Avoid spending time decorating pages, making research look perfect or copying out long passages of text.

Key questions

Use these questions to help you research a theme.

Art
Who are the important, relevant artists?
Are there artists who have responded directly to the theme?
Can you find unusual responses?

Non-art
Can you find connections in non-art such as literature, film, dance or music? Sophisticated responses can come from broad connections.

Context
Did the theme play a part in culture historically?
Are there places where the theme is of particular importance?

Society
Does it relate to anything in the media currently?
Are there issues and debates related to the theme?
Can you connect it to notions of equality or diversity?

You can use any **format** you feel most comfortable with to **collect** and **organise research**, such as a sketchbook, journal, folder, notepad or diary.

Sample notes extract

I can collect information by:
- visiting my local library and finding books about Nam June Paik
- looking online for more artists who explore the theme of 'Transmission'
- visiting a gallery
- printing images
- collecting objects.

I am interested in fashion so I'm going to focus on creating a head-dress based on code in response to ideas about 'Transmission'. I'm going to create my own specific brief with tight constraints.

Setting a **brief** can help to focus your research, developed piece of art or design and written commentary, whatever your specialism. Setting some **constraints** will speed up the process of **recording** and **development**.

Now try this

Try and find three connections to the theme of 'Transmission' from: history, another culture, media.

Defining a brief

To define a specific brief and set up some constraints, make initial decisions for each of the below questions.

☑ What specialism would you like to follow?

☑ What piece of developed art and design would you like to create and what research will this need?

☑ How will you demonstrate visual communication of the theme in at least three different ways, e.g. through style, medium, technique, interpretation?

☑ Look at pages 22 and 23 to consider presentation of research and use of annotation.

☑ How will you plan your time for roughly half on research/recording and half on producing a fully developed piece of art or design?

Visual recording and communication of content

When understanding the way that practitioners visually record and communicate, consider the **content** of a piece of art or design. This includes the theme or ideas that the practitioner was exploring, any brief they were working to, and any contextual factors that influenced them.

Theme

Sometimes the theme of an artwork is inherently obvious, for example if the subject has been presented representationally or if it has been transformed intentionally. But other artists may use very subtle and even subversive methods of communicating.

Ideas

It is worth looking at whether the artist is trying to engage in an issue or debate about issues such as religion, politics, morals, ethics, race, gender or ethnicity. Looking at interviews, statements or videos about the work by artists is a great way of getting further information.

Paul Nash 'Void of War' (Litho) (1918) / Private Collection Photo © The Fine Art Society, London, UK / Bridgeman Images

Paul Nash's print *Void of War* (1918) automatically reminds us of things we have seen. Because of their intentional transformation, he connects the work to discussions about conflict, war, disaster and the environment.

Questions to ask yourself

Use these questions to help you work out the content:

Theme	Ideas	Context	Brief
What is the title? Does it relate to other areas of culture or society? Do other works by the same artist share similar themes?	Does/did the artist have any strong beliefs or views? Are/were they part of an art movement? Do they use symbols, analogy or metaphor?	When and where was it made? What politics might have influenced it? Is/was the practitioner part of an art movement or collective?	Was there a brief or client? What was the brief? Who is the target audience? Where was it meant to be seen?

Context

The context in which an artwork was created has an impact. This includes when and where it was created. Looking back historically, it is possible to use work to reflect on the socio-political climate at the time. For example, work can be used by a political establishment to influence society, such as propaganda. Alternatively, many artists use their work to make a stand against traditions and authority, for example Ai Weiwei's *14,000 Lifejackets* (2016), which provoked governments to do more for migrants.

Brief

Artworks are often seen outside the situation they were originally intended for. Works of art as commodities get bought, moved around and taken out of their intended context. Knowing what the work was originally intended for can help understand what the artist's intentions were. Sometimes they will have worked to a brief from a client; at other times they will have worked independently and set their own loose brief.

Now try this

Find:

- a real example of propaganda, such as the Uncle Sam poster by James Montgomery Flagg
- a piece of work that uses styles similar to propaganda, such as a work by Shepard Fairey.

Write a paragraph to explain the differences in content of your chosen pieces.

Understanding and exploring form

When analysing the work of other practitioners you need to consider the **form** of the work, including formal elements, use and purpose.

Formal elements

When looking at a piece of work you can break it down into isolated aspects called **formal elements**. Sometimes work will specifically rely on a single formal element, e.g. its texture or pattern. At other times, artists will use a combination of formal elements to communicate. You can ask yourself: how do the formal elements contribute to the work? How would it look and communicate if the formal elements were changed slightly or radically? What can you learn from each of the formal elements in the work?

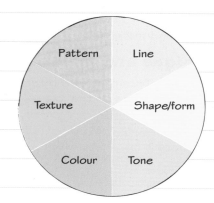

Scale and proportion

When looking at any piece of artwork you must understand how the artist has used **scale or proportion** to visually record or communicate. Scale can be central to artwork and many artists use it to create an impact just by adjusting the scale of objects. Proportion might be used in artwork to create a physical impact because the viewer automatically compares the work to their own physical size or to objects they have seen in the past.

Composition

Composition refers to the layout and combination of elements within space. When discussing composition, artists refer to terms like organisation, layout, arrangement, symmetry, asymmetry, balance, negative space, the golden ratio and the rule of thirds.

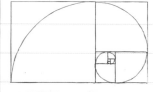

Many works take the form of the golden ratio.

Transient form

Some works change their form over time. For example, Antony Gormley's *Field for the British Isles* (1993) is an example of a piece of artwork that changes depending on the exhibition space.

Anthony Gormley, 'Field for the British Isles' (1993) Installation view, Irish Museum of Modern Art, Dublin, Ireland, 1994 Arts Council Collection, England © Anthony Gormley

Use

The use of formal elements within artwork will depend on what the artist is trying to achieve and observe. For example, a quick line drawing will gather important detail, while a two-tone drawing might help identify the negative space of an object and reflect its form.

Purpose

The purpose of an artwork can dictate its form. For example, architects and interior designers may use specific formats for their drawing, such as isometric records. These methods use codes and conventions so that others can understand them.

Now try this

Consider a piece of art or design that you know. Write one comment about this piece relating to each of the six formal elements.

5

Understanding and exploring process

When understanding the ways that practitioners visually record and communicate, consider the use of **process**, techniques and materials.

Process, technique and materials

The terms 'process' and 'technique' are often mistakenly used interchangeably. Process refers to the journey the work has gone through from start to finish. During this journey, the piece might have many different techniques applied to it. Similar techniques can be applied to different materials, which also changes the way the work communicates.

Historically, process is particularly important where the use of materials is perishable or transitory, but also in any work that changes over time, such as performance or interactive work.

Abstract expressionism

This was an important movement which focused on process, or the actions of the artist, rather than the visual outcome.

What stages has the work gone through?

Is the process more important than the outcome?

Was the work done rapidly or did it evolve over a long period?

Is process central to the ideas within the work?

Process

Have traditional or non-traditional processes been used?

How has the image or artefact changed from the starting point?

Did the artist want the audience to see how it was created?

Is the action used by the artist visible in the work?

Process in recording

This refers to the connection and use of multiple stages of recording and processing. For example, if you take a photo and then trace lines from the photo, you are using a two-stage process that uses different techniques: photography and tracing.

Process for communication

This refers to the stages of an idea's journey from inception to production. The process combines stages from the design cycle including:

- reviewing the brief
- recording from other art and design practitioners' work
- own primary recording
- own secondary recording
- developing own visual communication
- evaluating.

Now try this

Some artists associated with process art include Jackson Pollock, Eva Hesse, Michael Landy, Bernard Cohen and Richard Serra. Research a piece of work by one of these artists and write a paragraph about why the process is more important than the outcome.

Understanding and exploring mood

Understanding how mood is used by practitioners to convey meaning and creative intentions means you can learn from it in order to develop your own **visual language**.

Mood

Mood is related to the feelings and associations the audience is provoked into experiencing. Understanding how the mood is communicated in a piece of work will help you communicate a specific and intended mood through your own work.

Context

The communication of mood in an artwork will change depending on its context in time and place. For example, in China the colour yellow has historically been connected to power, but the same colour in the US is connected to cowardice. Your experience of the mood of the work may not be the same as the artist's intentions.

Questions to ask

Artists and designers use techniques to communicate mood:

- Colour – are the colours from a specific area of the colour wheel or are they often associated with certain feelings?
- Gesture or process – has the artist treated the work in a way that reveals certain feelings?
- Material, texture and form – does the material reflect a certain state or feeling?
- Composition – are the components connected in a way that suggests an experience through scale or position?
- Historical connection – does the place where the piece originates have a connection to a colour or symbol?
- References to popular culture – can you see a connection to popular culture such as comedy or tragedy?

Pablo Picasso, 'Blue Nude' (1902) © Succession Picasso/DACS, London 2018 Photo: Private Collection/Bridgeman Images

Blue Nude (1902) by Pablo Picasso was painted after the death of a close friend. His use of one colour, blue, accentuates the mood of despair.

Application and communication

Notice how the application of materials, techniques and processes impacts on the communication of an image. For example, Anselm Keifer uses unusual materials such as dirt, plants and clothes mixed with paint to reference the past. By contrast, Gary Hume uses clean and precise paint in a way that reflects consumer society. Both are painters, but use the medium differently to communicate.

Mood and the artist

The term 'mood' within art doesn't simply relate to feelings like happiness or sadness, which could be the resultant experience of an action or situation. For example, if a work is highly ordered, the audience might feel the mood of the work is sombre and sterile. Yet the artist or designer might take great pleasure in its simplicity and detail. It may be important to separate the feeling the audience has from the feeling the artist was experiencing or tried to achieve.

Ambiguity

Some works subvert our ordinary experiences of moods. For example, look up Yinka Shonibare's *Spacewalk* (2002). It juxtaposes unexpected colours and objects that may not easily be categorised, and makes us look differently at a situation.

Now try this

Find three artworks that you think represent each of the following moods: control, loss, conflict.

Understanding and exploring formal elements

To explore visual recording and communication in the work of art and design practitioners, you need to identify and record the formal elements. You can use a variety of written or visual methods to do this.

Identify

When identifying formal elements in the work of practitioners, consider:

- line
- tone
- form
- texture
- colour
- pattern
- scale
- perspective
- figure and ground
- composition.

They may only use one or they may use many to communicate their creative intention. Analysing the methods will help you to understand how an artist engages with their audience and will help you to select which formal elements and communication techniques to use in your own work.

Most artists and designers visually record in a sketchbook or journal. These are portable, and may be electronic, and are carried around at all times.

Record

There are many ways to visually record formal elements and the work of others. You have to make quick decisions about which method will be the most useful for you to refer to at a later date, for example:

- ✓ mark making
- ✓ modelling
- ✓ written annotation
- ✓ photography or video.

Most artists and designers combine methods to get the best results.

Mark making

Mark-making techniques can include:

- tracing
- detailed study
- rubbing
- linework
- colour study
- contour exploration
- exploded diagram
- continuous line
- drawing from touch
- negative space.

Modelling

Modelling techniques can include the use of clay, wood, wire, card, paper or anything else which helps to explore the formal elements used by an artist.

Written annotation

Written annotation can be useful to support visual records. It can describe observations of things that cannot be recorded visually, such as the experiences you have, sounds and contextual information.

Copying
Don't worry about the idea of copying from others at this stage. Use visual recording of other art and design practitioners' work as a means to learn about visual communication and to develop your own recording skills.

Learning
Artists and designers have had time to practise their visual recording skills and you can benefit from their experience by observing and practising techniques in their work.

Photography and video

Artists and designers rely heavily on photographs and video for visual recording. However:

- only rely on cameras and videos when you cannot observe in other ways, e.g. by drawing (this might be the case if you are recording a performance or temporary piece)
- there is a risk with photographs and videos that you won't scrutinise the scenes, artefacts and objects being recorded as closely as if you were drawing them.

Now try this

Select an artwork and create three different studies of the work. In each of the studies, use a different drawing technique to draw out a specific formal element such as the line, pattern, texture or shape.

Informing your own practice

Exploring how art and design practitioners develop their work can help to inform your own practice.

Recording with purpose

The main intention of recording from other art and design practitioners' work is to inform your own practice. You can learn from their techniques and find out how their work communicates. Remember:

👍 use a broad range of artists, not always from the same specialism

👍 use other practitioners' techniques in your own recording

👎 avoid making time-consuming reproductions.

Specialised recording

Each artistic specialism has specific technical methods of recording. Sometimes these are used to demonstrate how something works or to provide technical plans. Examples of specific methods include:

* silhouettes in fashion
* exploded diagrams or cutaways in product design or sculpture
* thumbnails in graphics
* storyboards in screen-based work
* wire framing in web design.

Recording from non-art

Your recordings look at others' art and design work, but will also benefit from looking at wider cultural artefacts and specimens. For example, on the theme of transmission, you could consider historic images of radio waves in science manuals, or different symbols used in languages around the world.

During the recording

When recording, ask yourself:

* What techniques has this professional used?
* Can I find their preparatory work?
* What techniques will give me useful records?
* Which media can be manipulated rapidly to enable quick drawing?
* Who produces work similar to my ideas?

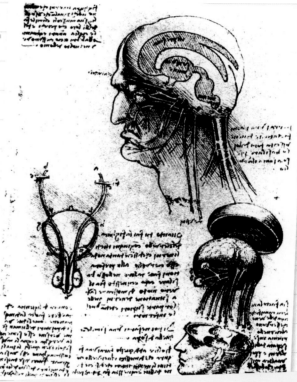

The Weimar sheet anatomical drawings by Leonardo da Vinci (early 16th century), demonstrate how artists explore things through visual recording as part of their development.

How others record

Looking at the techniques used in other art and design practitioners' developmental work can be more useful than looking at outcomes. Depending on their discipline, different artists and designers will practise recording by exploring objects and spaces in different ways.

Conventions

Depending on the specialism, technical drawing may need to adhere to specific conventions. This makes the visual record easier to understand through:

* measurement units
* type of material or surface
* abbreviations or notation systems
* visual styles and layouts – such as mood boards.

Now try this

Find an example of an artist or designer, such as Rachel Whiteread, who has made preparatory studies, and explain how they have used the studies to develop the outcome.

Using visual recording and communication skills

Consider the quality of your research into visual recording and communication and the use of formal elements in the work of art or design practitioners. Your understanding and exploration will inform your ability to communicate the theme visually in different ways.

Development time

Once you have settled on a direction to work in, you will need to focus quickly on finding art or design pieces relevant to the theme. Your choices should help you understand and explore visual recording and communication, and the use of formal elements. You can then apply your findings from other practitioners' work to your own practice, learning from it through visual recording processes.

Demonstrating your skills

You will need to demonstrate how well you understand how recording is used to communicate visually in the work of others through:

1 an understanding of formal elements and visual language in the work of others

2 an understanding of contextual factors and intentions in the work of others

3 a connection between the work of others and your own work.

Sample notes extract

In this extract from research, repetition of visual recording from other practitioners' work is well structured. It has enabled exploration of different formal elements within a piece of work as a method of development.

It may be useful to include more annotation than purely the different media used. Try using evaluative comments about the formal elements and discussing intentions and contextual factors.

The exploration of the image on different surfaces demonstrates how the learner has tested techniques to synthesise with their own direction and not purely copied them. This connects the work of others to the learner's intentions.

Sample notes extract

I am going to contextualise my visual recording by including:

- similar images from different contexts such as botanical drawing and nature magazines
- annotation of relevant facts and analysis that relate to theme
- images of culture from the same period including packaging and textiles
- printing images by artists that draw on nature
- collecting objects such as leaves and bark.

This extract from research notes demonstrates planning work logically and methodically towards an outcome. It's easy to get side-tracked by recording formal elements in the work of others.

You need to be explicit in your descriptions of the purpose of the visual recording by explaining why you are doing the visual recording.

Use visual tools to make connections to your own work, such as arrows, lines, circles and physical connections between the work and your annotation.

Reflection and notes

Keeping a record of reflective notes during research helps you to keep track of the creative decisions you take. These can help inform a written commentary on your choices and how research has informed your work.

Now try this

Generate two studies of a single work by another artist, each using a different media.

Developing visual recording and communication skills

To develop visual recording and communication skills, you need to explore observational recording from primary sources and the use of secondary sources for visual recording.

Primary observation

Where possible use primary observation (e.g. visit a gallery to view works of art first hand) to see details and context, and to explore the work from different angles, getting a real feel for the materials, techniques and processes.

2D work

You could take forward 2D recording from primary sources in the following ways:

- Create a thumbnail of the formal elements that stand out the most.
- Record the work more than once – using different media each time. This will help to identify different formal elements.
- Move closer and record small details as well as the bigger picture.
- Make notes about the way the audience interacts with the work and its scale within the space.

 Links To revise 2D and 3D recording in more detail, see pages 12 and 13.

3D work

You could take forward 3D recording from primary sources in the following ways:

- Move around and observe from different angles. Try to get unusual perspectives of the work.
- Record with and without the surroundings to contextualise it.
- Make notes and visual studies of the materials through texture, writing and colour swatches.
- Products should be recorded on their own and also when being used, operated or in action.

Exploring secondary sources

Secondary sources are generally used when you can't make a direct observation of the real thing. For example, if you can't access a landscape, you might record it from an image in a book or on a screen. However, consider what you might miss through this type of experience. How can you record the full spectrum of the space or object without connecting to it physically in some way? Combining both primary and secondary observation is ideal.

Techniques for recording

The way you choose to record the work of other practitioners depends on what you are trying to achieve and the nature of the work.

Form, structure and space	Expression, gesture and abstraction	Landscape	Time-based art and product design
▼	▼	▼	▼
Perspective drawing, line study, negative space, isometric study, floor plan, contour study	Watercolour study, continuous line, quick sketch, imitation of mark, mixed-media work	Tonal study, contour study, multiple perspectives, reproduction, tracing, rubbing	Simulation, storyboarding, overlay, diagram, observational study, multiple perspectives, layering

Now try this

Record the work of Anselm Kiefer on page 4, using three different media such as pencil, pen and charcoal.

2D recording from primary sources

When exploring observational recording from primary sources, there are different techniques you can use for 2D recording.

2D recording

Once artists and designers have identified a theme and analysed the work of others, they will move on to finding their own subjects to visually record from. You can record using:

- varied mark-making techniques
- technical and experimental materials
- different surfaces
- both precise and rapid processes.

Unusual methods

While observational drawing is the most common method of 2D recording, different situations allow for a wider range of methods:

- ✓ rubbing
- ✓ printing from objects
- ✓ cutting and collage
- ✓ mixed media
- ✓ typographical note
- ✓ measuring
- ✓ technical drawing.

Primary sources

You may have to be quite imaginative when identifying primary sources:

What can I access?

Is there a way of recreating or simulating the subject?

What observable things relate to my theme?

Primary sources

If I can't access the actual subject, could I observe something similar?

Could I travel somewhere in the time I have?

2D mark making

Before 2D recording, artists use warm-up or practice techniques to learn about 2D mark making.

Techniques

Artists and designers use a range of techniques to get a fuller picture.

In this extract from research, the learner has recorded a similar image using very different media.

Now try this

Choose a piece of 2D artwork that you are familiar with. Create a table of warm-up marks exploring the techniques used within the work.

3D recording from primary sources

3D observational recording from primary sources can be used in a number of purposeful ways. Take a photograph of any 3D work and include an indication of scale.

3D recording

This will generally take more time than 2D recording and needs to be exploited for a specific purpose, for example:

- **technical** – to develop skills in measuring, scaling and spatial awareness
- **creative** – exploring the object to experiment with materials and identify new processes beyond perfect reproduction
- **skills development** – learning techniques from observation to apply them later in your own work.

Sculpting

Sculptors have traditionally used quick-forming materials such as clay to develop skills in reproducing form that connects touch and sight.

Clay sculpting can be used during a life class.

3D interpretation

Making 3D interpretations of 2D visuals is quite common. This process is useful if you can't have the subject in the studio or if the subject won't stay still for long enough. Lines are a formal element and will demonstrate observation of form and contour within form.

Historically, before art forms like painting and photography were prominent, relief was widely used as a form of recording information.

Wire can be used for modelling. Look up the artist David Oliveira to see how he uses wire to look like scribbled 3D pencil drawings.

3D recording logistics

The materials involved in 3D recording may exclude artists and designers from making observations in the field because they take too long to manipulate or to dry, or they are too cumbersome. Ways around this include:

- ✓ collecting materials for later studio work
- ✓ recording using a lens from different perspectives
- ✓ preparing materials in advance
- ✓ combining primary and secondary observations such as your own drawings with photographs.

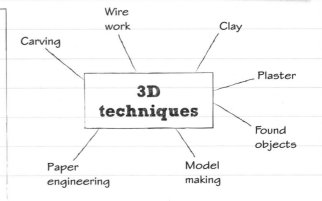

Carving · Wire work · Clay · Plaster · **3D techniques** · Found objects · Paper engineering · Model making

Now try this

Find one artist or designer that uses 3D recording as part of the creative process.

13

Primary recording with camera and film

In some circumstances, image recording with a camera or film can provide further insight into the subject. For example, sound, time-based qualities or movement may be needed as part of an observational recording from primary sources.

Image recording

This can be done with **any type of camera** such as a video camera, mobile phone, digital single-lens reflex (DSLR) or film-based camera. The immediacy of recording this way makes it very appealing, but it needs to serve a specific purpose for a variety of reasons:

- A subject won't be accessible for long.
- Lots of records need to be made.
- Very detailed and accurate records are required.
- Reproduction through a lens provides images that cannot be captured any other way.

Video

👍 Recording a moving image provides the benefit of being able to move around an object or see it change through time.

👍 You will be able to pause and observe things you might miss when just photographing.

👎 Image quality isn't the same as still photography.

Eadweard Muybridge's Animal Locomotion photos (1887) have inspired artists to look at images in motion.

Manipulation

Artists and designers may manipulate conditions when recording with a lens, for example:

- lighting conditions
- differing viewpoints
- macro and depth of field
- juxtaposition.

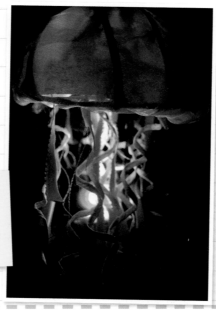

This practitioner has transformed everyday materials into something else through the use of light.

Controls

Most cameras on automatic settings such as mobile phones will make adjustments that change the image. When using a camera for accurate observation, you should use manual settings and adjust the:

☑ **aperture** – this controls the amount of light coming in to the camera and affects the focal length and depth of field

☑ **shutter speed** – fast-moving objects may appear blurry without high shutter speeds

☑ **focus** – the focal point and centre of interest within an image should be in focus

☑ **ISO settings** – with low levels of light, cameras will increase the ISO. However, this impacts on the grain of an image.

Workflow

Unless you are expecting to create a photographic outcome, recording with a lens usually combines with other records and serves to fill in the gaps.

Primary 2D records: notes, drawings and observations **+** Image recording with camera for later reference **=** Analysing both to get a fuller picture

Now try this

Interrogate an object by photographing it:

- from two different angles
- against two different backgrounds
- under two different lighting conditions.

Recording from secondary sources

Secondary sources can include the internet, books, magazines, journals, film, photographs, animation, video, music and audio.

Secondary sources

Artists and designers record from secondary sources to help them develop their own skills. Secondary sources should be selected because they relate to your work through:

- the subject matter
- the style
- the use of materials, techniques and processes.

Broader information

Secondary sources can enable you to find broader information on a topic, where information has been translated or interpreted. This often comes in the form of more abstract details relating to a topic, e.g.:

- information graphics
- flow charts
- data
- exploded views
- diagrams.

Interpretation

Some artists reproduce images from secondary sources to create their own work. These are not considered copies, but personal interpretations because they may use a different media that communicates differently to the original.
It is important to state the provenance of the original image (i.e. its title and who it is by).

Jane Perkins recreates *Girl with a Pearl Earring* by Vermeer in found objects.

Internet search engines

The use of search engines has radically simplified how artists and designers access secondary images, but you need to use this resource strategically:

✓	✗
Adjust settings on image searches to get larger images.	Do not only use image searches in search engines.
Allow time for research to find the right image.	Do not only use top-ranking images.
Access reputable sites focused on the topic and which give more insight than just the image.	Do not rely only on internet search engine results.

Appropriation

Some artists and designers visually record and communicate using other people's images. This may be through altering the images such as by collaging, combining or working over them. Again, it is important to be transparent about the provenance of the original image.

Techniques

There are valuable techniques for recording from secondary sources, for example:

- tracing
- copying specific formal elements
- extending images with own materials
- layering images
- interpretation
- appropriation.

Now try this

Find an image of a work by Louise Bourgeois and use techniques to record from the image, such as tracing, copying formal elements, layering or extending.

Visual recording and communication of recorded sources

When demonstrating your ability to record from primary and secondary sources in relation to a given theme, make sure you present your findings **visually**. This will be easier if you have used a variety of visual recording techniques during your research.

Recording in response to a brief

If your response to a brief on a given theme requires figurative and representational images, more time will be required on studying the subject through visual recording. Responses to the brief that are more abstract and experimental may need more time developing personal techniques and visual communication methods.

Relevant sources

It is important that you identify, research and record from relevant sources that relate to the theme. Make sure that your work includes observational recordings from primary sources. Ask your tutor or look at the Sample Assessment Material on the Pearson website to make sure that your records are relevant and meet the requirements for your actual assessment.

Sample response extract

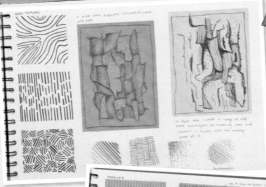

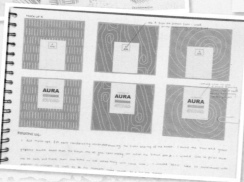

In this extract from visual recording, opportunities have been made to record natural textures. These are important for the response to a brief, and could be used in a presentation.

Strengths: this extract from visual recording has demonstrated applied studies as well as quick sketches. These develop the technique of mark making systematically. The application of techniques is also processed through stages and is clearly building towards a purpose when compared to the outcome. There is consideration of alternative mark-making processes for the recording from observation and some use of different media.

Areas for development: this extract from recording could be developed by combining recording with photography or more experimental processes such as rubbings from primary sources. There are also opportunities to extend this process by looking at other artists who have used natural textures, and learn from their techniques. Early colour studies may have had a more direct impact on colour choices in outcomes.

Self-assessing recording progress

At different stages of responding to a brief, you should self-assess the quality and exploitation of visual recording and how it relates to the theme and your choices. You can do this through annotating your work. These annotations could be useful if selecting work for a presentation. It is useful to ask yourself questions to help assess your progress.

Are there sufficient important artists related to the theme?

Have I obtained good-quality broad information from secondary sources such as information graphics?

Assessing your progress

Have I used tested technical and experimental approaches?

Have I applied both primary and secondary methods?

Have I made inventive use of primary recording?

Now try this

Find two primary objects that you could make a visual record from and record them in two different ways in response to the theme of 'Transmission'.

Breadth and variation in recording

You should use a variety of recording techniques in response to your given theme. This page shows two very different responses to the theme of 'Covering'.

Consider the theme

- Does the theme present any materials that could actually be used to draw or paint with, e.g. natural objects, foodstuffs, oil, colours or printable media?
- Have any practitioners worked with the theme in very unusual ways?
- Can I recreate or simulate the event or scenario?
- Could the marks themselves replicate the theme?

Sample response extract

This extract demonstrates qualities of recording in response to a brief. The theme of 'Covering' is interpreted by creating a packaging for a design product. This learner has moved beyond traditional mark-making techniques like drawing and photography. The literal application of nature to make marks demonstrates their use of lateral design thinking. The page is also positive in its demonstration of how the ideas are useful to the project's intentions by showing mock-ups of visual communication ideas.

Commitment

Show commitment and passion about the subject by demonstrating you are willing to travel, and put effort into finding the right material to record visually.

Think beyond the obvious

Using the internet, carry out research to find an image of Christo and Jeanne-Claude's *Wrapped Trees* (1998). You will see that this artwork connects to the idea of 'Covering' in a very unconventional way.

Now try this

Consider how you might respond if exploring postage and letters in response to the 'Transmission' theme. List at least six different media you could use to draw on, or with, that have a literal connection to mail letters.

2D ideas generation

You need to extend your own visual recording and communication skills through experimentation and investigation. One way of doing this is through 2D ideas generation.

Ideas generation

Artists need ideas as a way of moving away from simply recording towards creating their own original work for communication. At this stage, work doesn't need to be complete, but often takes the form of rough thumbnails, product sketches and manipulated observations.

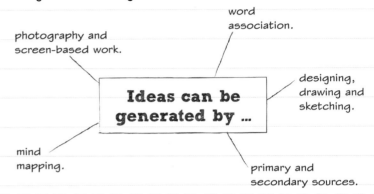

photography and screen-based work.

word association.

Ideas can be generated by ...

designing, drawing and sketching.

mind mapping.

primary and secondary sources.

Practical approaches

Most ideas generation will normally start with a mind map or brainstorm of ideas, but some artists prefer to move quickly into production as they feel that actually experimenting with media will help generate ideas. You might make mistakes by taking an experimental approach, but you can learn from them and might even create something new and unexpected.

Critical approaches

At this stage artists need to use imagination, critical and divergent thinking and synthesising of ideas in order to develop their ideas rather than imitating those of others. One of the best solutions is to consider several alternatives, reflect on the opportunities of each one and choose which direction to take.

Dos and don'ts when generating own ideas

👍 Carry out close primary and secondary analysis of visual recording in the work of others.

👍 Settle on an idea and follow it through.

👍 Critique and critically debate ideas early on.

👍 Use a project proposal or personal brief to structure your project and set constraints.

👎 Avoid taking too long to decide on a direction and avoid changing ideas frequently.

In Gustave Caillebotte's sketch for *Paris Street; Rainy Day* (1877), the focus is on creating a quick sketch to develop ideas for colour, style and final composition, rather than on details.

Now try this

Use either a mind map or word association to generate ideas around the theme of 'Transmission'.

3D ideas generation

Generating 3D ideas will help you to experiment and investigate as you extend your own visual recording and communication skills.

Working with 3D ideas generation

Generating ideas in 3D can be useful for any type of art and design practitioner. Some people may work in 3D and then move back into 2D. However, because of the time it takes, 3D ideas generation is most often done by sculptors, or product and spatial designers, whose outcomes will be three dimensional.

3D modelling with software programmes like Maya, 3ds Max® or SketchUp allow quick generation of ideas because materials, surfaces and forms can be explored easily.

3D ideas generation process

Most artists and designers expect to create many more models and test pieces than they do outcomes. As the process requires reflection and evaluation of ideas through practical testing, models are usually created using quick and easy 3D materials rather than materials that may take a long time to dry or set.

Rapid media you can use include:

* paper and card
* foamboard
* plaster
* clay
* found objects.

This maquette for a figure of a washer-woman (plasticine) by William Hamo Thornycroft demonstrates the type of rough ideas you can generate using 3D media.

William Hamo Thornycroft, 'Maquette for a figure of a washer-woman (plasticine)'© Leeds Museums and Art Galleries (Leeds City Museum) UK / Bridgeman Images

Typical creative ideas generation approaches in 3D

✓ **Exploring** – playing with materials

✓ **Connecting** – combining and making relationships

✓ **Metaphor** – using materials to reflect or represent

✓ **Examining** – trying a traditional process in a different way

Reflection on 3D ideas generation

Reflecting on practical ideas generation is critical to moving art or design forward. Remember to make notes on each sample:

* What has gone right?
* Has anything gone wrong?
* What techniques have you used?
* What was the material?
* What process did you use?
* Do you like the effect?
* How could you use it in your work?

Now try this

Identify two 3D techniques you could use to generate ideas in response to the theme of 'Transmission'.

Experimenting to record visually

Audiences expect artists and designers to use different, often unusual, materials, techniques and processes to record visually.

Experimentation in visual recording

Practical investigation into the use of unusual and non-traditional materials, techniques and processes to visually record can significantly enhance ideas generation and visual communication.

Anthony Gormley, 'Brick Man' (1986) © Anthony Gormley

By recording the form of the human body in brick, Antony Gormley in his maquette for *Brick Man* (1986) is able to relate the two together and provoke questions about their relationship. Bricks are traditional media, but not common in the arts and rarely associated with the body.

Form and material

The audience expects things to look a certain way. They will automatically connect a form and a material because of their expectations and life experiences. Practitioners often capitalise on this presumption and use it to surprise the audience.

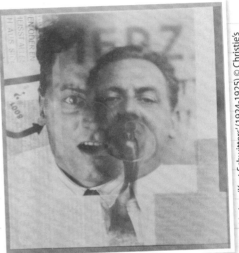

Eliezer Lissitzy, 'Kurt Schwitters' (1924-1925) © Christie's Images / Bridgeman Images

This photograph of Kurt Schwitters (1924/5) demonstrates an experimental approach to recording through photography and multiple exposure. The technique of photographing is traditional, but multiple exposures are experimental.

Form and technique

If an unusual technique has been used to record, the viewer of the work will ask why that specific technique has been used. The reaction is often manipulated by artists to provoke a response; for example, a delicate drawing of a solid form.

Dürer studied and drew everyday solid objects around him using very delicate and precise drawing techniques. These pillows were drawn in 1493.

Albrecht Dürer, 'Six Studies of Pillows (verso)' (1493). Licenced under CC0. The Metropolitan Museum of Art

Association in recording

Artists and designers often use a material, technique or process associated with what they are trying to communicate. In 1991, the artist Mark Quinn used his own blood to create self portraits. He was interested in regularly recording his image as Rembrandt did in paintings and drawings but Quinn used sculpture and blood to do so. Every six weeks he extracted one pint of blood until there was enough to fill a hollow sculpture of his head. The sculpture was then frozen and displayed.

Now try this

Using the internet to research your answer, explain two different ways that the use of blood in Marc Quinn's *Self* impacts on what it communicates.

Manipulating for creative intentions

Artists and designers explore manipulation of materials, techniques and processes to communicate their creative intentions.

Communication intentions

At this stage of the creative process, artists and designers do not have a completely set idea of their outcome, but they are deliberately working towards communicating intentions. This means they have an idea of what they want the audience to feel when their work is encountered. This experience in the audience is not accidental, but controlled and prepared by the artist well in advance of making the final outcome for exhibition, publication or delivery.

Structure

Practitioners often learn about how materials and techniques communicate differently through a structured approach. Rather than taking a risk, they will apply tests of different techniques and materials to the same image and review the quality of communication.

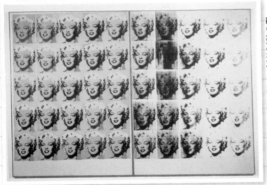

Andy Warhol, 'Marilyn Diptych' (1962) © The Andy Warhol Foundation for the Visual Arts, Inc. / DACS/Artimage 2018

In Andy Warhol's *Marilyn Diptych* prints (1962), it is clear that he is celebrating the fact that each image is subtly different from the others.

Selecting techniques

A written process like the one below can be used to help select appropriate techniques or materials.

Initial idea	Testing reproduction	Reflection
Image or artefact	Print	Commmunicates a very rough representation
		Too messy
	Collage	Perfect: tidy, commercial and witty

An example of the thought process at this stage of the creative process.

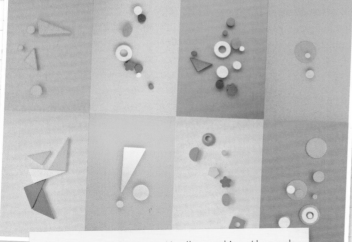

This artist is systematically working through background colours and compositions in order to communicate the right message.

Controlling the communication

Artists and designers cannot completely **control** what is communicated to the audience. However, when they select materials and techniques they can:

- consider what they have in common with the audience
- use codes and conventions such as colour
- use a material or process that is associated with issues and debates in the public sphere and media.

Now try this

Look at the *Marilyn Diptych* print reproduced above. Identify how Warhol has used techniques and processes to communicate his creative intentions.

Considering presentation of research

When demonstrating your skills in research and visual recording, select evidence carefully. Make a plan of what you will be assessed on (see also page 8) and the space available for presentation. You can then determine what content to include and ways to present it.

Selecting work

Ask your tutor or check the Pearson website to establish details such as the size and number of presentation sheets and what you will be assessed on in your actual assessment.

Sample response extract

The records you keep of your development work will directly impact on the quality of evidence, such as presentation of research, a developed piece of art or design and a written commentary. Visuals may include the original ideas, e.g. drawings, sketches, doodles, mind maps and mood boards. Also include your 2D visual experiments, observations and tests, as well as photographs of 3D work and working practices, models and maquettes.

Avoid lots of decoration of the pages and titles. Concentrate instead on demonstrating the quality and breadth of your research and showing evidence of your ability to manipulate materials, techniques and processes to communicate your messages.

- Use Photoshop or similar to touch up any images where possible.
- Be systematic and allow time for recording.
- Avoid using poorly lit photographs with distracting objects in the background.
- Don't throw things away that you don't like. Even if you weren't happy with it, you can use it to demonstrate the development process.

Show **processes** wherever possible as these will demonstrate visually how you work.

Equipment

If using digital approaches to present research and records, the equipment might include:

- ✓ Digital SLR and SD card
- ✓ Memory stick or storage device
- ✓ Well-lit white infinity curve
- ✓ Access to image software

Use an **infinity curve** made out of card or paper with some light to increase the quality of photographing 3D work.

Now try this

Make a list of things you should record during the research and preparation.

Using focused annotation

If using annotation to present research and visual recording, make sure that it is purposeful and focused. Your annotation can also help inform any written commentary and developed piece of art or design.

Sample response extract

Use **information graphics** tools like arrows, circles or lines to relate annotation to specific aspects of an image. These help the viewer understand what you are annotating.

Use a formal reflective log process as you progress through the preparatory stage to keep track of creative decisions. You can use these to support your research and recording, and any written commentary you might have to produce. Try to have a system for this and stick to it.

Annotation on the pages should discuss technical aspects of recording, evaluation of communication potential and opportunities for building on learning.

Annotation issues

✓ Produce simple, focused text using technical and objective language.

✓ Relate the annotation back to the theme and the communication intentions for the project.

✓ Spend time on your annotation – it is an important means of considering creative opportunities.

✓ Keep annotations up to date and never try to complete them at the end of a project.

✓ Avoid lengthy descriptions of activities. This wastes time and looks backwards instead of forwards.

Now try this

Annotate a piece of your own work, ensuring you cover technical aspects of production, what your intentions were and the effectiveness of your response to the brief.

Producing art or design

When considering how you would use your research, recording and development to produce a piece of art or design, you need to demonstrate:

- your response to the theme
- your use of materials, techniques and processes
- your ability to communicate your creative intentions.

Considerations for final piece

For your actual assessment, ask your tutor or check the Sample Assessment Material on the Pearson website for details relating to whether the piece can be an **extension and development** of work produced during the research and recording stage, or a **stand-alone piece of work** informed by the research and development.

Sample response extract

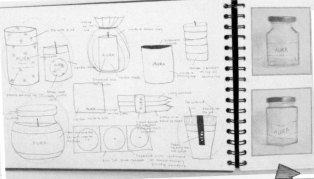

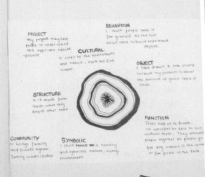

Early ideas combining writing as well as doodles and thumbnails help show ability to communicate creative intentions.

Research and recording demonstrates, for example, use of formal elements, materials, techniques and processes.

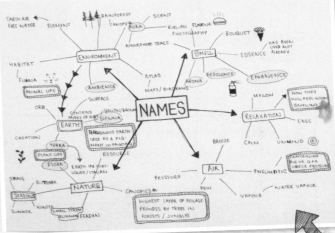

Contextual, primary and secondary research, as well as research into the work of art or design practitioners, contributes to how you respond to the theme.

Visual records and mind maps of logical ideas development show response to the theme and can combine with recording from primary and secondary sources and development of ideas to show the breadth of research and recording.

Now try this

Choose a piece of art or design you have produced recently. Explain what you did to help you settle on that particular idea.

Applying skills for creative intentions

When producing your own piece of art or design you will need to apply visual recording skills to communicate creative intentions. This involves selecting the appropriate materials, techniques, processes, tools and equipment.

Research

When selecting appropriate tools and methods for communication, it is critical to know how tools, materials and methods relate to art and design.

☑ Identify if there is a precedent of using the same tools, materials and methods in other art and design practitioners' work.

☑ Investigate the history of the media and how it evolved.

☑ Assess if the practice has been applied in radically different ways in the past.

Factors to consider

When thinking about which materials, techniques, processes, tools and equipment to use, consider:

- cost
- availability
- permanence
- strength
- durability
- malleability

- personal knowledge
- ease of use
- precision
- historical precedent.

Creative techniques, such as coiling in ceramics, have developed over time. Coiling is recognised as an appropriate method of creating pots of a certain shape. Makers would select this method because they have the knowledge that it works.

Historical precedent

Many forms of visual recording have a precedent for how they are used. This comes from how the media has evolved over time and how it has been developed and refined into craftsmanship. In many cases this is due to testing and development of technologies. Artists and designers may follow these rules because they enjoy working with them, or simply because the methods have been tried and tested over time. A precedent is also important in terms of communication, as the audience will read an artwork and often expect it to follow codes and conventions.

Critique

A good way of identifying the appropriate method is to use critique. Artists and designers will discuss their results with others and listen to constructive criticism on the craftsmanship, looking for tips and ideas for improvement.

☑ It is important to avoid being defensive.

☑ Leave time for valuable critique.

☑ Consider who will be able to give you the most valuable feedback.

In the context of assessment you may need to work independently and critique your own work only. Ask your tutor or check the Sample Assessment Material on the Pearson website for details of assessment.

Reject convention

Sometimes, visual communication is based on an artist or designer rebelling against convention. For example, they may be trying to ask questions about how an artwork is expected to be.

For example, historically, sculpture has been made of permanent materials like marble or metal, but Marc Quinn's *Self* (1991), creates a fragile and temporary sculpture, using 10 pints of the artist's own blood, which needs constant freezing to stay intact.

Now try this

Identify two artists who have used unconventional materials, and suggest how their choice of materials helped them communicate their artistic intentions.

Refining ideas

Practitioners refine their ideas. This can happen before they begin producing a work, but can also be part of the ongoing creative process. Make sure you record any refinements you make to your work as you go along.

Ideas

The term 'ideas' is used liberally within the arts. It isn't just used to describe an abstract conceptual thing an artist is thinking about, but relates to their overall approach. Ideas are the backbone of any project and evolve over time.

Making final decisions on elements of the work such as placement, colours and surface are a critical part of the refinement process. This needs close inspection and methodical assessment.

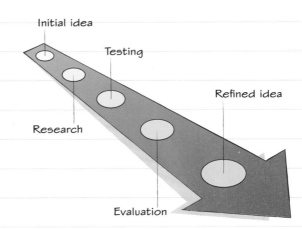

Initial idea
Testing
Research
Refined idea
Evaluation

Refinement

Artists and designers spend much of their time refining ideas. Whole careers are built on refining an idea further and further. They refine ideas by considering:

1 use of imagery – does it communicate what you expect it to?

2 contextual factors – is there a history of the use of the material or image that you haven't considered?

3 material manipulation – are you using the most appropriate method?

Refinement will take place across all scenarios of art and design towards the end of a project to ensure all details are right.

Scenario 1:
Time-consuming outcome
- lots of work already put in before long refinement phase – for example a figurative painting which takes a long time to create.
- final refinement touches still needed before completion.

Scenario 2:
Easy outcome to produce
- lengthy testing period – for example, a packaging design which goes through several stages of refinement but is then easy to print and make.
- needs only minor last tweaks before production.

Connecting the idea and the outcome

Outcomes by artists and designers will not always use all of the ideas that have been tested. However, it is generally expected that there is a clear and legible connection between the original idea and the outcome. Looking at the evidence of their research and exploration, you would expect to see some explanation of how the project has been refined.

Refinement in industry

Some areas of art and design have clearly defined refinement stages that should be followed:
- Web design – alpha and beta
- Product design – functioning prototype and simulation testing
- Fashion – first cut
- Graphic design – proof

Now try this

Within your specialism, list the five key areas of refinement that might take place after you have carried out the final prototype or test.

Refining your work

Make sure that you allow time for a stage of final refinement of your piece of art or design. Record the choices that you make, as this will help inform any presentation and written commentary.

Refining

You should set aside a specific period of time for refining your work. All art and design should go through this stage. You will need to demonstrate aspects of your project, which involves stages of refinement such as:

- checking the quality of individual parts
- scrapping elements that don't support the whole
- making small adjustments to outcomes.

You can keep notes on developments, revisions and their creative process in a journal or a reflective log. This makes it much easier to have a holistic view at the end.

Setting time

The simplest way to work out how much time you need is to work backwards from the end of the project. If you know when the deadline is, you can set time for each stage. This is a list of tasks that may need completing:

- ✓ recording from artists
- ✓ primary and secondary recording
- ✓ prototype or test
- ✓ period of refinement
- ✓ production of the outcome.

> Work backwards from the end date of the project, and set completion deadlines for each of the preceding stages.

> Produce **colour tests** for the outcome that demonstrate your ability to visually **communicate** the **theme** in **different ways**.

> This learner has used subtle variations of **texture and method** for the **outcome**, suggesting a **systematic** exploration and **refinement** of their own **visual language**. At this stage, these are not dramatic shifts in idea, but make the effort to ensure that each element is as good as possible.

Mistakes with refinement

It is most common that too little time is left for the refinement of the outcome. This is usually due to:

- 👎 leaving it too long to settle on an idea
- 👎 setting a vague and broad project that could result in anything
- 👎 making dramatic changes, rather than working on each individual element within the visual communication.

> Small refinements might include very specific choices and testing such as the colour palette.

Now try this

Make a time plan for a research and preparation period that includes a section for refinement.

Planning to mount your research

When you have made a careful selection of your research and preparatory work to demonstrate the required skills (see also page 22), you need to consider how to mount it.

Selecting your research

Consider how the work you select to display from your research and preparatory stage shows:

- your ability to visually communicate the theme in different ways
- exploration of ideas, imagery and visual language
- exploration of materials and methods of recording including at least one observational recording from a primary source
- research into art and design practitioners
- the contextual factors you investigated.

Demonstrating your skills

Consider how your selection of work demonstrates:

- the quality of your research into art and design practitioners
- the quality and breadth of your visual recording and research
- your understanding and application of contextual factors linked to the theme.

Breaking it up

If you are presenting your work on three presentation sheets, for example, make sure that your communication is clear and simple. Break your work up and let it stand out by using elements such as titles, simple fonts, sub-headings, sections and a grid.

Decide on what needs to go onto each of the presentation pages. One way of considering the content of your display is shown opposite.

Presentation requirements

Ask your tutor or check the Pearson website for the most up-to-date **Sample Assessment Material** to find out how you should present your work. The details of the actual assessed task may change so always make sure you are up to date.

Presentation sheet 1
- Initial research in response to brief and theme
- Contextual factors
- Ideas generation
- Primary recording
- Secondary recording

Presentation sheet 2
- Focused recording
- Focused practitioner research
- Experiments with materials and images

Presentation sheet 3
- Prototypes
- Testing
- Development of own visual language
- Testing of different communication types
- Refinements

Photography and scanning

To avoid cutting up all of your work, you could digitise it by scanning and photographing.

☑ Scanning: 300dpi for A4–A3 scale pages, 600dpi for smaller (this is excellent for flat drawings or where no studio lighting is available).

☑ Photographing: 12 megapixels minimum for A4–A3 scale images (this is good for 3D or highly textured work).

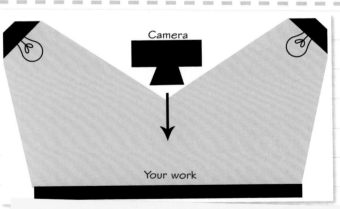

When taking a photograph, use a **copy stand** with **balanced lighting** from 45 degree angles to achieve the best results. Set the camera to maximum quality setting, low ISO and correct **white balance**. With lights, have diffused flash and no reflections or shadows.

Now try this

Photograph three pages of a sketchbook using the methods outlined on this page.

Creating narrative flow

Consider how you will position work selected from the research and preparatory stage. For example, you could help interpret your intentions by leading through the presentation sheets, to show how the pieces relate to each other and respond to the brief and theme as a whole.

Type size

Consider an appropriate type size. For example, a type size smaller than 11 point can be hard to read. Using larger sizes for titles and headings can help lead through your selected research.

Creative layout left to right
Ideal if you don't want to use a rigid structure, but it is important to organise the images logically so the viewer understands how they are connected.

Horizontal flow
The traditional model of left to right. This will be easily accessible, but can be adapted with different sizes of image and number of rows on the page.

Vertical flow
A simple structure to use that moves away from the tradition of left to right, but you amy want to use numbers, sizes of image or arrows to indicate direction.

Overlapped layout
A format that offers ways of connecting images that may reflect close ups, but care needs to be taken to ensure the viewer can interpret the flow.

The viewer must understand the **direction** and **chronology** of your selected research. Structure the sheet logically to help them.

You can be creative with the structure by placing images imaginatively or overlapping them, but the viewer must understand how the images relate to each other and the overall response to the brief and theme.

While you can be creative with the design and the layout, you need to make sure that the images are clear and present all of the work effectively. Avoid using lots of **effects**, **fonts** and **styles** as this will detract from the work itself.

Sample response extract

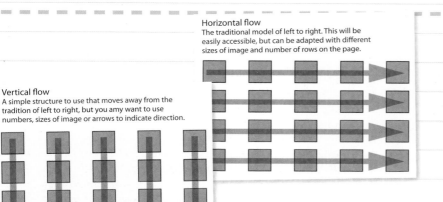

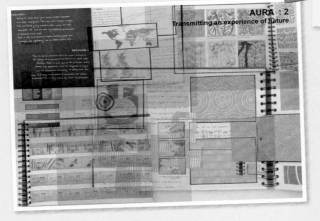

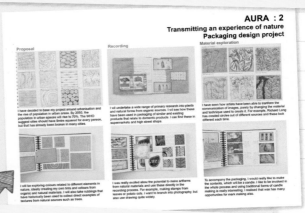

Putting some text with individual images may help the viewer interpret what is taking place in the image. Use **clear titles** and **hierarchy of information** with **scale** and **font weight** to identify information. You could keep to a maximum of two fonts per page, for example.

Now try this

Take nine images of an old sketchbook and organise them on a page in two different ways. Write a short sentence for each of the images to help the viewer.

Producing presentation sheets

Consider the factors involved in producing your presentation sheets.

Traditional or digital processes

You can create your presentation sheets using digital or traditional processes.

Digital
👍 Easy to edit
👍 Can create a template to use across all presentation sheets
👍 Can manipulate images digitally
👎 Need to know the software

Traditional
👍 Don't need to know the software
👍 Opportunities to use mixed media and more textures
👎 Needs more planning ahead
👎 Difficult to edit once made

Software packages

Software packages include: InDesign, Photoshop or Illustrator. You can create a structure on the pages using guides, columns, margins and gutters.

Sample response extract

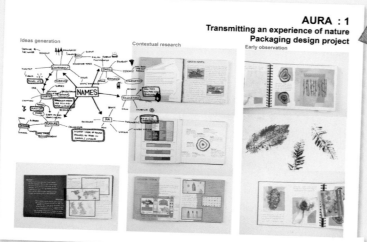

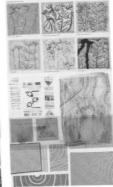

This learner has used clear and consistent titling across the presentation sheets that clarifies each of the sections. Headers for each of the subsections on the sheets are identified. Columns and grid have been created and then used consistently across both of the sheets. Any further type, such as explaining the response to the theme, has been added digitally. Image manipulation, such as the layering of the mind map, has been kept subtle so as not to distract the viewer. This learner has created sections to show progress through the research and preparatory phase and used space throughout to focus attention on the work.

You should pick out the most important parts of the research and development, rather than present everything. Keep fonts to a minimum and as neutral as possible to communicate information rather than decorate the page.

Now try this

Create an A2 file in Photoshop and define the grid structure, title font and header font. Use this to make an A2 presentation sheet using other people's images as a practice run.

Presenting art or design

When presenting your one fully developed piece of art or design that responds to the theme, it may be an extension or development of work produced during the research and recording stage, or a stand-alone piece of work informed by the research and development.

Demonstrating your skills

The work produced will need to demonstrate your:

- interpretation and communication of the theme
- ability to manipulate materials, techniques and processes
- ability to communicate your creative intentions.

Submission of images

Ask your tutor or check the latest Sample Assessment Material on the Pearson website for the requirements for submission of your work in your actual assessment. Details of assessment may change, so always make sure you are up to date.

Considerations might include the following, for example:

✓ The selection of images – these should be of sufficient size to show the quality of the work.

✓ Work that is intended to be accessed digitally should be submitted as PDF documents.

✓ 3D and larger pieces must be photographed and should include an indication of scale.

Sample response extract

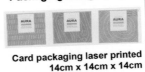

AURA : 4
Transmitting an experience of nature
Packaging design project

Card packaging laser printed
14cm x 14cm x 14cm

Check the Pearson website for the most up-to-date **Sample Assessment Material** to find out how many photographs you can submit, and size requirements. There may be specific requirements for 3D work. Consider the maximum number of photographs, showing the work in its entirety and images of different angles, possibly focusing on different details.

This presentation includes 3D work. Four images have been included: a large image of the overall outcome and three further images of details, including the net and the faces in flat of the fully developed piece. There is also a clear indication of the **scale** and **media** of the outcome.

Now try this

Create a presentation sheet that uses four images of a 3D object following the guidelines above.

Evaluating outcomes in relation to intent

Reviewing the creative process is an essential part of developing your art or design work. Here are some stages you can use to help you review the quality of research, outcomes and experimentation in relation to the outcome.

Review

Review the creative process in a structured way. Break it up into separate components and look at these individually to help determine where issues arose and what the impact was on the outcome. A review is not descriptive and doesn't try to tell a story of the project – instead it:

- is critical and not afraid to mention any weaknesses
- demonstrates the ability to identify issues
- considers each aspect of the project as equally relevant and important
- uses technical and creative vocabulary where possible.

The different areas of practice during the project and areas for review overlap, and each has an impact on the other, but they should be looked at separately.

Ideas generation, selection, refinement and development.

Contextual influences, purpose, meaning and intention.

Justification of creative decisions, materials, techniques and processes, imagery, visual language, formal elements.

Reviewing ideas generation

In order to review how you generated your ideas, look back to the start of a project and ask yourself:

- Was it a structured process?
- Did I use a broad enough set of approaches?
- Did I build on previous learning?
- Did the process delay the project unnecessarily?

The practice of keeping notes on developments, revisions and the creative process in a **journal** or a **reflective log** makes it much easier to have a holistic view at the end.

Reviewing development and refinement

Look at the **narrative** of your response to the brief and theme and how it evolved over time. Ask yourself:

- Can an audience see the way the project evolved?
- Was my development methodical?
- Did it meet the expected schedule?
- Did slow development impact on the quality of the outcome?
- Did the final idea come too late to be refined?

Reviewing selection processes

Consider the appropriate selection of materials, techniques, processes, tools and equipment. Ask yourself:

- Was craftsmanship affected by poor selection?
- Did the production take longer than expected due to poor choices?
- Were there any issues during production?
- Were there other, more suitable, methods?
- Have others done things differently?

Now try this

In a single paragraph, review the initial stage of a previous project and use the questions on this page to highlight one area for development and one strength.

Reviewing the meaning of work

When you are reviewing your work, it is important to evaluate its meaning. The key areas to look at are:

- what your original purpose was
- what your intentions were for the work
- the contextual influences you have used within the development.

These all contribute to its overall meaning.

Fitness for purpose

All art and design work fulfils a purpose and practitioners look back at the original purpose as part of their evaluation. This may have been included in a statement, proposal or personal brief at the start of the project. When reviewing the work's purpose, ask yourself:

- Did it fulfil the original purpose I set out for my artwork?
- Does the work meet the audience expectations?

Intentions

Intentions relate to both what you wanted to create practically and what you wanted the impact on an audience to be. Within art and design, the focus of review is based more significantly on what the intended impact on the audience was. The questions to ask are:

- What did you want the audience to experience?
- How did you want the audience to change in behaviour?

Contextual influences

While it isn't possible to know the full breadth of art history, you need to feel confident you understand how your own work sits within the context of **culture** and **history**.

👍 Ensure your project is well contextualised and has looked at a broad range of references before making decisions.

👎 Avoid using sources which are not really connected to the work (meaning that it has been generated in isolation).

Jasper Johns, 'Flag Above White with Collage', 1954 © Jasper Johns / VAGA, New York / DACS, London 2018 Photo: Kunstmuseum, Basel, Switzerland / Bridgeman Image

It would be a mistake to assume that Jasper Johns' *Flag above White with Collage* (1954) would have the same impact now as when it was produced, because there have been many political changes since the 1950s. You need to use contextual references in your work to support your intentions carefully.

Meaning

Individuals experience the meaning of a work differently. This makes it impossible to control the meaning of your work. The meaning of a work also changes with place and time. However, practitioners normally try to communicate something general as opposed to something specific. Getting feedback on the general communication of the work will enable a review of the meaning and how closely it meets your original intentions.

Remember

In the context of assessment you may need to work independently and critique your own work only. Ask your tutor or check the Sample Assessment Material on the Pearson website for details of assessment.

Now try this

Write three key questions you will use to review the meaning of your work.

Critical review of outcomes

Practitioners make judgements through a critical review of the outcomes and creative decisions they have made.

Review

A critical review of outcomes means justification of creative decisions. In order to do this, practitioners look at the work as a whole and specifically at materials, techniques and processes, imagery, visual language and the formal elements that make up the artwork.

Materials
- Are the materials suitable?
- Would professionals have picked something else?

Techniques
- Is there a good level of craftmanship?
- Does the technique help the communication?

Processes
- Were there more suitable alternatives?
- Did the process maintain the quality of visual communication?

Formal elements
- Do these communicate efficiently?
- Do they enhance the work overall?

Visual language

Practitioners review the visual language employed within their work by relating it to who the audience was intended to be and their perceived needs. They compare it to the expectations of the audience and the codes and conventions the audience are used to.

Justification of creative decisions

At each stage of any project, creative decisions are made. There may be reasons for decisions that are out of the practitioner's control. Practitioners generally avoid stating these and first explain that every reasonable effort was made and every alternative was explored prior to a decision that reduced the quality of the outcome. For example, imagine that a graphic designer could not afford the printing process. Rather than blame cost as a reason for the quality loss, they will justify their decisions through researching creative alternatives to achieve the same impact.

Justification

A common mistake of practitioners is to see justifying as an opportunity to state how the work is exactly 'what they wanted to create' to describe how successful it is without validating the argument. The best justification is one which remembers that the work is not intended for the practitioner but for an audience. Justification actually requires significant testing on the audience or scenario, so that the practitioner can judge if their work has achieved its aim.

Work in distinct specialisms can be tested in many different ways including:

- ✓ product design – simulation testing
- ✓ painting – feedback from viewers
- ✓ graphic design – focus group feedback.

Remember that, in the context of your assessment, you may need to work independently and critique your own work only.

David Shrigley could obtain qualitative feedback on the success of his *Really Good* (2016) sculpture in Trafalgar Square by interviewing viewers and checking if their experience was similar to his intentions.

Now try this

Write five key questions you will use to review your outcomes.

Identifying development needs

To improve your visual recording and communication skills, you need to identify developmental needs.

Developing visual recording

The quality of visual recording will have an impact on the quality of your art or design work as a whole. Identifying opportunities to improve visual recording, using both traditional and experimental methods, should increase the success of final outcomes in the future.

Contribution of visual recording

Visual recording to create a piece of art or design contributes in many ways. It will help you to:

- practise how you generate images
- study something in depth and learn about its characteristics
- develop a synthesis between materials, techniques and processes when recording.

Evaluating visual recording

The evaluation of visual recording in a final outcome means looking at three related areas.

Theme		Research		Recording methods
• Observations • Awareness • Insight	▷	• Primary • Secondary	▷	• Materials • Techniques • Processes

Primary and secondary

All projects will need **primary** and **secondary** visual recording in order to demonstrate a good level of awareness and insight into the subject.

- Could you have made more effort to find sources, including artefacts?
- Would broader visual recording have improved the quality of the outcome?
- How central and relevant to the project was the recording ?

Building confidence

The artist has placed images using different tones next to each other to be able to compare them.

Having tried and tested the materials for recording in a structured way, this artist can feel confident about using the correct materials, techniques and processes during visual recording.

They have made notes about qualities in each to show their thought process.

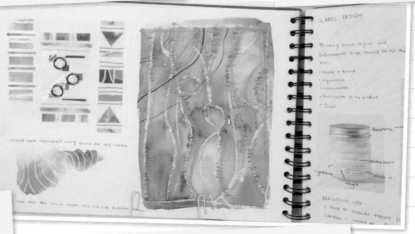

They have started small and got more and more confident with the types of marks being made.

The artist has made various attempts to create a visual effect and then expanded on one they feel is more successful.

Now try this

Write a paragraph explaining the relationship between recording and communication.

Evaluating visual recording and communication

You need to identify developmental needs in your visual recording techniques.

Identifying developmental needs

Practitioners will look logically at their communication development needs and then summarise them into priority areas at the end of the project. Some practitioners might use evaluation tools to help identify their needs. Below are two methods that could be used, for example:

- **SWOT** – this is a **situational analysis** tool for evaluating projects.
- **SOAR** – this tool enables future **motivational planning**.

This learner has produced packaging in response to a theme of 'Transmission'. They've completed a SWOT and SOAR analysis to help identify developmental needs.

Sample notes extract

SWOT

- **Strengths:** An innovative response to the theme of 'Transmission'.
- **Weaknesses:** I would have liked to consider the opportunities for creating my own natural colours in order to transmit more effectively the experience of nature.
- **Opportunities:** There would be an opportunity to synthesise more traditional and digital processes and even incorporate the textures of fabrics or natural materials.
- **Threats:** I tended to stay safe and use mark-making media that was familiar, and this limited the breadth of exploration.

Try to use as much technical vocabulary as possible.

It is important to be honest and critical with opinions to create a balanced evaluation.

Sample notes extract

SOAR

- **Strengths:** Mixing traditional and digital media has really paid off and built on both of my strengths.
- **Opportunities:** An area that could easily be built on is the relationship between the publicity and the product as these could use more coherent visuals.
- **Aspirations:** The areas of the project to build on would be the subtle hint of nature that is being transmitted within the designs. The techniques have worked really positively here.
- **Results:** Reviewing the communication of the product by creating templates and mock-ups before the final outcome showed the messages were clear.

Describing methods of measuring quality shows awareness of practical and tangible analysis.

Evaluating visual communication

☑ Look at the outcome and identify which of the visual communication methods employed were the **most** and **least** effective.

☑ Identify which points within the project could have had the most **detrimental** impact on the quality of visual communication.

☑ Reflect on how closely you met **communication intentions** and **impact** on audience.

Links See page 23 for an example of using a reflective log to keep track of creative decisions and review progress. This can help to inform a review of strengths and weakness, developmental needs and can contribute to a written commentary.

Now try this

Undertake a SOAR analysis of a previous project.

Written commentary

When writing a commentary, you need to include explanations of your interpretation of the theme and justify why you took this direction.

Demonstrating your skills

If you are asked to write a commentary to accompany the presentation sheets you have produced for your research and your developed piece of art or design, consider how you will show:

- your analysis of the use of visual language and formal elements in your own and other practitioners' work
- the quality and detail of your explanations and justifications for your decisions.

Extent of written commentary

Ask your tutor or look at the latest Sample Assessment Material on the Pearson website to establish whether there is a word limit for the written commentary. Details of the assessment may change, so always make sure you are up to date.

Focusing your commentary

You must ensure you include explanations of the following in your written commentary:

1 Your interpretation of the theme.

2 The art and design practitioners you researched and how they influenced your work.

3 The primary and secondary sources you used in response to the theme.

4 The visual recording methods and materials you used.

5 Your own visual recording and communication in relation to the theme, including decisions you made, as well as an assessment of your strengths, weaknesses and areas for improvement.

Sample response extract

From the outset, the theme suggested the idea of transmitting communication and information. Dictionary definitions of transmission describe it as the act of sending information from one place to one or more other places.

Research via search engines repeatedly presented data and binary code images. However, the idea of transmitting something tangible or physical rather than communication and information seemed innovative and challenging. Making sure there was use of non-art and wider cultural sources seemed appropriate. I found a quotation from the work of Leo Tolstoy that made me consider how art is the transmission of feeling that an artist has experienced.

After research into practitioners, it was clear that designers such as Nora Kaszanyi and Sidney Lim were using the idea of transmission with commercial design to visually 'transmit' an experience to the consumer through their packaging design. These designers needed to sell the idea of nature to the consumer using codes and conventions related to adventure such as maps the consumer could easily engage with.

Using facts, quotations, data or other reliable information is ideal in justifying your ideas as it shows a well contextualised project.

In this extract from a written commentary to accompany a presentation sheet, the learner has explained why they moved away from certain paths and how they tried to creatively interpret the theme by moving away from obvious solutions.

This learner has demonstrated that they are willing to look beyond obvious art and design sources to **inform their direction**.

The learner has introduced several names of practitioners and identified how they influenced their early direction within the project.

The learner has clearly explained why these designers relate to their interpretation of the theme and have justified this logically.

Use technical vocabulary related to visual communication and talk about the audience and their ability to engage with the theme.

Now try this

With reference to a previous project, write a paragraph explaining the development of your visual recording.

Sources, methods and materials

When writing a commentary, you need to comment on the sources, methods and materials you chose in response to the brief and theme, and include explanations to accompany your presentation sheets.

Structuring writing

It isn't necessary to write the commentary to accompany your presentation sheets from start to end in a **chronological** order. While the writing should lead **systematically** through the points to the end, it may be easier to divide up the time and focus an equal amount of time on each of the five areas you are explaining.

🔗 **Links** See page 37 for a reminder of the five areas of focus you should include in your commentary.

Checking your commentary

If you are writing a commentary under timed conditions, remember to:

- ✓ **connect** all of the parts
- ✓ **check** you have included the five areas of focus adequately
- ✓ **revise** any of your writing
- ✓ **proofread** and ensure everything is understandable.

Sample response extract

A simple solution to the brief on the theme of 'Transmission' was to consider the act of transmitting something outside of traditional information or communication and challenge myself to transmit nature itself through a design medium. With a need to transmit a feeling of nature into an urban space, it was obvious to engage with nature itself.

Initial observations included activities such as collecting leaves and making prints from these. However, this didn't develop any significant unique selling point that would help the product stand out on the shelf. To gain an awareness of the competition, primary research entailed visiting and analysing the shelves of retailers where packaging related to nature was photographed. This was topped up with a review of leading packaging websites such as lovelypackage.com.

A key element used across this type of packaging was pattern and shades of organic colours. This led me to move towards primary sources such as unusual plant cells, fossils, seeds and processes such as photosynthesis. Visual records from these would be subtle, but would communicate effectively to the audience because they would remember them from science lessons or documentaries.

You need to discuss the stages of primary sources you used and how they relate to the theme.

In this extract from a written commentary, the learner has justified why they selected certain primary sources by referring to their opportunities for communicating as a unique selling point and standing out from other work.

Considering similar and existing work shows reasoning in approach to creating your own work.

Listing names of relevant secondary sources used is better than listing sources vaguely such as 'the internet'.

This learner has introduced analysis of the visual language and formal elements in other practitioners' work and referred to visual recordings they have done from sources.

Now try this

With reference to a previous piece of work you have completed, select one artist you think relates to the theme and write a paragraph about their methods and materials.

Commenting on communication

You need to be able to comment on your own recording and visual communication in response to the theme.

Reflection and notes

Ask your tutor or check the latest Sample Assessment Material on the Pearson website to find out whether you can have any work carried out during the research and preparatory stage with you when you write your commentary. If so, the presentation sheets and the notes you have generated in your records of creative decisions will be helpful for identifying key points that had the most impact.

Further preparation

☑ List the points you want to cover for each of the five areas of focus (see page 37).

☑ Plan to cover all five focus areas and allow for each of these to have an almost equal share of any word allowance.

☑ Focus judgements on critical reflection based on your outcome and development process.

Sample response extract

A logical writing structure has been used to support the commentary.

In conclusion, the communication within the outcomes was significantly boosted by the fact the formal elements within the packaging still kept some of the details of the primary visual recording that took place very early on in the project, so the act of transmitting nature was more effective. While the images were heavily processed digitally, the audience could still see the hand-made feel of the marks. The substantial effort placed in early visual recording, drawing, mark making, printing and observational recording enabled the development of a subtle and sensitive visual language that reflected nature through a texture created by pattern and subtle tonal values. The fact there is a range of different packaging means the audience can read the difference in product even before they pick it up from the shelf. Considering there is so much competition within this type of product, I think I was able to make an individual and personal language that relied on recording and consistent visual communication.

Wider primary observation of unusual natural sources through microscope drawing and macro-photography or frottage could have presented further pattern creation opportunities. Along with the use of more advanced printing processes such as foiling, the packaging would become even more distinct from the competition.

In this extract from a conclusion to a written commentary, the learner has discussed what the product ended up communicating and how this related to the recording within the development.

The inclusion of an analysis of the impact of the methods within the overall outcomes is relevant.

Explaining how you have developed a visual language through recording means you are aware of communication methods.

Comparing work to others within the discussion shows contextual awareness.

The learner is critical enough to mention areas for development, without making excuses. There is also a clear use of technical terms and vocabulary for methods.

Now try this

With reference to a previous piece of work, explain a process you would take to move from recording to communicating.

Your Unit 2 set task

Unit 2 will be assessed through a task, which will be set by Pearson. In this assessed task, you will use your understanding of contextual research and visual analysis to critically analyse the work of art and design practitioners and improve your own practice as you carry out research and prepare a response to a provided brief.

Revising your skills

Your assessed task could cover any of the essential content in the unit. You can revise the unit content in this Revision Guide. The skills pages are designed to **revise skills** that might be needed in your assessed task. They use selected content and outcomes to provide examples of ways of applying your skills.

Investigate art and design practitioners whose work is linked to a given theme, using primary and secondary sources and providing a bibliography of your sources.
Revise this on pages 70, 76–77, 84.

Visually analyse the work of the creative practitioners, exploring their use of formal elements, visual language, visual communication and the connections with contextual factors and theme.
See pages 50, 62, 73, 76–77.

Investigate how contextual factors influence creative practitioners' work.
This is explored on pages 63–64.

Use specialist terminology and quality of written communication to justify your arguments, analysis and conclusions, supported by relevant evidence.
Revise this skill on pages 82, 92–93.

Set task skills

Compare the practitioners and their work linked to the theme, communicating independent judgements that demonstrate understanding of their work.
See pages 86–87.

Workflow

The process of investigating art and design practitioners and their work through research and visual analysis to form independent judgements could follow these steps:

1. Research practitioners whose work is relevant to a theme, using primary and secondary sources to make notes and visual records.

2. Keep careful notes and records in order to compile a bibliography of your sources.

3. Explore contextual factors which may have influenced the practitioners, and analyse their work.

4. Compare the work of the practitioners.

5. Justify the conclusions you reach through your analysis.

Check the Pearson website

The activities and sample response extracts in this section are provided to help you to revise content and skills. Ask your tutor or check the Pearson website for the most up-to-date **Sample Assessment Material** and **Mark Scheme** to get an indication of the structure of your actual assessed task and what this requires of you. The details of the actual assessed task may change so always make sure you are up to date.

Now try this

Visit the Pearson website and find the page containing the course materials for BTEC National Art and Design. Look at the latest Unit 2 Sample Assessment Material for an indication of:

- the structure of your set task, and whether it is divided into parts
- how much time you are allowed for the task, or different parts of the task
- what briefing or stimulus material might be provided to you
- any notes or initial research you might have to make and whether you are allowed to take these into your supervised assessment
- the activities you are required to complete and how to format your responses.

Planning the investigation process

When carrying out an investigation, you will need to plan your research carefully, taking a number of factors into account.

1 Setting aims and objectives

Set out your aims and objectives for contextual investigation clearly at the start, thinking carefully about what you are trying to achieve. Consider:

- What are you trying to find out? Define this clearly.
- How will you use the information?

You will become aware that there are a lot of factors to consider, such as:

- What themes are you finding out about?
- What is the work like?
- Who is the audience?
- How can I find relevant and reliable primary and secondary research sources?

Aims

Your aims are what you want to achieve.
For example:
I want to find out:

- what Monet's work was about
- how he influenced Impressionist painters
- how he still influences artists today.

Objectives

Your objectives are the steps you will take to achieve your aims.
For example:

- I will research from primary sources by visiting a gallery.
- I will draw directly from Monet's paintings, to visually record his use of subject and formal elements.

2 Make a plan

It is important to make a plan that is detailed enough and will provide a big enough range for your research. On it, you need to state:

- an outline of your intentions, e.g. 'I am researching <name of practitioner>' and the movement s/he is/was associated with
- your aims
- your objectives
- a timescale.

3 Timescales and action planning

Including timescales for your research (a series of short interim deadlines) will help you achieve your investigation and research objectives within a timeframe. Setting your own deadlines will also help you to monitor progress.

Leave a short time after the interim deadlines to make action plans. You may want to improve the depth of research, use different sources for your information, and so on.

4 Working SMART

You can use target-setting skills such as SMART targets for timescales and primary and secondary sources, i.e.:

S – Specific
M – Measurable
A – Achievable
R – Realistic
T – Time-related

 Links For more guidance on making a research plan, see page 49.

Thorough planning at the outset will help you use your time most effectively.

For more guidance on making a research plan, see page 49.

Now try this

Choose a practitioner you admire and who you would like to investigate. Write a list of aims and objectives for your investigation.

Identifying primary research sources

You need to identify relevant and reliable research sources for your investigation. Research sources are either **primary** (first-hand) or **secondary**. Some primary research sources are outlined below.

1 Viewing work first-hand

Original works of art and design are primary sources. Viewing a practitioner's work first-hand in a gallery, museum or studio is a primary source. Reproductions of art and design work are not usually considered to be primary sources. If you are researching a visual practitioner, try to view their work in person.

Gallery visits are one of the most important primary sources you will use.

> **Links** For more on how to record your observations through sketches and notes look at pages 50 and 51.

2 Visual recording

You can make **your own first-hand** visual recordings of art and design work, using any combination of drawing, painting, video or still photography, to:

- identify key parts of 3D pieces
- analyse site-specific work or view work in the context of its surroundings
- record any moving features in the work (which would be described as kinetic art).

Your own photograph of a detail of an original work is an example of primary research.

3 Interviews

You might choose to interview people as part of your primary research. Here are some examples of people you could interview:

- living artists
- art historians or experts
- curators or gallery employees.

You can record interviews directly or write notes during the interview.

> **Links** You might want to use interview questions as part of the investigation process. There is more about planning this on page 41.

Interview skills

If you want to interview someone for your research, you need to behave professionally and respect the fact that they are giving you their time and experience.

☑ Approach them politely by phone, email or letter.

☑ Explain who you are and that you are studying for a BTEC National qualification in Art and Design.

☑ Describe your research task and explain why you want to interview them.

☑ Ask if they are happy to talk to you, and when would be a convenient time.

☑ Ask if they are happy to be recorded. Make sure you get their permission in writing.

Now try this

Write a short email or letter requesting a phone interview with a local artist.

 Bear in mind the bullet points in the box above.

Identifying secondary research sources

Using suitable secondary research sources, when combined effectively with first-hand primary research sources, is an important part of your research. Some secondary research sources are outlined below.

1 Academic research

This is research using published books, articles, essays and information, across all the different secondary sources. Go beyond purely collecting facts and biographical details – use questions to interrogate the research information:

- What are you trying to find out?
- What themes or subjects are you looking into?

This will also help you to keep your research focused.

Annotation

Start annotating your research as early in the process as you can. Make notes on downloads, screenshots and screengrabs, and photocopied pages from journals. Use these to identify:

✓ how useful these sources are to the purpose of your research

✓ how you can use them, such as getting information on practitioners' ideas, or their working methods and processes

✓ if they give you any information about links with other practitioners.

Annotation means making notes and recording thoughts as well as drawing.

2 Art and design journals

Use journals to find:

- reviews of current exhibitions, projects and commissions
- information on contemporary trends in specific disciplines
- images and ideas
- information on practitioners' own ideas through printed interviews
- information on specific themes.

Remember there will be a theme in the set task brief for your assessment.

Art and design journals cover a wide range of practices. Many can also be found online.

3 Artists' blogs

Use artists' blogs to research specific examples of practitioners' work. You may be able to make direct contact with a practitioner as part of your research by adding comments to a blog.

Remember to present yourself professionally if you make contact with a practitioner. Explain who you are, what you are studying and what information you would like to research.

4 Websites

As well as using the websites of practitioners, you can also visit the websites of internationally recognised galleries. These include resources, such as:

- image galleries
- reviews of current and past exhibitions
- featured practitioners
- worksheets.

Now try this

Plan researching the theme of 'Our disappearing world' using secondary sources. List which sources might be the most effective for this task.

Recording and collating information

When carrying out an investigation, it is important to set up methods to record and collate the information from your research. Keep a record of all the sources that you use and also your thoughts and ideas. Some ways of doing this are outlined below.

1 Research folder

Use a ring binder or a folder with integral plastic sleeves with headings, dividers and an index to organise the information.

You will cross-reference information as you develop your research so set up a system that works for you, and which allows you to find and access the information you have collated.

2 Notebooks and blogs

Carry a notebook around with you – use it to record your thoughts, ideas and any information you find out about your research subjects.

You can also set up a blog, where you can upload images and your views and thoughts, as well as information.

You may be able to set this up securely as a blog on your intranet.

3 Sketchbooks

You can collage information into your sketchbook, such as typed information, relevant photocopies, highlighted extracts, postcards, as well as making your own annotation and studies.

Use page numbers in your folder or sketchbook with an index so you can easily find relevant examples when you need them.

4 Referencing

Effective research identifies its sources. You must use referencing systems, such as the Harvard system, for books in a bibliography (author, title, publisher, edition, year, ISBN). You should also make sure you include any website names as well as the URL.

Research takes time, so factor in enough time to look through your sources as well as simply identify them.

Links More information on how to reference your sources, and how to compile a bibliography, is supplied on pages 45–47.

5 Contingency plans

You may find information that doesn't fit neatly into your plan. Don't panic because you may well be able to use this, for instance to amend your original plan. But you may need to revise the focus of your research – so have a back-up plan.

- Look at other practitioners.
- Use different research techniques.
- Research the theme using a broader approach, and then narrow it down to individual practitioners.

Reflect on a regular basis – think about and write up your thoughts about practitioners and themes as you work through the process. Keep on top of the research tasks.

Write down your thoughts, views, insights and any conclusions regularly – it's difficult to remember all the points at the end of the research.

Now try this

Find out if you can set up a blog for collating research on your centre's student intranet, and make notes on how this would work in practice.

Referencing conventions

If you need to **reference information** correctly and compile a **bibliography**, there are academically accepted conventions. You could use a system such as Harvard, for example.

References and bibliographies

These list the **literature** that the writer has read and **cited** (mentioned) in their work.

- A **reference** section lists all the sources that have been cited in the text.
- A **bibliography** takes the same format as a reference section but lists everything you have read, or seen, about the topic, not only the sources you have mentioned in your written work (see page 47 for an example).

Correct referencing is important:

✓ You should always acknowledge the source of any information (**plagiarism** is using information without correct attribution).

✓ Good referencing increases the validity of your work as it shows that other researchers have published supporting information.

✓ The reader should be able to access any source material that you used – good referencing will help them find your sources easily.

✓ If you know how to read reference lists, you will always be able to find more references around a topic of interest.

Following conventions

Be aware when reading texts that some authors may use the terms 'references' and 'bibliography' differently. The definitions in this book are conventionally accepted ways of using the two terms.

Referencing systems

There are several referencing systems. The Harvard system is widely used and followed in this guide (see page 46). If you need to use references and compile a bibliography, use a conventional system consistently and correctly.

Notation system: footnotes

When reading texts, you need to understand the **notation system**, which is a small superscript number inserted next to the relevant text, like this[1].

[1]Authors give the reference as a **footnote** at the bottom of the page, preceded by the matching number. Footnotes are often given in smaller text.

Notation system: endnotes

Endnotes[2] are referenced in a list at the end of the section of text.

[2]An endnote looks very much like a footnote.

Whether footnotes or endnotes are used, there will also be a **full reference list** at the end of the work.

Plagiarism

Plagiarism is quoting other people's work without giving them credit. You can fail some courses for plagiarism. To avoid plagiarism, you must cite and reference correctly.

✓ You can use quotation marks to show that you have used someone else's words, and you include the reference:

> Galotti (2011, p.400) states that the analytic system is 'more deliberate and explicit'...

✓ You can paraphrase (use your own words) and provide a reference:

> Galotti compares the analytic and the experiential systems (2011, p.400).

Now try this

1 Why is it important to cite references correctly, whether in text or in reference lists?

2 What is the difference between a reference list and a bibliography?

Referencing print sources

You will need to understand and use a conventional referencing system for articles and books, such as the **Harvard system**.

Referencing journal articles

Here is an example of a reference for a journal article:

> Ball, L. (2012) Midwifery education: making sense of the current challenges. *British Journal of Midwifery*, 20(7), pp.516–520.

The information appears in this order:

1. author, last name first, and initial
2. date
3. title of article
4. journal title
5. volume (and issue number)
6. page numbers.

Note how the journal name appears in *italics*. In handwritten references, underline the title. The use of punctuation, such as full stops, commas and brackets is also important.

Referencing a book

Here is an example of a reference for a book:

> Sacks, O. (2011) *The Man Who Mistook His Wife for a Hat*. London: Picador.

The information appears in this order:

1. author, last name first, and initial
2. date
3. book title
4. place of publication: publisher.

Note how the book title appears in *italics*. Always use a colon (:) between the place of publication and the publisher's name.

Referencing a chapter in a book

This is how you reference a particular chapter in a book:

> Sen, A. (2000). Social justice and distribution of income. In: Atkinson, A., and Bourguignon, F. eds. *Handbook of income distribution*. Amsterdam: Elsevier, pp.59–85.

Citing references in text

This is how you would cite a reference in the body of your work:

> Ball (2012) argues that the challenges experienced by those undertaking midwifery practice have impacted on their ability to do their job.

or

> Current research suggests the challenges experienced by those undertaking midwifery practice have impacted on their ability to do their job (Ball, 2012).

Multiple authors

This is how you would cite a reference by more than one author:

> Bryant and Bradley (1985, p.24) argue that the educationalists are not …

or

> Some research argues that educationalists need to do more (Bryant & Bradley, 1985, p.24).

If there are three authors, give all names:

> Clark, Kemp and Howard (2016, p.189) argue that …

If there are four or more authors, give the name of the first author, followed by **et al.**, which means 'and others'.

> Jones, et al. (2016, p.189) argue that …

Note that '&' is used in the brackets but 'and' is written out in full in the main text.

Now try this

Choose any book and reference it using a conventional system.

You could use the system above. Make sure you include the correct information, punctuation and italic (or underlined) text.

Referencing online sources

You need to reference electronic sources carefully because websites change and you may need to find the information elsewhere. The conventions shown below use the Harvard system.

Referencing online journal information

If you are referring to a web document or journal, use the systems described on page 46. After the publisher, or instead if there isn't a publisher, give the name of the website of the organisation responsible for providing/maintaining the information: http://internetaddress/remotepath, and the date it was accessed in square brackets, e.g.

> Dalrymple, J. and Burke, B. (2006) *Anti-oppressive practice: social care and the law.* 2nd edn. *Dawsonera* [Online]. Available from: http://www.dawsonera.com [Accessed: 28 January 2009].

Referencing a web page

When referencing a web page, it is important to include all the information, e.g.

> University of Oxford (2006) Plagiarism [Internet], Oxford, University of Oxford. Available from: http://www.admin.ox.ac.uk/epsc/plagiarism/index.shtml [Accessed 19 January 2010].

Referencing e-books

URLs can be very long, and they can also be unstable (likely to change). If that's the case, it's best to give the URL of the main site, e.g.

> Neville, C. (2007) The complete guide to referencing and avoiding plagiarism [Internet], Maidenhead, Open University Press. Available from: Netlibrary http://www.netlibrary.com [Accessed 15 Oct 2017].

Referencing emails

If you reference an email, you need to include the email address of both the sender and the recipient, along with the date and subject, e.g.

> Bodley, M. (mark.bodley@pearson.com), 14 October 2017. Re: Escher study day. Email to S. Barley (simon.barley@pearson.com).

Example of a bibliography

When you compile a bibliography, you must arrange your list of references alphabetically by author, using the surname and initial.

> Gompertz, W. (2013) *What Are You Looking At?: The Surprising, Shocking, and Sometimes Strange Story of 150 Years of Modern Art.* Reprint edn. New York: Plume.
>
> Gombrich, E. H. (1995) *The Story of Art.* 16th edn. London/New York: Phaidon Press.
>
> Phillips, S. (2013) *...isms: Understanding Modern Art.* Reprint edn. Milford: Universe.

 Links See page 45 for an explanation of what a bibliography is.

If you visit a gallery to carry out research, and you want to reference your primary sources, you could do it like this:

> Drawings and notes made from Jasper Johns, *Fool's House,* 1962, Oil on canvas with objects attached, on 6th December 2017, at the exhibition 'Jasper Johns: Something Resembling Truth', Royal Academy of Arts, London.

Now try this

 You could use the system above. Include the correct information, punctuation and italic (or underlined) text.

Choose any article from an online journal and reference it using a conventional system.

Understanding a task brief

When you have received a task brief in your assessment for Unit 2, make sure that you understand what it requires of you. Some key points relating to your assessment are outlined below.

Assessment of Unit 2

Ask your tutor or look at the latest Sample Assessment Material on the Pearson website for an indication of what the actual assessment involves. Pay attention to whether the task is in parts, whether you can take any research notes into your supervised assessment, and whether you need to write within word limits. The task is different each year and the format may be different. Details of assessment may change so always make sure you are up to date.

Set task brief

Your set task brief will outline the task and might include the following kind of information, for example:

- Information about the theme on which the task is based, for example 'Identity'.

- Names of two art and design practitioners, for example Cindy Sherman and Yinka Shonibare. You select one of these practitioners and another internationally renowned practitioner, of your own choice, who also addresses the theme.

- An image by each of the provided practitioners. You select an image for your chosen practitioner which you can visually analyse.

- A briefing sheet with more information in relation to the theme and images.

Making notes

☑ If you find you can take some preparatory notes into your assessment, choose them carefully to ensure they contain the information and prompts you need.

☑ Ask your tutor or check the Pearson website for the most up-to-date **Sample Assessment Material** to get an indication of the structure of your actual assessed task, whether you can take in notes from the research and preparatory stage into the supervised assessment and, if so, any explanation or restriction for the kinds of notes.

☑ Make sure your analysis, conclusions and justifications address the theme.

☑ You need accurate information on all of your sources if referencing information correctly and providing a bibliography.

Responding to the brief

In responding to the brief you might need to do the following, for example:

- prepare copy to be used in a given context, e.g. an information guide for an exhibition on a theme such as 'Identity'.

You would need to include:

- the contextual factors that have influenced the practitioners and their work

- a visual analysis of two pieces of Art and Design work – one from each of the practitioners you have investigated

- how the practitioners have addressed or used the theme in their work.

- a bibliography of your primary and secondary research sources used in your investigation.

You might also need to prepare a communication (a letter or an email, etc.) to explain your conclusions from your research, justifying your views. For example, if asked to research a theme for an exhibition that includes two practitioners, you might need to explain which one would have an image on the front of the catalogue, justifying your choice by explaining how they represent the theme best.

You would have to put forward a balanced argument with justifications for your opinions and, for example:

- synthesise the visual analysis and contextual factors to form judgements

- compare the practitioners and their work linked to the theme

- justify your arguments with relevant evidence.

Now try this

Explain what is meant by 'contextual influences' on practitioners and their work.

🔗 **Links** This Revision Guide contains sample extracts of notes and responses. The following pages show key examples of using research when preparing to write about practitioners and their works (pages 57, 61, 80, 82, 84) and to write a supportive document (pages 87, 92–94). For formatting a bibliography, see pages 45–47.

Planning your research

When you receive the set task brief for your assessment, you will need to plan your research carefully and make sure your aims and objectives are clear in your mind before you start.

Below there is an example of an outline planning page from a learner's sketchbook.

Sample notes extract

PLANNING MY RESEARCH

My outline plan

For my task I am researching <u>Gustav Klimt</u> and the movement he was associated with – the <u>Vienna Secession.</u>

Aims

I want to find out:

- what his work was about
- how he influenced symbolist painters
- his influence on artists today

Objectives

In weeks 1–2:

- I will research from primary sources by making at least one visit to a gallery or museum.
- I will draw directly from Klimt's paintings, to visually record his use of subject and formal elements.
- I will support this by researching using secondary sources, i.e. in libraries and recognised gallery/museum websites.

In weeks 3–5:

- I will develop my visual analysis of Klimt's work by evaluating his use of formal elements and visual language through making studies of his work.
- I will use studio sessions to write up what I have found and to reflect on what I have learned.
- I will research web-based/printed articles and writings about his work, and make links between his work and the work of others.

 Clearly state your aims before you start.

 Objectives are the steps you take to achieve your aims.

 Think carefully about timescales.

When you choose your self-selected practitioner for your set task, ensure that they are internationally recognised, and that there is sufficient scope to carry out your research into them. Include this in your planning.

 You won't be able to progress your study if the practitioner is hard to research and you can't find information on them.

Now try this

Outline a plan for research into an artist or designer of your choice.

Annotating imagery

If you have to visually analyse two pieces of work, one from each of two practitioners you are investigating, you can use annotation to help you deconstruct imagery and show your personal views.

Sample notes extract

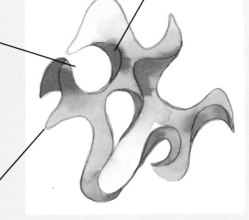

Single red colour emphasises form; red is bright and clear, solid colour gives modern feel.

Cellular forms are constructed using organic shapes.

There are internal and external shapes in the piece – the external shapes flow into the surrounding area and make use of negative space to create a visual effect.

This links in with the artist's exploration of form and construction techniques and explores the potential in making techniques, ceramics, slip casting.

Annotate by adding arrows to relevant sections and labels which include a description of formal elements and your analysis. The annotations here identify the overall composition and components in the image.

You can also analyse elements such as colour by making small colour studies of the image. Drawing an image may help you understand it better. Annotating can tell you how an image is constructed.

Use the correct terminology – this will ensure you communicate your response to the set task in the correct language.

Check the Pearson website

Find the most up-to-date **Sample Assessment Material** and **Mark Scheme** to get an indication of the structure of your actual assessed task and what this requires of you. The details of the actual assessed task may change so always make sure you are up to date.

Use it how you want

Try out different ways of annotating during your research. Discover which ones work best for you. For example, lay tracing paper over an image and trace the outlines of the main elements in the picture – this will give you a diagram that shows how the composition is constructed.

You can then make notes about the types of materials, techniques and processes that have been used. You can go on to use what you have learned about visual work as you develop your conclusions in draft. This is all part of the process of visual analysis.

Now try this

Take one of the images you are researching and use different recording techniques to highlight key visual components and annotate these using correct terminology.

Organising your notes

Organising your research and gathering information carefully will help you to use it in an assessment task.

Sample notes extract

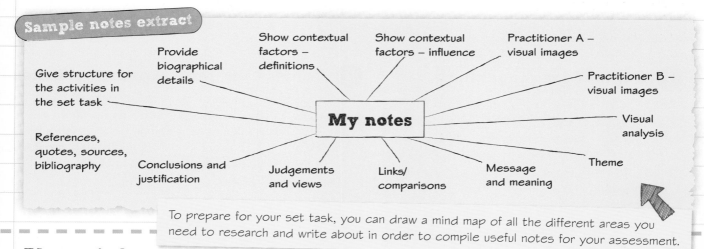

Give structure for the activities in the set task

Provide biographical details

Show contextual factors – definitions

Show contextual factors – influence

Practitioner A – visual images

Practitioner B – visual images

Visual analysis

My notes

References, quotes, sources, bibliography

Conclusions and justification

Judgements and views

Links/ comparisons

Message and meaning

Theme

To prepare for your set task, you can draw a mind map of all the different areas you need to research and write about in order to compile useful notes for your assessment.

Plan or index

Use an index to give your responses a structure – this will help you organise the information you gather.

Sample notes extract

Index

Any preparatory work for set task activities

Practitioner A and Practitioner B

Theme

Research sources

Contextual factors

Contextual influences

Comparisons and links

Visual analysis

Message and meaning

References/sources/Bibliography

Judgements

Conclusions

Drafts and write ups, and notes

Practice drafts for tasks

Be organised and manage carefully any research time that you may be given.

Produce a clear plan or index and use it to organise your information based on the key aspects of your research – this will help you structure your research as you develop it.

Sample notes extract

I've organised my notes as bullet points which are under headings. I can use the notes I have about visual analysis and contextual influences in part of the set task. I have picked out the main influences on both practitioners and made comparisons between them. I have made good notes about the image I am selecting for the practitioner in the paper. I still need to come up with another image for my self-selected practitioner – this is on my to-do list. I've got an idea as to how I can present the writing, and explain my conclusions. I've made notes on the kind of language used, which I have filed.

It's good practice to reflect on your organisation and notes. You need to do this on a regular basis. It's a good way of making sure you are organising information properly and identifying what needs to be done. This type of regular review of progress should be carried out as often as possible.

This learner has already identified the way to approach their tasks – be sure you understand the activities in the assessment as the emphasis in each one is likely to be different.

'To-do' lists are a good way of keeping ahead of tasks.

Now try this

Make an initial plan for organising your notes on a practitioner. You could draw a mind map or compile an index.

Developing content – vocational scenarios

You need to become skilled in researching and generating copy which can be used in an art and design context or vocational scenario.

1 Content for magazines

Reviewers and writers use research to inform their writing in art and design journals. The articles might be:

- reviews of exhibitions
- case studies
- interviews
- historical or contemporary studies.

2 Content for practitioners' websites

Practitioners use research to provide factual information on their websites – this can be about some of the contextual influences on their work, or about the work of a fellow practitioner. It might also provide supporting justification for the ideas in their work.

Practitioners' websites vary in the balance of visual and textual information they show.

3 Leaflets and exhibition graphics

Leaflets and graphics in exhibitions can show:

- themes or ideas that link the practitioners shown together
- biographical information
- description of techniques
- information about historical or contemporary movements
- how the works on display are linked, for example through subject, treatment, use of materials, techniques and processes.

Information helps visitors understand and enjoy exhibitions.

4 Interactive and online guides

Many galleries, events or trade fairs use interactive guides for visitors. The information must be user friendly, present the main points, ideas and themes, provide directions and offer users the opportunity to explore the information in different ways.

5 Pitches, proposals, personal statements and briefs

Use research to support information about work when pitching for exhibitions, commissions or entering competitions. You will need to write detailed copy when proposing a new work or exhibition.

Most competitions or exhibitions that are open to artists and designers will require an in-depth personal statement.

Commissions for clients also require clear written briefs to keep a project on track.

6 Preparing for interviews

Artists and designers ordinarily prepare for an interview through methodical research into their own practice by contextualising it and by researching the company or organisation conducting the interview.

Links Personal statements are explored in depth on page 53.

Now try this

You have been asked to produce the copy for a short leaflet advertising the launch of a new photography exhibition. List five important pieces of information you might need to include.

Developing content – personal statements

Personal statements are a tool to support career progression. They are used by practitioners to explain the ideas, influences and creative intention in their work.

Purpose

Personal statements are designed to communicate a practitioner's reasoning and methodology. They are sometimes called 'statements of intent'. They can provide clues and references for the reader to gain an insight into what the work is about. Where visual work is deliberately open to different interpretations, personal statements can act as a bridge between the viewer and the work.

> Artists' statements can include images – in this extract, the statement is outlining the ideas behind a suite of drawings.

CONVERSATIONS

This was both our first project and probably the project that has taken the longest time to execute, as we are learning how to trust each other and to exchange drawings and work on them. The project began in earnest as a series of musical compositions, that is, CD anthologies of swapped tracks – lined up in as effective a mode as we could orchestrate. We made many CDs, but the drawings come out of two eighteen-track compilations that we then used to stimulate our drawing conversations. 'Time past' and 'the movement of time' have been revisited in many of the drawings and often harnessed metaphorically through water-related imagery. Chance events in the drawings often elevate a slice of time that can subsequently just as easily be erased or reactivated, in order to foster fresh consideration. Sounds, words, nuances and expressions in the music acted as triggers for memory and drawing dialogue that meant the imagery often evolved in unexpected ways.

The project began initially with a *seven-drawings per song* format, but subsequently we found that we could form our responses in four. There was no logic to this other than a visual and intuitive logic; in effect, the evolution of making decided the final strategy. On completion of all the drawings, we began the arduous task of grouping the different sets of four and exploring the nature of what format to use. The drawings were chosen to be together, based on setting up the most pertinent conversation dynamics between any given set of five; although various alternative formats both more and less than five were also considered. *2010–12, Mixed Drawing Media on torn Saunders Papers, individual drawings 19/20 cm square, complete panels 137 cm h x 105 cm w.*

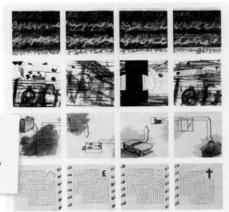

Structure

Personal statements follow a logical sequence.

- Begin with an introduction to the project, body of work, or person.
- Outline details of specific works and methods, as well as ideas and supporting research.
- Include aspects of justification and expression of personal views.
- End with some form of conclusion.

Restrictions and content

Personal statements need to be concise, meet any guidelines for word count and the number of images, and must consider:

- audience needs
- ideas, influences and inspirations
- relevant details about production, e.g. materials, techniques and processes
- practical aspects, e.g. consideration of budget
- description and evaluation of the outcome
- key visual aspects, use of colour, scale, etc.

Career progression

Personal statements are an integral part of applications for work and the interview process. The depth of information required will vary according to the purpose. Students in creative subjects usually have to provide personal statements as part of their application for further study.

Now try this

Imagine you have to write a short personal statement about a project you have recently worked on. List what type of information it should contain.

> Remember that a personal statement can contain images.

Developing content – analysis

Analysis is used in vocational contexts to explain, justify, support content, and educate viewers and users. It forms a key aspect of this unit.

Defining analysis

Analysis is used at different stages of creating a work. Where a practitioner is researching a brief or subject, they may research previous examples where others have tackled the same theme. The results of this analysis can then inform the direction they take in their own work. This is often presented as information on practitioners' websites.

Galleries and museums will have online guides for exhibitions that use analysis to inform the viewer about the exhibits.

Analysis as a tool

Analysis is used to deconstruct art and design, and to look at the underlying themes and ideas in visual work. Analysis is an important aspect of the viewer's response in conceptual art. The work can require 'decoding' – the viewer has to 'unlock' the meaning, idea or message using their own analysis techniques.

Artists' and designers' statements often contain elements of self-analysis to point the viewer towards an informed reading of the work.

What does analysis look like?

Analysis is in action when explanations are provided, and when individual work and themes are being broken down – taken apart or deconstructed – to show the ideas behind them. You will see this in:

- descriptions of visual work and the ideas behind them
- introductions to exhibitions
- proposals for commissions and competitions
- statements of intent
- justifications of working methods, and selection of techniques and materials for production.

Developing analysis

Analysis is often presented as a series of facts supported by quotes or accepted statements, which are then used as a basis for the critic, reviewer or practitioner to develop their own viewpoint about themes and visual work.

When to analyse

Analysis has to become a part of what you do when working on this unit. You will need to apply it when you are:

- ✓ looking at influences on practitioners
- ✓ looking at specific examples of work
- ✓ comparing different practitioners
- ✓ explaining a theme
- ✓ reaching your conclusions.

Now try this

Visit the website of a well-known museum or gallery, for example the V&A Museum, and identify places where you can see analysis being used to explain examples of work.

Developing content – presenting text and images

Vocational applications use images and text differently according to their purpose. So an interactive website will use a different approach from that of an information leaflet.

Making images work

Images have to be selected carefully so that they make best use of the available space and budget. The balance of image to text will vary according to the purpose of the context. An online gallery will generally contain a lot of images, whereas an exhibition plan or magazine article will probably use fewer images.

Image selection

Images will generally be selected to:

☑ represent the practitioner's work and be the strongest example of a practitioner's style or subject matter

☑ show the practitioner's methods and production techniques

☑ support a viewpoint being discussed or written about.

Websites

Websites can allow for some user interaction, for instance zooming in on images and varying the viewing of pages according to the user's preference. Some websites have galleries and separate pages with information about the work; others have images and information displayed on the same page or screen.

See how writing is used to provide information on websites, and the way the viewer's journey through the site is structured, for example with headings.

Sequences

Information is often presented sequentially. Where a practitioner's work is being reviewed or shown in series (e.g. in an exhibition or retrospective) the sequence will be chronologically arranged. Where more than one practitioner's work is being compared or reviewed, sub-headings may be used to structure the information across all the practitioners, for example:

- influences
- working methodology
- subject matter.

Telling the story

Sometimes information is used to explain the journey of a piece of work or set of related works. Sometimes the progress of individual sets of works are shown and discussed. This is particularly true of pitches to clients and proposals.

 There is more on sketchbooks on page 44.

Sketchbooks can show the development of ideas.

Now try this

Choose a journal, website or leaflet. Analyse how the images and text support each other and how they have been used to present the information in the most effective way.

Developing content – information

Information is a key element of content. You can use it to put a practitioner's work into context, explain ideas and themes, and justify conclusions.

How is information used?

Information should show the key ideas and influences on an artist's life, and how their work relates to themes. It can also be used to support descriptions and analysis of key works.

Information provides a structure and context, and can be used in art and design publications, such as journals.

Accuracy

Information about specific contextual influences must be researched before it is used in vocational scenarios. Ensure that any information you present as a fact, such as the list of influences on a practitioner's work, is correct.

Leaflets and exhibition catalogues will often present a lot of factual information about exhibitors, movements, etc. and it must be accurate. Writers and contributors will always check their sources.

Headings

Headings and sub-headings can focus the reader or viewer's attention on specific areas and provide a recognisable structure for a piece of information. Useful headings might include:
- ✓ Influences
- ✓ Audience
- ✓ Materials and processes
- ✓ Themes and ideas
- ✓ Conclusions
- ✓ References and sources

Personal views

Some readings of practitioners' works – and the influences in them – may be a personal view or interpretation by the writer.

However, information can support personal views, readings of the work, and explanations. It can also inform conclusions about the work, for example using direct quotations. The specific context will dictate the amount of information and how it is presented alongside personal views.

Fact versus opinion

Some information used in vocational contexts is factual and some is opinion.

✓ Where information is an opinion, it can still be used as long as the writer or author of the opinion is clearly referenced.

✓ If a practitioner's work is deliberately ambiguous, the researcher has to make clear that the information they present on themes of the work is their own opinion.

✓ Writers will use words like 'may' rather than 'is', and phrases like 'could be interpreted as...'.

Now try this

Suggest five sources of information you might use if you were going to write a short article for a journal about an artist and the early influences on their work.

Contextual influences – themes

Practitioners are influenced by a variety of contextual factors, including themes which might be found in literature, developments in science, environmental issues – and many other spheres.

Messages in themes

A theme can provoke ideas or topics that pervade and recur in the work. Practitioners explore themes through their work; they develop ideas and communicate messages that are often intensely personal in response to themes. These themes then dictate the direction for their work, as well as providing visual stimulus for future ideas and imagery.

Themes can be explored through a body of work or a series of related images.

The notes opposite are one learner's initial response to a piece of art by Richard Billingham, *Untitled (RAL 28)*, *Ray's a laugh*, Colour print on aluminium. The learner explores how Billingham has approached the theme of realism in his work, and is using one image to begin their analysis.

You can see this image on the internet by searching for 'Richard Billingham Ray's a laugh' and finding the photo where a cat appears to have been thrown in the air.

Sample notes extract

Theme: Realism

- Richard Billingham uses documentary photography to record aspects of the everyday life of his family in his book 'Ray's a laugh', 1995.

- Billingham's themes – based around the nature of his family, and also a study of the reality of working-class life in the UK at this time.

- In this image the chaotic nature of the family home is shown through the main character – Ray – how he treats his home and the people in it.

- The bottle of alcohol on the left hand side + the expression on Ray's face + the fact that he seems to have just thrown a cat across the room, invite us to consider if he is under the influence of alcohol.

- All adds to the way the image shows an everyday scene with dysfunctional characters.

- Image also has a surrealist twist – does the way the cat is caught in mid air reference the image by Dali?

Interpreting themes

Many works that explore themes also bring the viewer's response into the equation. When we look at images like the one explored above, how do we react? Are we being encouraged to pry voyeuristically into the lives of others?

Some works have multiple themes and communicate more than one idea; the viewer is encouraged to reach their own conclusions about these. Artists' statements can provide information and pointers about their work and the themes they are exploring.

Remember

✓ When interpreting themes there may be more than one 'correct' reading.

✓ You as the viewer may be encouraged to reach your own viewpoint.

✓ There may be visual codes in the work that you can compare with other work.

✓ Themes can overlap – think about cultural identity and realism.

 Links For more on analysis and viewpoints see page 89.

For more on analysis and viewpoints see page 89.

Now try this

Think of a theme you would like to explore in an art and design context. What is it about this theme that interests you?

Contextual influences – culture

Practitioners use different aspects of contemporary culture as a basis to develop their ideas and work. For example, fashion and film can be a source of inspiration.

Imagery

Referencing culture is one of the ways practitioners reflect their own lives and aspirations as well as commenting on society. Fine artists can reference culture through the images and subjects in their work. Designers will often take a key visual motif or code from a cultural idiom and use it in their imagery to invigorate their work.

This garment represents Gaultier's ideas about challenging female and male stereotypes in dress. It references power dressing as well as the contemporary music scene in the figure of Grace Jones, whose music and public image as a powerful and challenging woman were designed to confront viewers. Gaultier is bringing together fashion and music – taking inspiration for visual work from a different aspect of culture.

Jean-Paul Gaultier, Look 1, Spring collection, 2013.

The self

Artists and designers may use the idea of the self in their work, reflecting their own cultural identity, and its constraints and characteristics. They might explore ideas about place, race, family, nationality, sexuality and personality through their use of subjects that resonate with cultures or across cultures.

Daily life in Athens, 2016.
In this photo of a record shop, there are two examples of album covers on the left where artists have been involved in the design and imagery – can you identify the covers and artists involved?

Some practitioners become involved in the branding and personality of musicians and their work, while others can be further involved through an active engagement with aspects of live performance, such as Jamie Hewlett and his work with the Gorillaz project. There is always the potential for art and design, fashion, music technology and so on to overlap in cases like this – the work isn't only seen in museums and galleries.

Culture as comment

Art and design work can celebrate cultural ideas as well as criticise them. Practitioners can use their visual work to bring to life aspects of their culture in a positive way as well as highlighting negative aspects of culture.

More than one source of inspiration

Contextual factors can overlap – it is unlikely there will be one single influence on a piece of art and design work. This is particularly the case with contemporary work, where we are exposed to a wealth of information and visuals, all of which can act as inspiration.

Now try this

Select one example of art and design that you feel references specific cultural influences or ideas, and describe these.

Contextual influences – embracing technology

Historically, technology has offered artists and designers the chance to break traditions and to work in new ways. Comparing these with traditional works and understanding how they were received at the time provides insight into how art and design has evolved.

The effects of technology

Practitioners have responded to the potential offered by advances in technology in different ways. The Impressionists were able to take painting outside their studios and into landscapes when tin tubes of paint were invented. The development of acrylic paint – primarily for exterior murals in the 1930s – allowed artists to work with political themes on a grand scale.

During the advent of photography and its embrace by artists and designers, there was a fear that it would replace painting. Looking at art history shows how painting evolved to become less about literal representation of the world, which enabled abstraction and expressionism among other movements. Photographers and artists used photography as the medium to record and document the unfolding dramas and events in the 20th century. In this example, *Migrant Mother*, by Dorothea Lange, 1936, photography is used to record the hardships of a mother and family in the Great Depression with unflinching clarity.

Exploring technology

Some practitioners have seized the potential to explore technology in producing their artwork. Designers have embraced computer-led technologies across fields such as graphic design, photography, moving image and animation. Technology is a powerful aspect of contemporary practice – think about its use in commercial photography, animation and filmmaking.

Interactive designers harness technology to provide users with experiences in commerce and entertainment.

Design which uses technology will still harness the potential of formal elements and visual language, e.g. as in the use of perspective, shape and colour in this design.

Audience needs

Designers use the potential in new technology to develop their products to meet audience expectations and needs. Technology is ever evolving, so the opportunity offered for innovation in art and design seems endless. Examples of new technology used by practitioners are visible across all aspects of contemporary practice, from fine art to interactive games design.

Now try this

Write a short paragraph explaining how the advent of a new technology enabled one of the following: Andy Warhol; Bill Viola; Nam June Paik.

Contextual influence of politics and society

Historically, art and design has been highly influenced by the politics of the time and by social conventions.

Politics and society

Art and design can be used as a political or social tool and it is important to understand the links between the work and the politics of the time. Artists and designers who work for the state, large organisations or companies will inevitably be influenced by the pressures of these institutions. While much of this appears historical, illustrations of political use of design can be seen in patriotic presidential campaigning, for example. When you analyse work, you should ask who created it and consider:

- Does the work have any political or social intentions?
- Has politics or society changed since the work was created?

Soviet propaganda was political and social, presenting ideas through bold and simple compositions, which have had a huge influence on art movements such as constructivism.

Propaganda

Propaganda has been used by almost all political parties in history, especially when trying to influence society to commit to their changes and proposals, whether they are revolutionary, social or military.

Propaganda can take many different forms beyond posters. For example it has been reflected in architecture, film, theatre, events, literature, music, painting, murals and sculpture among other creative forms.

Benito Mussolini, leader of Italy between 1922 and 1945, constructed the Palazzo della Civiltà Italiana, a huge complex of buildings celebrating his fascist ideals in architectural form.

Influence

Instances of creative work used to inform or persuade society are all around us. On television there are social awareness adverts about drink driving or diseases. In public places there are monuments to historical events and figures. It is important to remember that art and design can be used to influence and change people's behaviour.

Art and design in society

The state is also involved in areas of design that try to serve the community. An important example is Harry Beck's famous London Underground map from 1933, which still influences graphic design and the arts today.

Now try this

Research one political poster and make notes on the contextual influences on the practitioner.

Contextual influences – reaction to politics and society

Artists and designers frequently use art and design as a means to react to the status quo within politics and society.

Imagery

Practitioners have used images from politics and society to communicate their ideas – in doing so, they often force the viewer to consider and sometimes rethink their own understanding of society.

Practitioners will often take an image (appropriate it) and use it in a different way.

This can create tension between its original purpose and the practitioner's idea.

Find out background information (factual or biographical details) about the image and the practitioner – this will help you understand their ideas in more detail.

Andy Warhol, Ads: Van Heusen (Ronald Reagan) (1985)
© The Andy Warhol Foundation for the Visual Arts, Inc. /
DACS/Artimage 2018.

Sample notes extract

- Ronald Reagan by Andy Warhol – uses technique of placing an advertisement image as the central subject, in this case the then President Ronald Reagan (advertised products in print-based advertising in the 1950s and was a B-movie actor in Hollywood).

- Warhol attracted to the world proposed by advertising – 'of the moment' as well as more 'perfect' than the real world, a make-believe world where everything was glamorous.

- Warhol explored obsession with celebrity culture in similar images – another theme in his work, and again one that references contemporary culture – in the society of his time (and today) there was/is an obsession with celebrity culture.

- A recent example of this approach = the Shepard Fairey image of Barack Obama in the 'HOPE' printed stencil series.

- Made this image because he believed Obama's 'power and sincerity as a speaker would create a positive association with his likeness'.

- He added the word 'Hope' to reinforce this – other versions use the words 'Change' or 'Progress'.

- Emerged in the 2016 presidential campaign, sometimes with negative overtones.

Shepard Fairey

☑ Fairey was a street artist, illustrator and activist at the time of making his poster 'Hope, Printed stencil poster, 2008'.

☑ It depicted the then American presidential candidate Barack Obama.

☑ It was originally handmade in a small-scale operation and was eventually adopted by the official presidential campaign.

Now try this

In a short paragraph, explain how one of the following contemporary artists has tried to respond to politics or society: Ai Weiwei or Guerrilla Girls.

Explaining themes and ideas

When researching a practitioner, you should explain how they address the theme and ideas you are exploring.

Start with the facts

✓ Gather information, quotes and views about the practitioner and the theme. You can use them to support your own views.

✓ Make sure you record all your sources.

✓ Trawl through their writings or comments and find any direct mention of the theme.

✓ If so, use this as a reference point. If not, are you looking in the right place or at the right work?

✓ Refer to any image you are given in the set task brief – it's likely to be a source of information which you must use.

Building your explanation

✓ Develop your explanation in bullet points.

✓ Make lists of key works, formal elements, visual communication, how they have used processes, and so on.

✓ Start linking the theme and the practitioner – how have they done this? Is it via subject matter, formal elements and/or visual language?

✓ Develop by using appropriate terminology.

Sample notes extract

- Aim = develop my analysis and reading of the themes and ideas in the work I have researched.
- See photograph by the artist Richard Billingham showing two people eating dinner on a sofa (series of photographs entitled 'Ray's a Laugh') – shows an image of daily life with uncompromising, gritty realism.
- Image hints at dysfunctional nature of the people. Use analysis to explain how this has been done, supported with researched information – looking at the way formal elements are used, and visual language, in this image composition especially.
- My analysis contains personal views – I'm interpreting the image and its meanings.
- Working through techniques in analysis I've covered earlier to deconstruct the image.

Initial analysis points – in the image Billingham shows:

- family members eating in a very separate, disconnected way
- family members not sharing the meal, but being involved in their own worlds, distraction
- separateness reinforced by composition – picture is literally split down the middle, a gap between them
- the meal – precarious, balanced on laps
- type of TV dinner – people don't interact, instead rely on TV to be focal point
- a sense of grime and unhappiness
- some aspects of the dysfunction in this series of images.

A visitor to a gallery viewing a video by the shortlisted Turner Prize artist Richard Billingham in 2001. (A series of Billingham's photographs, 'Ray's a Laugh', was published in 2000.)

This learner:

- has started by isolating the main points read in the image
- is using points rather than connected sentences
- is showing they have recognised the subject matter, theme and compositional devices.

They are also relating this to wider cultural aspects connected with perceptions of 'dysfunction'.

Think ahead – if explaining your choice of practitioners in relation to the theme, it's important to get to grips with what it means early in your research.

Now try this

Find another image that interests you and use this technique to start developing your explanation of its theme/s.

Using bullet points to 'get going' is a useful way of getting over the 'blank page' feeling.

Explaining contextual influences – compiling notes

Explain how contextual factors have influenced the practitioners you have researched. Begin your research by compiling notes.

Sample notes extract

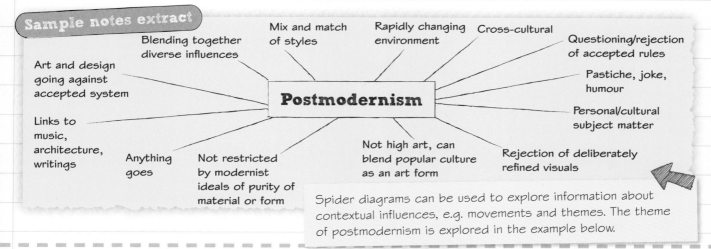

Blending together diverse influences

Mix and match of styles

Rapidly changing environment

Cross-cultural

Questioning/rejection of accepted rules

Art and design going against accepted system

Pastiche, joke, humour

Postmodernism

Personal/cultural subject matter

Links to music, architecture, writings

Anything goes

Not restricted by modernist ideals of purity of material or form

Not high art, can blend popular culture as an art form

Rejection of deliberately refined visuals

Spider diagrams can be used to explore information about contextual influences, e.g. movements and themes. The theme of postmodernism is explored in the example below.

List the factors

- Break down the influence into component factors or sub-headings. These can help you start to develop your explanation.
- Visual diagrams are a great way to start this – they enable you to see the different aspects together.
- You can also draw arrows or chains across from one box to another if you think they are linked in some way.
- It can be easier to see how factors interrelate if it's done visually.

Start by listing the sub-headings or factors and see if they have individually influenced the practitioner.

Not all the headings will necessarily apply to all the practitioners you look at, or to the same degree – this will really depend on the theme and the practitioner – it's up to you to find, record and justify it.

Remember that you will be carrying out most of your contextual analysis during any preparation, so it's a good idea to get thinking about this as early as possible.

Linking the factors

Sample notes extract

Link specific factors to the influence they have on graphic design (my specialist pathway) + research practitioners in this field. Initial points:

Visual elements: mix and match of styles: graphic designers could combine different elements traditionally associated with 'set' rules or constraints, i.e. typefaces with certain associations used alongside imagery that just didn't fit.

Anything goes: the idea of rules in design broken up – e.g. article on Bryan Ferry where David Carson reproduced the text in Zapf Dingbats symbols so was completely illegible. (Carson – article so boring couldn't see the point in anyone reading it – so in his own way made sure that at the time no-one could.)

Humour: links with idea of humour as valid element in post-modern design – where 'seriousness' of high design can be replaced by more irreverent set of ideas.

As part of your assessment, you may need to prepare copy, e.g. for an information guide or leaflet. You will need to understand how the writing will work, but you may not need to produce layouts, columns, artworks, photos, etc.

Now try this

Select a contextual factor, e.g. recession or religion, and develop a spider diagram showing the different ways it might influence practitioners.

Explaining contextual influences – practise writing copy

Once you have outlined how contextual factors have influenced the practitioners you are researching, you can practise expanding your notes and building up copy. Practising like this will help you when you come to expand any notes you are allowed to take into your set task.

Sample notes extract

<u>Postmodernism – influences on graphic designers – summary of my main points</u>

Postmodernism allowed graphic designers to move away from accepted ideas on legibility and content. Some designers became deliberately provocative by questioning whether legibility was even a requirement for this field – see Carson and to a lesser degree Brody. This allowed them greater freedom in their work, and they created images that were startling because they looked more like fine art pieces than graphic communication that was meant to be consumed by its audience. The whole idea of legible, informative writing and copy was pushed to one side in favour of a compositional and design ethos that allowed them to put text and image in their layouts where they wanted to.

 Get used to developing your explanation – pick a factor and summarise the main points on how it has influenced this particular field.

 You can say how the influence has affected aspects of working practice directly.

 Use two practitioners to highlight and reference examples of this in practice – developing the explanation to show a justification in the way the two designers saw what they were doing.

 The phrase 'compositional and design ethos' covers a lot of ground – so needs breaking down as the explanation really develops.

 The statements are written clearly, and would form a sound basis from which to develop content that was more in-depth.

Although it's in a summary form, the copy does sum up how the influence has affected this field.

What does the message say about the influence?

Many practitioners respond to influences by tackling them head on in their work – they become the subject. This can form their response to the influence, and may be positive or negative.

Choose your second practitioner wisely

In your supervised assessment you may be asked to identify and explain the importance of specific contextual influences on practitioners. If you have to select a practitioner from any given options (plus another practitioner of your own choice) make sure you can research the contextual influences they have responded to. The influences on their work will vary and the effects may not always be obvious.

Now try this

Select a contextual factor, and write a paragraph, using full sentences and appropriate terminology, explaining how this factor might influence practitioners.

Contextual factors – form and style

Practitioners can use form and style to communicate their contexts and historical influences.

Form

You should understand 'form' as including all artwork and even less tangible forms such as sound or performance. The term has continually evolved as new practices within art and design have been adopted. When you research practitioners you need to make explicit links between the forms artists use and what this communicates about society and history.

Practitioners will often use multiple forms together to communicate about contexts and issues. For example, many modernist practitioners combine materials from different areas of culture, such as Kurt Schwitters who combined found photographs with text from different sources. The text takes on new meanings by being combined, while still suggesting references to its original context.

Kurt Schwitters, *It's Terrific!* (1944) © DACS 2018.
Photo © Christie's Images / Bridgeman Images

Kurt Schwitters, *It's Terrific!*, 1944.

Sample notes extract

Grayson Perry, The Rosetta Vase, 2011

- Image = vase that references a classical pottery form.
- Methods used to apply the imagery are also traditional, but style of images is not classical.
- Themes within illustrations are contemporary and relate to modern living and modern issues. Grayson Perry is juxtaposing multiple contexts to communicate new meaning and in innovative way, but through references to different contexts.
- Use of coloured glazes – bright yellow background and modern phrases painted in way that reference a historical feel – give tension and quirkiness asking viewer to consider it in detail.
- Perry exploring themes common in other pieces – humour, identity, importance of cultural references + juxtaposition.
- Themes amplified and presented using formal elements and visual language – can be identified pictorially through visual analysis.
- Perry has linked influences on his work to themes he explores = visual devices, motifs and imagery he uses to present and communicate them.

Use the internet to research Grayson Perry's *Rosetta Vase*. Study the images you find in relation to what this learner has written about it.

Style

Artists and designers will often reference a style or multiple styles from history within their work. When contextualising, you need to be aware of how and why these are being used and what they are trying to communicate. Sometimes the style will simply be the actual style of the era that is influencing the artist. Historically, it may have been difficult for practitioners to escape the trend or look of a style of working. More recently in modern art, the practitioner may be making a comment about the style, such as rebelling or reinterpreting it. Style can be separated from the form of work in that artists and designers may apply a style using a form that is not normally associated with it. For example, Jeff Koons creates sculptures that reference the style of balloon sculptures for children, but these are actually made of metal.

Now try this

Choose another piece by Grayson Perry and summarise in bullets the contextual factors it references by the form and style.

Contextual factors – time and place

Many practitioners respond to contextual factors from a unique time and place.

Time/era and place

Time and place are often connected. Think about the influences of specific geographic locations and cities in the work of certain movements: the different Bauhaus schools, the Impressionists and the abstract expressionists. It is not only the location but what is happening there. For example, Paris in the 1850s and 1860s was being redefined by the civic planner Haussmann, with wide boulevards, great sweeping structures and interrelated civic spaces. It felt new and modern, and attracted creative people who saw Paris as the centre of a new, modern way of life including writers, intellectuals, scientists, engineers, poets, painters, designers and businesses. When the Impressionists started to paint the urban spaces where they worked, they were reflecting this excitement.

Tim Noble and Sue Webster, *Dirty White Trash (with Gulls)*, 1998.

A record of reality

Practitioners in painting, photography and film have recorded moments of great crisis and drama in their work. This sense of recording reality rather than legend or fable became central to much 20th century art and design work: practitioners saw it almost as their duty to record and show reality as it was.

Responding to the zeitgeist

The image above, *Dirty White Trash (with Gulls)*, is made by a pair of artists who belonged to the Young British Artists or YBAs of the late 1980s and 1990s. Practitioners in this group responded to the challenge of making their art and design by using what some described as shock tactics, and the leftovers or rubbish from everyday life as raw materials. Their work seemed to fit with the emergence of a new and more upbeat political movement in the UK at that time.

The moment itself

Time itself became a subject for some practitioners as they tried to explore actions or temporary events and move away from the idea of lasting artwork. Examples included Yves Klein's *Anthropometry* from the 1960s which used performing bodies to paint canvases, or Richard Long's 1967 *A Line Made by Walking*, where the artist simply made a line in the grass by walking. Both of these focused on the event rather than a lasting outcome.

A sense of era

The moment can relate to an **era** and there may be other contextual factors including:
- ☑ conflict
- ☑ political change
- ☑ cultural changes
- ☑ stability
- ☑ technological advances.

Now try this

Describe three factors that influence your practical work that are unique to this time.

Contextual factors – reacting to technology

Practitioners may respond to technological advances and question their impact on society.

Relationship with technology

Practitioners can make social comments about how technology changes our behaviour in powerful ways. Look at why a practitioner has used that particular piece of technology and the context within which it is normally used. Sometimes it is, or has been, used socially or commercially, or for entertainment, security, military or other reasons. The context provides important information about the work. Practitioners often question the ethics surrounding the use of technology because it is always developing and often exploited by commercial and political forces.

Rafael Lozano-Hemmer, 'Zoom Pavilion' (2015), Art Basel Unlimited, Basel Swizerland, 2016 © Rafael Lozano-Hemmer. Photo by: Sebatiano Pellion

In his 2015 installation, *Zoom Pavilion*, the artist Rafael Lozano-Hemmer uses technology usually associated with computerised surveillance equipment. Robotic cameras use face recognition to focus on individuals, zooming in and creating a piece where their faces become the subject. This uses technology to provoke questions about our relationship with technology that is used for surveillance.

Technology over time

Things that are taken for granted now may have had significant influence in the past. When researching the influence of technology on practitioners, make sure you understand how it affected them at that time.

Rejecting technology

Some practitioners choose to ignore technology, returning to more craft-based or 'hand-made' ways of working. Look at the technological context within which this has taken place historically: for example the Arts and Crafts movement in the early twentieth century was a rejection of the industrial revolution taking place at that time.

Pastiche and context

Some work might seem to fully embrace a type of technology but may be subversive in its use. For example, Andy Warhol used mechanical print reproduction techniques to make artworks that would at first appear like a celebration of commercial technology. Warhol even had a studio to produce work that was called The Factory. However, in context, the artworks provoke questions about the influence of commercial technology on our day-to-day lives.

Now try this

Identify five technological influences today; rank them according to how important you think they are, with number 1 being the most influential.

Key works – visual language and themes

A key work exemplifies the approach of a practitioner and has become associated with their style over time.

Key works

Key works are representative examples of a practitioner's work, in terms of:

- themes and imagery
- materials
- techniques
- processes
- formal elements
- visual language and style.

 Links Formal elements will be explored on pages 71–73.

They are often used to explain a body of work, or referred to when reaching a conclusion about a practitioner.

Chair B3

This piece uses aspects of visual language to communicate themes – in this case the form in the piece is directly related to the functionality of the piece. There are a series of angles and planes that show the geometric influence in the design idea. Breuer was inspired by the lightness and manufacture of a bicycle he had, and this influenced his use of tubular steel frames in furniture. The design is refined – there isn't any carving or arbitrary surface decoration to detract from this.

The Model B3 chair designed by Marcel Breuer in 1926 and manufactured by Standard-Möbel, Lengyel & Co., Berlin.

Identifying characteristics

There is often more than one reason or justification for calling work 'key'. When you look at examples, analyse the visual characteristics – you can do this through annotating/making notes.

Analysing visual language and themes

Practitioners and exhibition organisers sometimes use artists' and designers' statements to highlight themes in their work. Researching themes allows you to gain a deeper understanding of the ideas practitioners are communicating.

How does it fit?

Think about a key work that shows the development of a new way of working – Pablo Picasso's *Les Demoiselles d'Avignon*, 1907, is considered a key work, as it brought his experimentations with cubism, African art and his own personal vocabulary to a conclusion and opened the way for other work. When identifying key works, research why they are considered key.

Why is it key?

Works may be key for a number of reasons. They may:

- ☑ mark the beginning or the end of a style, period or process
- ☑ bring the practitioner's explorations and visual enquiry to a conclusion
- ☑ sum up a practitioner's style or output
- ☑ be a break with tradition
- ☑ be innovative.

Now try this

Select one work that you think can be called 'key' for Damien Hirst or a practitioner you have studied, and state three reasons why.

Key works – materials, techniques and processes

Looking at the materials, techniques and processes that practitioners have used in their key works can give you an insight into the themes they are exploring.

Materials

Key works may display an innovative approach to materials, possibly linked to the form or the function of the piece. In Breuer's Model 3B chair, the materials and their application provide the visual dynamics of the piece.

Processes

You might research a range of sources to find out about processes. Some practitioners explain the ways they work in detail; others leave the viewer to work it out. You could explore:

- how physical resources are used and developed
- the technologies used to create a piece
- the mechanical processes used to develop work
- combinations of different processes – drawing and print, photography and paint, digital and analogue.

You may be able to email practitioners to request information on their processes.

This detail of the Breuer chair shows the use of line in the tubular steel frames of the seat and back, and these create strong open shapes – the interior of the chair is as visible as the outer.

Techniques

Used when applying materials, and working with processes, techniques can vary across key works. A practitioner's output may contain many different key examples. They may also work across disciplines, exploring a common theme. Research the way techniques have been used – it will vary depending on the pathway or discipline.

Details

Focus on specific details when researching key works. You can make sketches and drawing studies directly from primary sources, as well as photography. If researching aspects such as texture and specific techniques, you could draw and photograph the texture, and make notes about the materials, techniques and processes used to make the work.

Recording your thoughts

You can use a blend of drawings, annotation, photography and research from secondary sources in your analysis and research – record your thoughts using sketchbooks, notebooks, blogs and folders.

 Some recording methods are shown in detail on page 44.

Remember

☑ The use of materials, techniques and processes can dictate the form of a piece.

☑ It is not always obvious how processes have been used.

☑ You can find information in practitioners' statements, or in gallery information.

☑ Regular evaluation and analysis are a key part of this unit – and will help you gain a better understanding of works.

Now try this

Choose a practitioner you have researched and make studies of a key work they have produced, looking in detail at the materials, techniques or processes they have used.

Investigating key works

If you have to analyse an example of a visual work by a practitioner for your set task, choose a key piece which demonstrates their approach to the theme.

Sample notes extract

Recording ideas about key works –
Claes Oldenburg

- Examples of Claes Oldenburg's re-interpretation of household or everyday objects on a different scale, e.g. lipsticks in Piccadilly Circus.

- Looks like postcard showing science fiction towers (sort of homage to consumer culture many pop art practitioners involved in).

- Oldenburg asking questions about what constitutes sculpture – not necessarily accepted works of art, bronze casts, etc., but everyday consumer items.

- Having drawn them, they are interesting shapes and actually work as towers – but always going to be lipsticks.

- Work references aspects of surrealism – scale and juxtaposition of different objects used to show heightened, alternative take on reality.

- Piece could be used as key work to show Oldenburg's concerns and use of visual and tactile devices to communicate his ideas.

- Talking about his practice and those around him Oldenburg said:

'We don't copy the objects, we try to transform them and we hope they go on transforming as you look at them. The idea of a public dialogue … visual dialogue … is very important to us.'

Is it key?

The work you select must exemplify the practitioner. You need to:

- visually analyse the piece
- explain how it is key
- identify the contextual influences on the piece and show how they affected it
- be confident that you can use it effectively
- be sure it references the theme in the set task brief
- double check all of the biographical details about the key work – some websites may contain misleading information.

Don't limit yourself to one image initially – choose a few and gradually narrow this down to the one you will use in the supervised assessment.

This learner uses a combination of drawing and written analysis to look at 'Lipsticks in Piccadilly Circus, London' by Claes Oldenburg (1966).

Well-observed visual examples are used, as well as factual information, supporting quotes and personal views.

The research format is used to develop a more in-depth piece of writing which could be produced in the supervised assessment.

Remember that the key factor of a key work is that it must be representative.

The learner has picked out key quotes by the practitioner to support their investigation.

Now try this

Identify one image from one practitioner that you believe is key, and write a short paragraph, justifying your choice.

Identifying formal elements

Recognising and understanding formal elements is a key aspect of analysing and deconstructing art and design images.

The Black Bow by Georges Seurat (1882–83).

Georges Pierre Seurat, 'The Black Bow' (1882–1883)
Photo © Private Collection/Bridgeman Images

Formal elements

These are:

- tonal values
- colour
- texture
- pattern
- form, shape
- line
- technical details, e.g. measurements, medium, title.

Identifying formal elements

This image by Georges Seurat uses formal elements in a very deliberate way. When deconstructing images, you should begin by describing what you see – sometimes this can seem obvious, but it is a sound introduction and first step in the process. You can use drawing as a tool when deconstructing images.

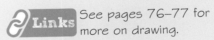 See pages 76–77 for more on drawing.

Visual analysis is a skill that you can practise by looking at other images and identifying the formal elements you can see.

Interrelationships

Formal elements are rarely used in isolation. The different formal elements will often overlap and reinforce each other. In *The Black Bow*, Seurat has used composition to place the figure centrally, and developed a strong relationship between the way light and dark are used, especially around the edges of the figure, to accentuate contrast. Together, the formal elements combine to communicate visually.

 For more on visual analysis, see Unit 7, page 147.

Analysis

Analysis takes time and practice. It's not always obvious what a piece of work might be about, or what the artist or designer is trying to say. By breaking the image down and deconstructing it – identifying its components – you can start to see how it has been made, and gain an insight into the thinking behind the piece. This image could have been made in colour – but the artist has made a deliberate decision not to, and to focus on black and white to explore his ideas about contrast and light.

Now try this

Take a work by a practitioner. Identify and list the formal elements in the piece.

71

Deconstructing formal elements

You can analyse the formal elements a practitioner has chosen to use in more depth by reproducing samples or extracts from their work.

Ben Copperwheat,
Heart Explosions,
printed paper, 2010.

Analysis in action

To deconstruct images you may need to apply your art and design skills. It's useful to be flexible about how you can record your analysis – this example uses drawing to record the specific colours in one of the hearts in the image above.

Detail of *Heart Explosions* recorded by a learner using pastels.

Dig deeper

When deconstructing visual work, be prepared to carry out the same task more than once. In this print, the formal elements are at first glance straightforward enough to see. There are bright colours, shapes and a complex pattern of overlay. Now, look again and revisit those formal elements: can you describe the colours exactly – their hue and saturation?

You can also apply understanding from other units you have studied on your course. Using your knowledge of colour, are the colours harmonious, discordant or neutral? Go beyond the obvious when deconstructing formal elements in order to reach a clear conclusion.

Remember

 Formal elements are often combined.

 You have the potential to refine your deconstruction and make it more in-depth.

 Think about how formal elements can communicate an idea or message – what does the image on this page say to you?

Now try this

Record some of the formal elements in the image above using text and drawn imagery.

Recognising formal elements

Recognising formal elements is an important part of your research. You will be doing this in detail as you prepare for your supervised assessment.

List the elements

- Use your analytical skills to list the elements in the image.
- Some may be immediately recognisable, others less so.
- The elements will certainly overlap – and there may be many, depending on the image.
- Don't worry if your notes mention some of the points shown under visual language on pages 74–77 – again, these will overlap.
- Make basic notes on exactly what you see – you will develop this in more detail through analysis of visual communication.

 Links Remind yourself of the elements you need to study by referring to the list on page 71.

 Links The extract from sample notes below explores the formal elements of the image shown on page 71.

Sample notes extract

Formal elements in *The Black Bow* by Seurat:

- monochrome/black and white
- tonal values – there is some contrast
- texture
- form and shape of the woman.

My study of image by Georges Seurat helps me understand how he has used formal elements in his work.

- Will develop my initial analysis on monochrome and tonal values in more detail – the formal elements that really stand out for me.
- Composition is simple yet powerful – figure placed centrally, with little other detail, focusing attention on her.
- Use of light and dark – a strong interplay between dark background on right and light on figure, which is reversed on the left-hand side, where figure becomes dark and background lighter.
- Deliberate pictorial device to create drama and a sense of mystery, as well as exploring interplay between light and dark.

- Vary your techniques – for recording your thoughts you can use visuals, such as studies.
- You may find a balance of these and written notes interesting to do.
- Sometimes making studies can give you a deeper insight into just how a work is made.

 You need to analyse each practitioner's use of formal elements as you are working through your research for the set task.

You can develop your awareness of the similarities and differences between practitioners by looking at how each one uses formal elements.

 Your analysis might not always be sequential; you may have to return to formal elements again and again.

 Remember – you will be conducting your analysis when you are making notes which you may be able to take in to your supervised assessment.

Now try this

Choose an image of work by a practitioner. Use drawings or diagrams to identify the formal element/s within the piece.

Understanding visual language

Visual language is the combination of formal elements into broader aspects, such as techniques and processes.

Visual language

Consider:

- scale and size
- composition, viewpoint and framing medium
- materials
- processes
- production methods
- techniques
- other elements used in visual language: use of text, time-based and series.

The medium is the message

Practitioners use formal elements and visual language to speak directly to the viewer – their response is dictated by the specific and targeted use of these elements and language. In conceptual work, the message is often linked to the way the work is presented – formal elements may not be so obvious if it's a minimal piece of work. Some form of visual language will be present – viewers may have to interpret this.

Atomic bomb testing in Nevada, 1957.

Understanding how visual language works

To understand any message in a piece of work, you need to read it. Begin by describing what you see. Focus on details to isolate areas of the piece, and narrow down your analysis.

You might need to 'drill down' into an image to understand it fully. The image above shows a dynamic and menacing scene, where contrast, composition and shape are employed to create tension. The distant mushroom cloud has become a symbol of the destructive nature of atomic weapons, and we immediately read this in the image – a warning, a sign of potential danger, of menace. In the foreground, the figures are silhouetted against the light, all actively involved in carrying out the recording of the event; they are animated, crouched, studying equipment. The interplay between the distant cloud and the foreground, the contrast between the dark figures and brighter sky, all work to communicate through using visual language – relating to the landscape, the environment and the figures.

In contemporary practice, ideas and intentions are often made very visible – the formal elements and visual language are there to see. In historical work practitioners had to conform to accepted ideas and constraints, so often hid one intention underneath an obvious one.

Now try this

Make notes using bullet points, deconstructing the visual language in the photograph above.

Deconstructing visual language

You need to be able to analyse the interplay between formal elements and visual language in a piece of work.

Screen for Presentation, New York City, 2011, by Ben Copperwheat.

Sample notes extract

In this image I am analysing composition.

- Integral component = <u>composition</u> of main shapes, and <u>colour</u>, <u>pattern and rhythm</u> – most prominent aspects of visual language in the piece.
- Have reached conclusion by analysing way the image is constructed from different elements.
- Composition is reflected through format of the piece – long screen so an extended landscape format rectangle.
- Features rhythmic set of brightly coloured wavy shapes = a bright and vibrant feel. Contrast = jagged set of very sharp linear elements acting as a foil, an opposite to softer wavy flow of coloured shapes.
- Result = element of tension in piece, as these two aspects of visual language – softer pattern + harsher jagged elements – act against each other, creating vibrant and slightly uneasy feel.
- Almost as if wavy, happy rainbow has had harsher graffiti of jagged lines superimposed over the top.

Colour relationships

You must show you know how to separate the components of visual work. Here the relationship between the hues and saturations of the colours is also important. You can use colour studies to pick out aspects of the visual language in a piece – in this case the use of flat colour resembles aspects of screenprinting.

You can use crops to show details to support your analysis of visual language.

Isolating aspects of visual language

This means thinking about the message in the work. It will happen naturally once you start looking in detail at the work. You can combine techniques: drawn diagrams and annotations alongside written information can clarify what you are selecting and highlighting.

Different interpretations

☑ There is likely to be a wide range of responses when reading a piece of work.

☑ It is possible that there is no obvious right or wrong answer – but don't rely on it. For instance, the print on this page uses colour, shape, pattern, and positive/negative space through overlaid imagery.

Now try this

Summarise how the formal elements and visual language in the print on this page work together as a design.

Recording visual language

You can use different techniques to record visual language during your research and analysis for your set task. You can then go on to express and justify the conclusions from your analysis – some of these may be your personal readings.

Identifying visual language

Refer back to page 74 about aspects of visual language. As you analyse visual language you might stray into the content listed under visual communication but it's natural that these will overlap.

Techniques, production methods and processes

You may need to research extensively to find information on these aspects of visual language – some practitioners explain their working methods in great detail; others prefer to say very little.

If researching a living practitioner, you could email them via the contact details on their website and explain what you want to find out (remember to use a professional tone).

Sample notes extract

This learner has used drawing to record visual language in a complex image.

A pencil study recorded by a learner of *Figure 0* by Jasper Johns, 1959.

You can use any combination of writing and visuals – it's your study so take ownership and conduct it how you would like to.

- Worked in colour to see how complex arrangement of shapes and colours actually was.

- Felt the complexity in the painting was developed in an almost cubist way – where space was represented outside of so-called traditional perspective.

- Have also looked at compositional elements and techniques used to make the work.

- In some ways Johns is almost halfway between flat colour, poster imagery of pop art movement, and painterly qualities of cubists, who were using traditional techniques – oil on canvas – to explore new ideas.

Record what you have found out regularly – so you can generate viewpoints and judgements from these snippets of writing later on in your research and in your assessment.

- Looked at way Johns worked on these and other images – allows a very playful sense of visual language to emerge.

- In keeping with lots of pop artists at the time, Johns took everyday or so-called mundane objects as subject matter for his work.

- Different to many pop artists – developed strong sense of visual language by exploring potential for subjects to provide ideas.

- Uses elements of numbers and letter forms as integral components in his visual language – explores them in painterly images, prints and drawings.

🔗 **Links** There is more on viewpoints and judgements on pages 88 and 89.

Remember to make sure you are covering all the points in the set task brief and generating relevant information.

A colour sketch recorded by a learner based on Jasper Johns' *Figure 0*, 1959.

Now try this

Choose a practitioner and use visual recording to show how they use visual language.

Using visuals

There are many ways to deconstruct and visually analyse images as you prepare for your supervised assessment.

Photographs

You can take photographs in galleries to record primary sources – where permitted.

Alex Katz, 'Anna Wintour' (2009) © Alex Katz, DACS/Artimage, London/VAGA, New York 2018. Image: © National Portrait Gallery

Alex Katz, Anna Wintour, 2009.

Line drawings

Line drawings can show the basic components and composition in an image.

You can use this technique to pull out the main areas in a composition, especially if it's complex to read – it's a way of reducing it down to component parts.

<u>Alex Katz, 'Anna Wintour' – my analysis</u>

- Visual devices help me analyse images.

- Can use a wider range of techniques – not just words.

- Line drawing – helps to understand composition. Portrait is central but hair frames the area of the face – makes it more explicit in line drawing.

- Cropped examples – allow me to isolate details – like putting a frame around part of image. Detail of face shows influence of billboard + simplified advertising-type imagery.

- Colour swatch/sample – can examine type of colours – all fairly muted + overall pastel tint (influence of posters and adverts).

- Not trying to replicate traditional oil painting portrait – light + colour range simplified.

Your analysis will bring together your understanding of formal elements, visual language and communication.

Visuals can be an interesting and rewarding alternative to just writing information.

- You can use visuals to separate out formal elements as well as aspects of visual language.
- You can blend visuals like these into your research techniques and make the process very personal.

You can isolate details by cropping photographs to help you analyse a piece.

Isolating colours can show you the palette or colour range used.

Visuals can also be used to highlight different influences on images and to make links between the practitioners you are researching.

Now try this

Research another image by Alex Katz. Scan or photograph the image and increase the contrast dramatically to identify the tonal balance within the image.

Visual communication – imagery and subject matter

You must interpret how an artwork communicates visually to contextualise it.

Visual communication

Formal elements combine with subject matter to generate visual communication. Each element may draw from similar or different contexts and their combination creates meaning and communicates to the audience. The subject matter has an intended mood and emotional impact on the audience. Pay attention to any symbols and explicit or implicit messages, and balance alternative readings of the work.

Subject matter

The visual subject of this painting by Pablo Picasso is a musician dressed as a harlequin. For Picasso, the harlequin was a kind of alter ego, and was associated with power and alchemy. Picasso has explored themes he developed earlier in his cubist period, such as music and instruments in paintings, and used these in an inventive way. He seems to be combining elements from different contextual influences – surrealism and neoclassicism.

This initial description already suggests some of the aspects of visual communication that are being applied here.

Pablo Picasso, 'Harlequin Musician' (1924) © Succession Picasso/DACS, London 2018

Harlequin Musician by Pablo Picasso, 1924, oil on canvas.

Visual messages

When deconstructing visual work, the imagery will contextually relate to other visuals in culture and history; these are visual clues that convey overt or subtle messages. Research these by looking into the working practices of the practitioner and at any available web-based or published information and artist statements.

You can cross-reference your analysis by comparing it to ideas already discussed – either by the practitioners themselves, or by critics and reviewers.

Remember

Deconstructing imagery can often throw up more questions than it initially answers.
- Don't panic if this happens.
- Make notes about any questions – write them down – and then try and answer them using research techniques.
- This will help refine your research and analysis.

Now try this

Picasso's *Harlequin Musician* contextually references aspects of synthetic cubism, neoclassicism and surrealism – write a sentence that sums up the main characteristics of each of these contextual movements.

Visual communication – message and meaning

The message and the meaning of an artwork may not be obvious. It's your job to explore and explain what they might be.

What does it mean?

Your analysis should lead you to generate some ideas about the work – what you think it's about (its meaning), what it's trying to say (its message), and how it's doing this. Your conclusions may be tentative at first – just make sure you record them. You can then work on testing them, using quotes and researched examples of analysis for support.

You should express your views with confidence so practise writing out and justifying your conclusions.

It's all connected

As you consider how to deconstruct imagery, notice that the methods you use are all connected and that the process is not sequential – you will need to go back and forth looking at and reviewing these aspects. This takes time and requires patience – answers to questions are not always found immediately.

You can compare practitioners by looking at one piece of their work, and analysing the formal elements, visual language and communication.

Looking at details

Your research must be in depth and have a purpose. If you have two images that are related, you can compare/contrast them to find their message (whether it is explicit or implied) and meaning. You may have to look initially at the formal elements and visual language used in the details – so you can develop analysis by considering these factors and potential messages at the same time.

You can compare/contrast the two paintings opposite by posing a set of questions about them:

- When were they produced?
- In terms of subjects, are they similar?
- In terms of treatment of the subject (the way they are painted) how are they similar and how are they different?
- What do the positions of the heads suggest?

Portrait of Pablo Picasso by Juan Gris, 1912.

Juan Gris, 'Portrait of Pablo Picasso' (1912)
Photo © The Art Institute of Chicago, IL, USA /
Gift of Leigh B. Block / Bridgeman Images

Self-portrait by Roy Lichtenstein, 1976.

Roy Lichtenstein, 'Self-Portrait' (1976)
© Estate of Roy Lichtenstein/DACS/
Artimage 2018

Remember

✓ Themes in art and design can be complex, especially when practitioners are expressing several layered themes and influences.

✓ In the Lichtenstein image, is the artist saying something about influences on his work? If you researched Lichtenstein and pop art, you will be aware that they are part of an ongoing European development that took ideas and themes from other art and design movements, as well as the media and the culture of the day.

Now try this

Define what you believe is the message and meaning in Lichtenstein's painting, and record this.

Visual communication – symbols and symbolism

Symbolism in artwork can be understood as features used by a culture at a certain time. You need to be able to 'decode' symbols so you can uncover meaning in a piece of work.

Reading symbolism

A culture will invest certain symbols with meaning, which may be explicit and literal, e.g. a lavatory sign, or more abstract, e.g. a 'one way' sign. They can also be subtler, e.g. a colour used by a culture to symbolise a particular feeling.

Understanding how symbols are used in paintings

The painting by Ingres (below) shows a royal figure, resplendent in full regal clothes, sitting on his throne. It is an image that shows a symbol of power, wealth and opulence. The setting also symbolises historical importance, wealth and power.

The figure seems statue-like, and fixed in time, staring back out of the image. The fabrics and colours used are symbolic of wealth; the pose and position of the sitter display confidence – he is almost confronting the viewer.

The first thing you can do is make notes on these points as you develop your analysis. Note that, in the extract below, the learner has practised fleshing out the notes into full sentences.

Jean-Auguste-Dominique Ingres, *Napoleon I on his Imperial Throne*, oil on canvas, 1806.

Sample notes extract

Identifying influences and symbols

On researching Ingres's piece I learned that it had been intended to showcase Ingres's talents and to be a symbolic representation of the power of Napoleon I on his coronation throne. Ingres creates a still, fixed image, where he has used stylistically bold devices to frame the sitter, and this creates a strong sense of an artificial feel to the image. He has set the sitter straight on to the viewer, and used a limited perspective – the picture space is quite shallow. The figure itself has been painted as if it were a statue to reference earlier examples of art that Ingres may have seen in the Louvre. He seems to be using stylistic conventions from earlier European paintings. Napoleon had returned with treasures from war and handed these to the Louvre museum in Paris. Artists of the period would have had the chance to see art from wider afield for the first time, and they would have been influenced by the stylistic and visual language devices these works showed. Napoleon himself in this image is a deliberate symbolic device, as he appears reserved, almost wax-like, and distant.

Intention

Where something has been done deliberately, e.g. Ingres referencing other paintings, the practitioner is using this to promote/provoke a response through the associations with the older pieces. Uncovering information about these sorts of scenarios – the ideas behind a piece of work – is an important skill. You can support your ideas about the practitioner's intention by researching statements or articles about the artist and using quotes.

Now try this

Identify at least one example of contemporary art that has been influenced by the Ingres painting.

Visual communication – aesthetics, mood and impact

Practitioners can play with aesthetics in their work in order to have an impact on their audience, creating a particular mood.

Aesthetics

Aesthetics can be a set of principles that define what something looks like, or how it affects the viewer. It can also cover notions such as beauty and ugliness. When researching aesthetics, you must assess the aesthetic value of visual work: is it aesthetic – balanced, harmonious, proportioned, having some kind of beauty – or is it unaesthetic – deliberately harsh, jarring, discordant, unsettling? Sometimes these can overlap, so an unsettling image can still have a kind of stark aesthetic.

Detail of arm from *Napoleon I on his Imperial Throne* by Ingres.

Detail of leg from *Napoleon I on his Imperial Throne* by Ingres.

Mood and emotional impact

The aesthetics of a work will create the initial impact on the viewer. Some works are deliberately shocking or disorientating, while others are more subtle and sensitive. Neither is more powerful, but simply a tool used to generate a certain state or mood. Practitioners use contextual references to generate impact, such as the children's hands used to paint the controversial Myra Hindley painting by Marcus Harvey from 1995. Looking at the context of the work will help appreciate the intended impact on the audience.

Impact of technique

In the detail above, there is a sense of aesthetic beauty in the way Ingres has painted the sumptuous and heavily decorated fabric and light. Consider the impact of technique in the works you look at. For example, what kind of aesthetic is Picasso creating in his painting on page 78? If Ingres is creating an image whose impact suggests power and richness, how would you define the impact of Picasso's painting?

The principles of aesthetics and function

Be aware of the different factors of:

- aesthetic principles including: balance, unity, harmony, contrast, rhythm, centre of interest, direction and relationships
- functional principles including: ergonomics, anthropometrics, usability, life-span, safety, economy and life-style.

Conclusions

After analysing and researching visual work, you need to reach conclusions. Work towards this by answering these simple questions.

✓ What have you learned about the work you have researched?

✓ What factors have the practitioners explored?

✓ How have they communicated this to you?

Now try this

Take an example of a visual work by a practitioner and analyse the aesthetics in the piece and the mood they create/the impact they have on you.

Preparing to write about practitioners

For your set task you may need to make decisions about the practitioners you have researched – how you read their work, and their use of aesthetics. You can show this in your descriptions and analysis of influences on them, their work, and their approach to the theme.

Analysis techniques

You can use different techniquesfor analysis.

First level analysis

- Biographical details
- Contextual factors

Second level analysis

- Discussion of ideas and intentions
- Visual communication
- Your personal views about practitioners' work and themes

Sample response extract

<u>Practitioners: Gilbert and George: Theme – icons</u>

When Gilbert and George were studying they decided to challenge the nature of the art world. They made themselves into 'Living Sculptures', and began developing an identity for themselves as a pair – not as individuals – where they themselves became the central focus of their work, and aspects of their lives were woven into their pictures. They also used film and performance as vehicles to communicate their ideas. These media were much in use at the time, so they were using a contemporary art form. They were becoming recognisable as subjects, and subsequently as icons, displaying themselves in a variety of personas depending on their purpose. Gilbert and George use scale in their work as a powerful way of making sure it has a strong impact – <u>gridlines</u> reference religious or stained glass paintings, and they often present themselves as mock religious icons.

They use bright colours, often to link to specific ideas or <u>motifs</u>. In 'Jack Freak Pictures' Hamburg, 2011, the Union Jack (a potent symbol with a range of meanings, from nationalism and issues about national identity to imperial dominance) is an example of this. They also make their images shocking and garish – and this gives them a strong visual impact, so they grab the attention of the viewer. When this is added to the large scale they work at, the end result is images which can't be ignored. They exploit the media of photography and mixed media to combine visual elements that use ideas about colour and imagery. They are influenced by pop art, conceptual art and the real world, e.g. text from newspapers, graffiti and images of themselves in their environment. I think their work <u>confronts the viewer directly and starkly</u>, through portrayals of themselves as <u>icons for a disturbing, flawed world. Their use of imagery and symbols are taken from the establishment that</u> they then subvert and use for an altogether different message <u>or possibly to expose and uncover the inherent meanings in these symbols that we are all aware of, but would rather not face</u>.

This extract uses research to prepare copy about practitioners and their work, including contextual factors, how a theme is addressed, and visual analysis.

You need to be able to express your readings of your chosen practitioners' work, and justify your views.

The underlined terms in this extract demonstrate effective use of specialist language.

The way you use language is important – you should describe accurately and reference clearly: visuals, formal elements, visual language and visual communication. Use appropriate terminology correctly and explain and justify your own views.

Develop your own views about their work – this is second level analysis. You should still maintain an awareness of audience. You can explain your own views without saying 'I think…'.

Now try this

Select a practitioner you have researched, and write a few bullet points about their work and its aesthetic qualities using first level and second level analysis.

Summarising information

When drawing conclusions and forming judgements on the research carried out, you will need to summarise key information. You can do this through selecting relevant and reliable information, identifying key points and articulating findings and conclusions using a combination of written and visual information.

1 Selecting information and formats

You must use relevant and reliable information – accurately researched from reliable sources. You should also include all of your references and source information. If you followed the guidance on pages 51 and 45–47 about organising your research and referencing your sources, you should have a good idea where everything is. But it may be in several formats, including books, on your PC, phone, etc.

It's important to review all of the information before you decide what to use.

2 Key points

- Identify and bring together the key points in your research. Keeping an ongoing review or blog should make this straightforward – so you have a good idea of what your key points are.

- Start to summarise information by listing the key points separately – don't be concerned with word length at the moment – there are techniques you can use to condense the information.

- Get used to cross-referencing – often one piece of research can be applied to more than one viewpoint, justification or commentary.

3 Summarising techniques

Practise summarising information:

- Bullet points are a useful way of recording information. Notes don't need to be in running prose.

- You can use diagrams to make sense of some of the influences and their effect on practitioners.

- Drawings or annotated artworks can be used to support your understanding of deconstruction and visual analysis.

- Use a table to help you compare the work of practitioners (see page 86).

- Go over your summary statements until you are sure they say what you want them to say.

4 Using visuals

Your research is likely to contain many visuals. There may be a limit on how many images you can use in the supervised assessment, but you can use images in your notes if these help you.

If you can only choose one image for analysis by a practitioner, choose a key work – one that will support your analysis and response.

Think carefully about how your choice of visual relates to how your chosen practitioner's work shows the theme.

Using your notes

You may be allowed to take some of your preparatory notes into your supervised assessment time. If so, there may be restrictions on the length and type of notes that are allowed. Check with your tutor or look at the most up-to-date Sample Assessment Material on the Pearson website for information.

Now try this

Take a theme or idea you have researched and practise summarising it using some of the techniques described above, e.g. by using bullet points.

Making connections

When forming independent judgements, you should make connections between messages, themes, creative intentions and the visual elements that form the work. Make as many connections as you can initially, then you can select the most relevant ones.

Sample notes extract

Humphrey Ocean: Theme – Reality

Connections between theme, subject and treatment

- Humphrey Ocean has chosen a building as the subject – shows his interest in effect people have had on their landscape or where they have lived or worked.

- Says that he likes to 'paint where human beings have been, where they've done something to a place' – this shows what is presumably telephone exchange or office type building.

- Kind of detachment in way he paints – objectively but in a very subdued manner, with a muted palette in this image. (Definitely representational, but not in a heightened, photographic sense.)

- Ocean goes on to say 'people think my colour is drab but to me it's not, it's the colour that I see and I don't want to heighten it in any way'. Inspired to work from surroundings in a sort of detached documentary style, while recording colours exactly as he sees them.

- His pursuit of reality is very personal – shows the effects of people on their environment. His choice of viewpoint is as an observer who might be able to see the building – nothing fantastical about where we are as we look at this building.

- Work reaches out to viewer and convinces them of integrity of his vision. Documenting his surroundings, his reality in an observed and detached manner = continuing the tradition of artists being inspired to record their immediate surroundings – their reality.

Image and treatment

This is a straightforward piece of writing with an image – it outlines crisply what the image shows, as well as giving information about:

- the practitioner's trademark approach to recording their surroundings
- how they are interested in the effects people have on their surroundings
- their use of a subdued yet absorbing colour range
- their use of formal elements and visual communication.

> The introduction introduces the subject matter and theme.

> Quotes are used to support the discussion.

> The learner has looked at the treatment – the visual language and communication.

> Colour and intention is discussed supported by a quote.

> There is a concluding sentence, with a justification.

Now try this

Damien Hirst's work is often related to the theme of mortality. Look at some of his work and list three ways in which he connects his work to this theme.

Making links

Making links to other works can be an effective way of supporting your conclusions. You can make links between work by practitioners that explores the same subject but in different ways.

Types of link

Links can be created by any number of factors, influences or visuals. There are too many to list all of them, but they could include:

- technology, media and production
- society and audience
- themes and influences
- formal elements and visual language
- ideas and messages.

Make the links work by keeping them very specific. If you are using them to support the use of visual analysis, make sure you are providing the right information.

René Magritte, 'Decalcomania' (1966) © ADAGP, Paris and DACS, London 2018 Photo: Artepics / Alamy Stock Photo

Decalcomania by Rene Magritte, 1966.

Visual links

You can make links between individual works that explore similar subjects. In this case the two images on this page deliberately use a sense of illusion to each create arresting visual images – a kind of visual conundrum. They both present juxtaposition – two or more things, aspects, objects or elements that force the viewer to look again, in order to articulate the images. Magritte's painting features the exact silhouette of a figure cut out of a drape in front of a landscape (is it a window?) – and the same figure is standing next to the image. This arrangement confronts the viewer with an impossible scene, and demands further consideration. The Bailey image also presents an impossible situation, a regular pattern featuring birds and fish. As in the Magritte piece, the elements are referencing shape – the shape of the bird translating into the negative shape enveloping the fish. And again, this image forces the viewer to look beyond an initial glance and to consider the mathematical qualities and arrangements Bailey has explored.

David Bailey, *Bird and Fish 1*.
Source: http://www.tess-elation.co.uk/

By comparing and contrasting practitioners' use of formal elements and visual language you can delve deeper into the messages in their work, and this can help you reach conclusions.

Remember

☑ If using two images in the supervised assessment, you will need to use written language to describe any other examples of visual work. You will also need to describe their visual components accurately.

☑ You can make links between work by different practitioners that explore the same subject but in different ways.

Now try this

Write a short paragraph that compares Sherrie Levine's *Fountain (after Marcel Duchamp)* from 1991 with Marcel Duchamp's *Fountain* from 1917.

Comparing practitioners – summarising

You may need to make connections between two practitioners – and use them to reach conclusions as part of your set task. This page will help you to summarise the points you have made and to clarify your comparisons.

Make a summary

As you develop your writing and move towards making judgements and reaching conclusions, you should work through summarising the main points of your comparisons. The points you use in your summary can form the focus for any writing you might need to complete as part of your set task.

Sample notes extract

	Jenny Holzer	Alan Fletcher
Contextual factor – communication	Communication using technology, association with information, subversive messages, ability to question – is it an information notice or something else?	Communication – ability of the medium to create an additional representation, words/type can show the meaning or state of something, allowing type to become expressive, of an idea, a state
Formal elements	Used black and white in series, and then colour in series, strong use of contrast	Use of colour to make images look artificial, garish, plastic, fake and made up

Tables or grids are helpful when summarising the information you gather.

Summarise the contextual factors across both practitioners in a table format.

This type of table can be developed to include other points for comparison, such as detailed information about the images you use.

Comparing Jenny Holzer with Alan Fletcher

I have used this table to start to lay out the main findings from my research. This helps me to clarify the main points that I have gained from my research, as well as highlight the similarities and differences, common ideas and influences across both of my selected practitioners.

Compare relevant points including:

- formal elements, visual language and visual communication in the practitioners' work

- what contextual factors have influenced them

- how this influence is shown in their work

- how their work links to the theme

- what they communicate specifically about the theme – their interpretation.

Develop a table that shows the points you would compare for two practitioners of your own choice. Complete a comparison of two of the points.

Comparing practitioners – making connections

Before your supervised assessment, you need to get used to making connections between two practitioners and writing about your comparison. In the notes below, the learner has practised writing their notes in full.

Jenny Holzer, 'Monument' (2008) © Jenny Holzer, ARS, NY and DACS/Artimage, London 2018 Photo: Vassilij Gureev

Jenny Holzer, *Monument*, 2008 (detail) installation.

Holzer and Fletcher – a connection

Jenny Holzer and Alan Fletcher are two practitioners who explore the potential in using language and letter forms to communicate ideas and meaning. They achieve this by being creative with the way they use materials, techniques and processes to depict words, and how the meaning in these words relates to the context of their work – for example, Holzer's in installations and Fletcher's in graphic communication about typography.

Before you read the sample notes below, use the internet to view Alan Fletcher's, *Beware Wet Paint*, Limited Edition Print and book cover, from 1996.

Sample notes extract

Comparing practitioners

I've looked at the different ways that language and text can be used to communicate ideas – that go beyond the literal reading of the works and what they mean.

In Holzer's work she explores ideas about technology and the ways that art can be shown and viewed, as well as the power in language and words to promote a sensation or communicate a message. In 'Monument' she is specifically using one of the themes in her work that relates to technology – using twentieth and twenty-first century technology to communicate as an art form. This example uses the text that was used on the stock exchanges, and is often seen at stations or on transport networks, listing where trains and buses stop. As such it has connotations with providing information, but in this case it's a set of statements that can be taken as a warning or message to be heeded.

Alan Fletcher's work 'Beware wet paint' explores the ability of the medium used to create the words to communicate above and beyond the meanings. He has used plastic alphabet shapes to communicate ideas about the alphabet and typefaces. In this example he has shown the moment that the paint – all different colours – has been used and run down the wall or screen. It's a visual representation of wet paint running – and reinforces the nature of the meaning in the words. It also references Duchamp's statement about needing to let wet paint dry – in other words art and design pieces can take time to understand.

You may be able to include visuals in any preparatory notes – check the Pearson website for the most up-to-date **Sample Assessment Material** to find out.

You should refer to many visual pieces in your analysis of the practitioners. These will form the basis for your subsequent response.

Comparing practitioners who use the same subject matter, and considering how they do so, is really helpful in clarifying what it is you are trying to find out. This can offer a direct contrast between images.

Using key images can also provide points about the practitioners that go across their body of work.

Now try this

Use the table you have developed showing two of your points of comparison between two practitioners (see page 86). Write them up using two full paragraphs.

Forming judgements

To form your judgements you need to bring your research and summaries together.

Aspects to consider

There are a lot of things to consider when forming judgements, including:

- biographical details
- contextual influences
- contextual factors
- links to other practitioners

- materials, techniques and processes
- message and intention
- audience

- themes
- key works
- formal elements
- visual language
- visual communication
- questions

- summaries and notes
- visuals
- research sources
- references and bibliography.

Bringing it together

To form judgements you must consider all the information you have gathered. Summarising this information should help you start the process. Ask yourself questions, such as:

- How does each practitioner address the theme in their work?
- Which one communicates their ideas about the theme more clearly?

You should form judgements based on evidence and factual information, as well as explaining your own views through reasoned argument.

Make the connections clear

Set out your initial thoughts and judgements, making all the connections as clearly as you can. This may be a complex activity because there are a lot of factors to consider so you need to allow sufficient time for this.

This is where connections need to be made across all of your research.

Try to stay on track – it is easy to put in information that isn't important and doesn't actually help you in forming judgements – keep your judgements crisp. Ultimately, you will be working towards your conclusion, so make sure your judgements will support it.

Using supporting information

As you work through forming your judgements, make sure all supporting information goes into the notes next to your comment, view or idea. You can then make the support for your judgements clearly and give your judgements validity and depth.

Remember to use terminology appropriately to describe, explain, reach conclusions and form judgements.

Finally, don't forget to list the sources, journals and books you have used in your bibliography.

Remember

Justify your judgements and conclusions by:

- ✓ basing them on a blend of facts from research
- ✓ using visual analysis of artwork – how practitioners have used the components in visual communication to convey their message
- ✓ supporting them with ideas, comments and quotes
- ✓ giving clear explanations of the effects of contextual factors on the practitioners.

Your view is important – make it count by supporting it with evidence.

Now try this

Find an article on Damien Hirst's *The Physical Impossibility of Death in the Mind of Someone Living* from 1991 and use this to support a judgement you make about the work in a short paragraph.

Justifying your view

Justifying personal viewpoints is used extensively in creative practice, and provides one way for practitioners to explain and support the ideas behind their work.

Why justify?

Justification is a key aspect of contemporary practice – practitioners have to explain and justify their work. Where this work offers a direct challenge to the viewer's expectations, it becomes even more important, to:

- support a choice of challenging subject matter
- put a production method into context
- provide a rationale for working in a particular way.

You can use critiques (analytical and formal discussions about artwork) to practise generating conclusions and justifications.

Justification is used at all levels to support and explain choices and creative outcomes in art and design. Here a designer is presenting her ideas to a group.

Terminology

To justify effectively practitioners must use the correct terminology. There is a set of accepted and widely used terms for art and design practice. These include:

- formal elements
- visual language
- creative intention
- inherent qualities of materials
- conceptual
- context.

Using terminology correctly will help you make your copy concise and ensures it addresses all the points you want to make.

The benefits of justification

☑ Justification allows practitioners to support their visual work. It can provide information that validates their work in the eyes of their peers and viewers.

☑ Justification can provide grounding for innovative work.

☑ In design briefs, it is used to add weight to the creative solution: sometimes clients and practitioners don't know if a product will work, so they might justify their outcome's potential by referring to similar products, or audience feedback.

Justifying your views is a skill – you can practise it and gain confidence.

References

Practitioners use references to support and justify the conclusions they present in their work. These are widely used in academic writing and in vocational contexts, such as exhibition reviews, articles in journals and books on practitioners. See pages 45–47 for ways of referencing sources.

Quotes are used to make a point firmly, or support a conclusion – they can explain what the practitioner was doing or thinking and you can use them to reinforce your views and conclusions.

In summary

Justifying your views is an important part of contemporary practice. It is used to:

☑ explain ideas to clients
☑ support applications for progression, or for competitions
☑ support exhibition proposals
☑ encourage creative debate
☑ explain and support practitioners' choices of subjects, treatments and production.

Now try this

Justify how you have selected a material or technique in one piece of your work, using references to appropriate influences and contexts.

Communicating conclusions

Conclusions will complete your research, so they need to be clearly communicated – they may also be a key part of your assessment.

What was the question?

To draw your conclusions, you need to answer the original points and questions that were asked to bring the research and analysis to a close.

Use the structures you have explored in this guide to support you – summarising information, justifying and making links and connections.

Don't leave it to the end to revisit the questions. Keep going back to them to make sure your research and analysis are on the right track.

Be sure about what you want to say

If you have carried out your research and all the associated tasks effectively you should be able to structure your conclusion. The theme of your research will need to be highlighted. Be clear about what it is you want to say, and say it using plain English. You will be putting across your own viewpoint, so be sure of what this is before you start writing.

You can think about your response when you are preparing any preliminary notes. This will enable you to work out some of the structures and reasoned arguments you will put forward.

Justify your views

You need **relevant** evidence to back up your views and conclusions. This can include:

- quotes from practitioners, accepted commentaries and articles
- information from reliable web-based sources, e.g. the practitioner's own site
- your own primary and secondary research
- your visual analysis
- your ongoing evaluation of the theme.

Use of language

You will be assessed on the quality of your written communication so structure your sentences properly. Do not use slang terms or sloppy phrases.

Make sure that you use terminology associated with art and design effectively, as this will be one of the ways you can demonstrate the depth and intelligence of your research.

Try to use language concisely to make your points as succinctly as possible. Read your work through and see if it gives you a clear idea of what the practitioners' work is about.

Remember:

- effective writing is clear and focused
- language and terminology should be used appropriately
- you will need to apply descriptive language when talking about visual imagery.

Now try this

Choose a practitioner you have researched. Write notes for a conclusion on a theme and/or idea in their work.

 Remember that you should refer to examples and evidence when constructing your conclusion.

Preparing a supporting document

In your set task, you may need to write a document, for example an email or a letter, in response to a particular scenario.

> **Remember**
> Check the Pearson website for the most up-to-date **Sample Assessment Material** and **Mark Scheme** to get an indication of the tasks in your assessment. The details of the actual assessed task may change so always make sure you are up to date.

Preparing for a written activity

The document that you prepare for might be in the context of a vocational scenario.

Vocational scenarios might include the following kinds of communication, for example:

- an email to a gallery owner
- an email to a producer or company about the product
- a letter to an exhibition organiser.

Written language

Your writing should be formal and avoid slang or abbreviations. Try to write in the third person (he/she/it/they) and avoid the use of the first person (I) where possible. To practise, you could write in your normal way and then rewrite the copy more formally.

Try to use technical terminology correctly, e.g. when referring to formal elements, materials, techniques, processes and concepts.

Length

You may be given a word restriction for any written task, so you must be succinct. It is common for copywriters to draft longer text and then to edit (cut) any content that doesn't add to the central point. For example, you don't need to use the full names of the artists each time once you have introduced them.

Scenarios

Although there may be different scenarios, the main points that you need to cover are likely to remain the same.

For example, you may have to compare the work of two practitioners that you have researched and state which one, in your opinion, has used the given theme in the best way. You would do this by developing a balanced and reasoned argument.

Make sure you show your ability to:

- synthesise the visual analysis and contextual factors to form judgements
- compare the practitioners and their work linked to the theme
- justify your arguments with relevant evidence; reach clear conclusions.

The flowchart below shows one way that you might focus and structure your writing.

> Draft your text with an introduction
> ▼
> Discuss the artists using visual analysis of contextual factors
> ▼
> Compare the artists in relation to the theme
> ▼
> Justify arguments with evidence from own analysis and relevant evidence
> ▼
> Draw conclusions
> ▼
> Proofread and review

Now try this

Put together a list of bullet points which you might include in a letter to a curator recommending Antony Gormley to be included in a group show on the theme 'The Figure'.

Justifying your arguments

It is essential that you are able to put forward a balanced argument with justifications for your opinions and conclusions, using relevant evidence.

Sample response extract

Practitioners: Pablo Picasso, and Gilbert and George

Theme: Iconography

Pablo Picasso combined events from his own life in his paintings to create an autobiographical iconography. He referenced aspects of traditional painting in the way he blended religious iconography and characters from his immediate surroundings.

> In this extract written to justify a view, the learner has introduced the artist and the way they approach the theme simply – this establishes a strong beginning.

His icons are figures captured in situations showing extremes of emotion. He painted images that evoke an almost childlike happiness, or images that show suffering such as in *Weeping Woman* of 1937. Picasso took ideas about portraiture from Old Master paintings and used them as the basis to superimpose his personal interpretation of what a portrait can be.

> The learner develops the discussion to look at the effect of Picasso's uses of European painting traditions in portraiture.

Gilbert and George explore their own identity as icons through their consideration and communication about their (and in their view, society's) attitudes to belief, pain, sexuality and politics. Their iconography is a definite construction, yet is a powerful tool in their visual communication, in that it is recognisable, and through its repeated use they are able to explore themes in depth.

> The second practitioner is introduced here – linked immediately to the theme.

As Gilbert says, 'Our art has always been based on reaching people, attacking the viewer, in some way, with the thoughts and feelings that we have inside.'

> Quotes can be used to support arguments and justify views and conclusions.

Both sets of practitioners use iconography as a theme by referencing visual aspects of traditional icons. These might be connected to national identity – colours in flags being one example. Their work shows an ability to force the viewer to question their ideas about their accepted notions of order and a clearly defined, established set of ideas and rules.

> Both practitioners are now considered in relation to the theme.

Both practitioners use iconography to reflect aspects of their environment, personal identity and life itself. Both practitioners have used their own lives and influences as the basis for their communication.

> Similarities and differences can be discussed to show analysis – what you have found out about their work, how they use imagery, etc.

I would argue that Gilbert and George do this most convincingly, as their work has established itself as recognisable across a range of genres: painting, film and sculpture. Their work reflects a wide range of cultural iconographic details – the Union flag, London and religious motifs. These reinvented icons are recognised across the world. Picasso's personal iconography uses a more traditional format and has a significant, though in my view lesser, impact.

> State the conclusion, and justify it.

Now try this

Write an introductory paragraph on your interpretation of two practitioners you have researched.

Structuring your conclusions

Be aware of what you will be assessed on when you are structuring your conclusions and make sure this is included in your submission.

Reaching conclusions

Throughout any research, and during any assessment activities, you need to reach conclusions when:

- analysing practitioners' use of formal elements, visual language and visual communication
- working out just how contextual factors have influenced practitioners
- considering how practitioners integrate and express contextual factors in their work
- comparing the practitioners.

To reach a conclusion if comparing the work of practitioners and justifying a view in relation to a scenario, you must:

- synthesise (bring together) the results of your research into contextual factors and your visual analysis – to form judgements
- compare the work of each practitioner and the theme – how do they show the theme in their work?
- explain which practitioner in your opinion communicates the theme most effectively
- justify your arguments with relevant evidence.

Sample response extract

Practitioner: Gilbert and George

Theme: Iconography

Both practitioners explore the idea of icons and iconography as a theme in their work. Gilbert and George explore aspects of cultural and national identity, influenced by their appreciation of social factors around their London East End studio. They have used themselves as subjects or icons in many of their works. Their use of grid lines and panels makes reference to stained-glass imagery, which itself would often represent iconic imagery. They position themselves as icons within these formats and compositions to challenge the viewer's perception of iconography, especially as many of their images feature themes exploring sexuality and the body. They also explore the artificiality of the way cultures can be perceived and constructed by their use of iconic symbols and flags. In some ways, they are almost asking us to question our accepted beliefs about what is classed as iconography, through their juxtaposition of personalised imagery within European art traditions of religious paintings.

A basic fact is set out as the starting point. The learner then goes on to discuss the first practitioner's work – Gilbert and George.

The learner is careful to discuss the theme of 'Iconography' at regular intervals throughout, as the main thrust of the writing is to say which practitioner best shows the theme in your opinion, using balanced and reasoned argument. The learner has also included information about the subject matter.

You should carry on to refer to the second practitioner, drawing comparisons and justifying which practitioner you feel will best fit the task.

Check the Pearson website to find out if there is a word count for any of your written work. Be sure to stick to it.

Now try this

Using the notes you compiled for the activity on page 90, write a paragraph reaching your conclusion about a theme in the work of one practitioner you have researched.

Writing a supporting document

Below is a sample letter to a gallery curator, recommending the selection of practitioners for inclusion in an exhibition entitled 'Environment', and identifying which artist would be best to exemplify this theme.

Sample response extract

Dear _____,

I recommend Andy Goldsworthy and Robert Smithson as suitable for your 'Land as Art' exhibition. I believe both artists have produced significant works that allow the viewer to reconsider environment and place in a fresh and innovative way. There are similarities between them that I think reinforce the importance of the theme – while at the same time posing questions about the supposed timelessness of artworks.

Both practitioners use visual devices that promote a sense of wonder in the viewer. Goldsworthy's work attracts through its intricate use of delicate shape and surface, structure and form; Smithson's through the scale and ambition, and visual strength.

Both artists reference natural forms in their work. While Goldsworthy explores the potential of smaller-scale elements in his visual communication – leaves, ice, stone and pebbles are all transformed into structures that force the viewer to think about nature – Smithson uses scale and a sense of grandeur to reference archaeological structures and items that may be submerged or half hidden. His 'Spiral Jetty', 1970, is a significant piece of land art, and is still visible depending on fluctuating water levels. Can this be used to highlight how we are changing the environment through global warming?

Smithson was also interested in the idea of thermodynamics and entropy – this might make some interesting links with current concerns re renewable energy, although his work is mainly in photographic form so may provide a barrier to the viewers. Nonetheless, his ideas on decay and re-growth, and finite energy sources, would provide at least an interesting set of points for visitors to the exhibition to consider.

Goldsworthy's work would have a direct communication with the viewers through its use of hand building and crafted approaches to exploiting the inherent qualities of materials, and I think it is this directness and potential for audiences to empathise with the physical work that makes him an ideal choice for a central role in the exhibition. Although the ephemeral nature of some of his work means it too will be in photographic form, I do think it would be possible to install his work in the gallery by creating a set of single self-contained spaces. In terms of the theme of this exhibition, I believe Goldsworthy's work has the most potential.

 Address the points that will form the basis of the assessment. Ensure you keep within any specified word count.

 Use clear language to make your points succinctly.

Discuss formal elements.

 Discuss visual language and visual communication.

State personal views.

Introduce the conclusion clearly and neatly.

 Link conclusions and justifications.

Now try this

Write the first paragraph of the letter to a curator that you scoped out on page 91.

Your Unit 6 set task

Unit 6 will be assessed through a task, which will be set by Pearson. In this assessed task you will use your understanding of responding to a client brief in the art and design sector by researching the client, developing your ideas, and producing a presentation for the client that demonstrates your ideas in response to the brief.

Revising your skills

Your assessed task could cover any of the essential content in the unit. You can revise the unit content in this Revision Guide. The skills pages are designed to **revise skills** that might be needed in your assessed task. They use selected content and outcomes to provide examples of ways of applying your skills.

Clarify a client's product or service, target audience and what they need from you.
See page 96.

Research and select relevant information and material to inform ideas in response to the client's brief.
See pages 104–105.

Set task skills

Develop design ideas relevant to the brief.
See pages 108, 111–112.

Organise your ideas, information and practical outcomes for presentation.
See pages 119, 122–124 and 126.

Justify your decisions in relation to the brief, the target audience and the client's demands.
See pages 110 and 127.

Workflow

The process of managing and responding to a client brief could follow these steps:

✓ Research a client and any linked theme, purpose or focus, to inform your ideas.

✓ Research a target audience, to inform ideas.

✓ Develop and record your ideas.

✓ Select an idea which you will take forward to develop and present.

✓ Develop a presentation and speaker notes which explain and justify your ideas.

Check the Pearson website

The activities and sample response extracts in this section are provided to help you to revise content and skills. Ask your tutor or check the Pearson website for the most up-to-date **Sample Assessment Material** and **Mark Scheme** to get an indication of the structure of your actual assessed task and what this requires of you. The details of the actual assessed task may change so always make sure you are up to date.

Now try this

Visit the Pearson website and find the page containing the course materials for BTEC National Art and Design. Look at the latest Unit 6 Sample Assessment Material for an indication of:

- the structure of your set task, and whether it is divided into parts
- how much time you are allowed for the task or different parts of the task
- what briefing or stimulus material might be provided to you

- any notes or initial research you might have to make and whether you are allowed to take these into your supervised assessment
- the activities you are required to complete and how to format your responses.

Starting analysis and research

You will need to research and develop design ideas relevant to the client brief. Any information given to you as part of your set task will be the starting point for your research.

Understanding the brief

The task might ask you, for example, to:

- research a client and any linked theme, purpose or focus, to inform your ideas (e.g. the National Trust commissioning a redesign of its brand)
- research a target audience, to inform your ideas (e.g. ages 6–10 or 11–15)
- develop and record ideas (e.g. using your specialism)
- select one idea you will take forward to present
- develop a draft version of your presentation, explaining and justifying your idea.

You will then go on to produce a presentation for the client that demonstrates your ideas in response to the brief (e.g. using a set number of slides, with speaker notes).

The purpose and audience may be provided, or you may need to choose from a number of options.

Identifying the client

Use any information about the client as a starting point to learn about them.

A short history of the business, website content and images which give some background context about the client

Themes, issues or aspects of the client's business or the way it operates

Client information

An intention to be communicated, and the target audience

The business's house style, branding or colours to be used

Planning your time

You need to plan your time effectively so that you can research and develop your response to a client brief.

- Read the brief and choose which specialism you will use.
- Set yourself small deadlines.
- Have clear targets on what you need to have completed.
- Start planning the time across the task to help focus your research and ideas generation.

You may find some of your research and development tasks take longer than you expected. Write down any timetabling changes and make sure you can still finish your set task on time. The factors in the flowchart below may help with your planning.

Personal constraints

Making a list of personal constraints that may impact on the research and the task will help you plan. For example, if you don't have access to locations, then you won't be able to analyse or research data related to it. Other constraints will include:

- time
- budget
- personal skills
- available resources
- access.

Brief	Personal experience	Audience	Competition	Personal
• Client • Intentions • Outcome • Constraints	• First-hand experience • Scenario analysis • Personal view of company	• Feedback from the potential audience • Audience empathy • Compare company's own view to others' view of them • What are their expectations?	• Seeing what others do • Compare and contrast • Consider unique selling point (USP)	• Skills • Resources • Time • Access • Initial ideas

Now try this

Draw up a timetable like the one below for your research work. Show each task and how long you plan to spend on it. You can ask your tutor or check the Sample Assessment Material on the Pearson website to find out how much time you are allowed in your actual assessment.

You could use a Gantt chart to help you keep track of what you've done in the time you have available each week and what's left to do.

Research/development task	Time allocated	Completed

The client, audience and outcome

Before you can respond to a client brief, you need to know who your client is, the purpose of the brief, the audience and the outcome required.

Client

The client is a key element in this unit. They will have certain requirements for a brief, product or service. You need to be well informed about your client.

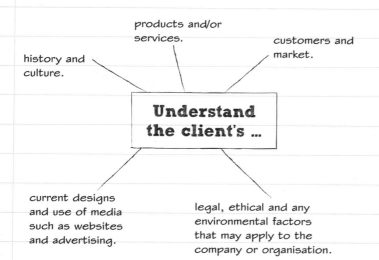

products and/or services.

history and culture.

customers and market.

Understand the client's ...

current designs and use of media such as websites and advertising.

legal, ethical and any environmental factors that may apply to the company or organisation.

Audience

The audience is the group (or groups) of people whom the client wishes to attract with their product or service. The audience is a key aspect of the brief and you will need to be aware of:

- the likely audience demographic (age group, gender, income, social group, geographical location)
- the likely needs and wants of the audience.

You will need to ensure your response to the client brief is suitable for the audience.

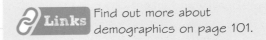 **Links** Find out more about demographics on page 101.

Purpose and outcome

The purpose is the key message the client wants to deliver to the audience. It informs your outcome and how you produce it. The outcome is your final product. It needs to meet the requirements of the client brief.

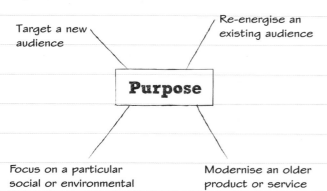

Target a new audience

Re-energise an existing audience

Purpose

Focus on a particular social or environmental theme

Modernise an older product or service

The pitch

This is where you present your ideas to your client. The pitch – your presentation – demonstrates how you have met the brief and shows the client your proposed solution.

You need to both explain and persuade in your presentation. Think about sentences that begin:

👍 I investigated the brief and possible ideas included...

👍 I set out to solve...

👍 My creative solution to the design problem is...

Find out about the history of the company, how it applies its environment policy to its factory and products, and identify its target market.

Now try this

You have been asked to design a washing-up liquid bottle for Ecover, an eco-friendly company which manufactures household cleaning products using only natural ingredients. Using the internet to research the company, briefly describe the client and the audience for your product.

Producing initial ideas

Once you've identified the client, audience and the outcome, you can get down initial ideas in response to the client brief.

What are initial ideas?

These are the first thoughts and ideas you have.

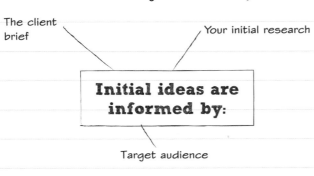

The client brief

Your initial research

Initial ideas are informed by:

Target audience

Initial ideas must also include your own creative personality and intentions.

 Links See page 106 for more help on how to generate new ideas.

Record your ideas

Keep a record of all your ideas. You could use:

👍 mind maps – these enable you to set out possible ideas or things to consider

👍 sketchbooks – drawings and roughs of, for example, processes or set-ups, can show a great deal of information; you can also work up ideas visually as they are developing

👍 annotation – critically analysing work, noting ideas and planning future ideas

👍 scanning or photocopying – 2D work, tests and experiments

👍 digital photos

👍 screengrabs

👍 blog or vlog.

As you build a response to a client brief, remember to show how your ideas have been **informed** by your research.

Use the information in the brief

Extract information on what you need to do. It will give you clues on what has to be included and what the constraints might be. Once you have read and understood the brief, you can use any visual clues in your initial ideas.

Annotating visual ideas

Use annotation to:

👍 record your thoughts

👍 record the progress of your initial ideas

👍 justify the choices you make

👍 explain how your initial ideas meet the requirements of the brief and the needs of the audience.

Time management and planning

When you are planning your response to the brief, you must be able to manage the task. This is achievable by:

- managing your time carefully. You can set mini-deadlines for different stages, such as research and visual recording.

- testing and using analysis. Have you built in enough time to allow this to happen and to think about what the results tell you?

- resourcing. Have you got the right materials, techniques and processes in place?

- having a back-up plan – creative tasks can sometimes take unexpected twists.

Remember

☑ Initial ideas must be linked to the audience and client requirements, as you understand them.

☑ Use visuals and annotation to help set out information about your ideas.

☑ Use mind maps throughout the initial stages – not just at the beginning.

☑ Strive to balance the technical requirements and constraints with your own creative ideas.

 Links To learn more about requirements and constraints, see pages 102 and 103.

Now try this

You have been asked to design a new logo for an established vegetarian restaurant in your town. Using a mind map, jot down your initial ideas and thoughts.

Analysing client information

When responding to a brief, you need to understand your client in order to be able to meet their needs. You can find information about the client from the brief, and from your own research.

Client identity

There are many forms of clients who might employ art and design practitioners.

Every client will have an existing **identity**. This is how the client is perceived by customers, groups or individuals. Understanding the existing identity of the client is important to providing a product or service which fits with their brand, intentions, tradition or audience.

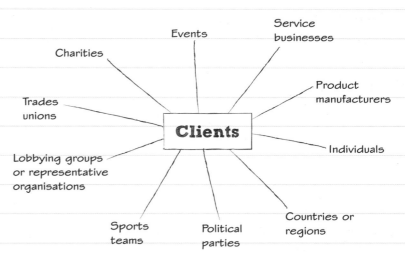

Charities · Events · Service businesses · Trades unions · Product manufacturers · **Clients** · Individuals · Lobbying groups or representative organisations · Sports teams · Political parties · Countries or regions

Colours, styles and branding

The client's **visual identity** plays a big part in the creation of products and services.

You can identify clients by existing designs, logos, images or colours. Artists and designers working to a client brief might incorporate existing branding, colours or styles, or be asked to update or alter these elements.

ALL BLACKS®

The logo and colour scheme of the All Blacks rugby team is very distinctive.

Client history

You can review past products and services offered by the client, and art and design elements that the client has previously used. This will help you to clarify the client's identity, product and audience.

Make sure you know whether the client wants you to fit in with its existing brand and identity, or to update or alter it.

Client's purpose

Clients may want to engage with a new audience, to move into a new market, or to provide an experience to a wider range of consumers. The brief should give you an idea of purpose and guide your research.

 Links Find out more about researching the client on page 96.

The client's message is an important part of its identity. Mission statements, straplines and advertising copy can help you find out about a client's identity.

Now try this

You have been asked to produce material for the Welsh Government's *Visit Wales* website that promotes tourism in South Wales.

- Use the internet to find two contrasting images which have been used to promote tourism in South Wales. Briefly describe why you think those images were used by this client.
- Read any text that appears in promotional materials for this client, and identify any common language or descriptions.

Getting the complete picture

Information gained from research gives you a full picture of the client. It helps to ensure that your ideas for an art and design solution address the requirements of the brief.

Investigating the client brief

The client brief is the starting point for research. After analysis of the brief, practitioners plan research to gain a wider picture of the context they are working in. Start with:

- a short history of the client – why it was set up, its purpose and main characteristics or ethos
- client's background – aims and objectives, products and/or services, target audience (customers) and unique selling point
- any important aspects or issues that you may need to take account of when fulfilling the brief
- visual references, e.g. images of colour schemes, branding, logos, building interior/exterior, products, uniforms, etc.

How does the client view itself?

Sources of information

These can include:

- Direct contact with the client and research visits
- Client's website
- Marketing and advertising campaigns, e.g. promotional materials
- Mission statement
- Press releases
- Direct contact with customers and user reviews
- Trade magazines
- National and local media
- Social media, e.g. Facebook, Twitter, Instagram, YouTube, Pinterest, blog, etc.

Common gaps in research

It is impossible to cover everything, but common gaps in research occur when simple insights into products, companies or services are neglected. So try to have a real experience through direct interaction with the product, company or service. It means getting a consumer perspective and trying things out using a scenario analysis, such as putting a product into extreme situations or looking at it from alternative perspectives.

Balanced view

There is often a difference between what the client believes it is projecting to the audience and the way the audience actually experiences the client. You must be able to assess this and try to create work that brings the two perspectives closer together. Once you have researched the client and understood its values, you can compare this with how it is viewed by its target demographic. You could do this through surveys, questionnaires or focus group discussions.

Gathering information

You need to gather broad forms of information and compare and contrast them. Collect your information in different ways such as:

- record interviews
- create a survey
- draw and sketch
- photograph
- collect ephemera.

Planning your research

Start by listing anything you can easily access to start the research.

▼

Make sure you get real experience of the product, service or location.

▼

Finally, balance primary with secondary research opportunities.

Links See page 101 for more on primary and secondary research.

Now try this

An online women's clothing retailer is expanding its product range to include children's clothes. Write a short research plan that includes five different stages in order.

Research could be endless. Setting targets and priorities is an effective way of managing it.

Analysing the audience

Demographic information, market research data and questionnaires can all be analysed to learn more about the audience so you can produce a design solution that works both creatively and functionally.

Who is the audience?

The brief will identify the target audience the client is trying to attract, such as a new group of consumers or widening an existing customer or membership base. You will need to research the characteristics of the audience so you can develop ideas for an art and design solution that the audience will want to engage with.

Market research data

Market research involves gathering information or data about the target audience. There are two types of research:

- **primary** – this is new research which is tailored to the needs of the task, for example face-to-face interviews, surveys and focus groups
- **secondary** – this may include data about the target audience already collected by the client.

What are demographics?

Demographic information relates to characteristics of a population or group of people. Clients use demographics to develop ideas about potential future target audiences as well as established ones. They often define their target audience – the **market** – using a range of demographic factors:

Age – different age groups have different needs and spending patterns.

Gender – different groups have different tastes and needs, and spending patterns.

Socio-economic groups – people of a similar social and economic status, often based on occupation, employment status and income.

Demographic factors

Geographical location.

Ethnic, cultural and religious background – these influence people's choice of food, fashion and styles.

Income – how much money people have to spend. People with higher incomes have different spending patterns from those on lower incomes.

These categories can be measured and statistical data produced. As you develop your understanding of the audience you will see how their characteristics fit into target demographics.

Surveys and questionnaires

Surveys are used to gather information. They may be carried out in person, online, by phone or by post, using a questionnaire which asks the individual a series of questions about themselves.

Responses to questionnaires can provide both quantitative and qualitative data which can be analysed and used to shape ideas for products and services in line with the needs of the audience.

Note that quantitative data is information about quantities, so it can be measured and written down with numbers. Qualitative data is information about qualities, so it can't actually be measured.

Focus groups

These are groups of people selected by a company or organisation to give their views and opinions on a particular product. A moderator conducts the discussion. The group's attitudes and reactions are used to produce qualitative research which is analysed to help the company or organisation to develop products and services that meet the target audience's needs.

Now try this

Think about the colour scheme, textures and materials that could be incorporated to help them feedback on experience.

A children's hospital is planning an outdoor play space in a disused walled area easily accessed from the children's outpatient department on the ground floor. The hospital believes that play facilities will help children to feel safe and happy. Design a questionnaire to find out what staff, parents and children visiting the outpatient department would like to experience when using the play area.

Technical requirements and constraints

A client's branding and house style are often central to its identity. The brief may also specify that your art and design solution should be based on certain sizes or materials and take account of environmental sustainability.

Identifying requirements

These are the aspects that the client believes are important in making them or their brand distinctive. Examples include the triangular packaging and logo of Toblerone chocolate, the interior branding of Nando's restaurants, or the uniforms worn by students at your local secondary school. These may make the client instantly recognisable within their market or area of interest. The client brief should specify any elements that are special requirements, and what needs to happen to them.

Identifying constraints

Clients may have special ways of making and marketing their products. The materials and production processes they use will be part of their identity, no matter how large or small their ranges of products. You may need to consider:

- the type of materials you are permitted to use
- specific formal elements such as colour schemes in logos
- size, scale and production methods
- legal and ethical factors that may apply to the company or organisation
- ensuring the design idea is sustainable and works to preserve the environment.

Practical considerations

A brief may require art and design ideas that have a practical application.

Functional aspects to consider could include designing work uniforms or an interior/exterior area.

Brand colours

Colours are an important part of the way consumers and users recognise and choose products, services and artefacts. For example, the iconic orange and white colour scheme of EasyJet makes it instantly recognisable. Sometimes a client may require the design solution to use their existing brand colours, or they may want them to be revamped.

BA crew members in uniform showing brand colours in the tie and scarf.

House styles

These are existing and very specific visual characteristics, such as a set range of colours or typography, e.g. the unique dark red lettering of Kellogg's cereals. Think about what makes brands instantly recognisable – would they still be so if you changed their house style?

Art-based pieces

A brief may ask for an art-based solution to a specific issue, such as a piece of sculpture for corporate offices. It will have to fit a number of themes or ideas the client wants the piece to communicate.

Now try this

Your local library is redesigning its children's section for the under-fives. You have been asked to put forward ideas to make the area user friendly for parents and young children. What are the likely legal and ethical requirements and constraints?

Working with constraints

Technical requirements and constraints given in the brief will include some direction on how visuals are to be used.

Visual constraints

These:

- include use of company logos, text and information
- can be key imagery that needs to be instantly recognisable to the viewers
- will vary according to the brief
- function in more than one way
- are informative, attractive and attention grabbing.

House design style guides

The designer of the brand visual identity will have developed the style guide with the client. The style guide will be published for any new designers to work with to ensure there is future consistency. You need to follow these rules, but also appreciate the creative opportunities they present. Some style guides go into great detail and cover elements such as:

- fonts – weights and styles
- colours and shades
- pattern and textures available
- positioning of logo, wordmark or slogan
- use of images
- other style elements.

Mini briefs

Each of the mini briefs will have their own constraints or technical requirements. These aren't always written within the brief, but you will have to reflect on that specific scenario and what constraints should be automatically applied. For example, if a product is to be sold in a gift shop, that application will automatically need to have no harmful aspects such as sharp materials or features. You will need to look at the particular application of the product and what constraints that would automatically incur, such as:

- size
- materials
- sustainability.

The style guide of any company will specify specific colours. The specific Pantone colours, RGB or HEX colours should be accurately applied. Creatively, you can identify which colours are used for accents and which are used for negative space or backgrounds and apply these to your own designs whether they are fashion designs, photography, paintings or sculptures.

Common specialism considerations

3D design	Fashion	Textiles	Photography
Strength, safety, durability, sustainability, finish, balance, weight	Sizes, washing, cost, sustainability, allergy, equality and diversity	Safety, durability, sustainability, hanging, presentation, hand-made or manufactured	Ethics, privacy, copyright, format, empathy, resolution, colour mode, printed or screen-based

Fine art	Graphics	Interactive design
Scale, weight, safety, material, durability, product application	Colour mode, resolution, copyright, stock vector or raster, accessibility	Compatability, file type, platform, audience ability

Now try this

Describe at least three constraints that would automatically relate to a product for 5–8-year-old children.

Analysing your research

Once you have gathered information and ideas, you need to analyse your research.

Analysis

Pull out facts and information that are relevant to your line of enquiry. Look for information to analyse and support your initial ideas generation:

👍 Use critical review to make initial judgements about your research.

👍 Establish a link between your research and visual ideas – this will help you to justify your decisions later.

👍 Reach personal conclusions. Make sure you can support them with facts from your research.

 Links See page 106 for initial ideas generation.

Ongoing research

Research and analysis within art and design don't start and stop at the beginning of a task. While the bulk of research may be undertaken at the start, it would be usual to continue to research throughout. Each stage of the task, such as initial ideas, development and refinement, can bring up further questions that need to be resolved. You should expect this and include some time contingency for further research throughout.

Practitioners use critical review to make judgements about research. Within an assessment context you will need to work independently. Outside of an assessment context, you could do it with others in a form of critique. (Often, discussing research with others can help a practitioner draw more succinct conclusions.)

Evaluate your research to identify gaps, and compare different types of research to determine what is most valuable. This can supply surprising results.

This type of evaluation should be approached with an open mind in order to avoid preconceptions of results. It is important that you see your own opinion framed within the context of others' opinions and no more or less important.

Any critical review should be logical and evidence based, using arguments to back up judgements.

Establishing a link between your initial ideas and the research as a whole is demonstrated by statements about how you will develop the task.

Sample notes extract

After undertaking analysis of the company and collecting different types of research, it was clear that the audience has an expectation of the company to maintain its traditional presence. While I would have liked to perform wider surveys, there was a clear response from my small sample. This was similar to my own personal view of the company and what I expect it to be on balance with a questionnaire that I put out to the potential audience of the product.

While I had hoped to break the mould with my personal designs, looking at wider competition that the company has, they all use a colour palette, fonts, styling and images that reflect a hand-made and artisan quality that should be included in any product solutions. Because of this, I would like to start by collecting samples of materials and textures to incorporate into the design that reflect this, such as wood, handmade paper and natural dyes. Looking at products that are commonly purchased by the audience demographic also confirms this. The colours preferred by 80% of the demographic, and confirmed within the survey of 14–20 year olds, were also more muted natural colours as opposed to the synthetic feel.

By assessing the survey you might find significant differences and strong evidence that confirms your initial inclination.

Now try this

Look at the National Trust website, and consider the design elements used across some of the pages. Draw informed conclusions in a short paragraph about how it is trying to present itself.

Recording your research

As you carry out research, record all your findings so that you can start to generate ideas.

Visual and written records

You will need to record your research both visually and in written format because:

👍 drawing and colour help to connect research into generating ideas

👍 visuals will help you to think of the issues involved in art and design terms; they may also help you engage with components of the brief

👍 you can use both text and images from this research stage within your final presentation (and any speaker notes you may have to produce) to demonstrate the full process you have gone through.

Organising your research

1 Keep your research in order by putting it under headings, e.g. 'history of company'.

2 Summarise key findings from your initial research under each heading.

3 Key data might be used in your final presentation to put your art and design work into context. Use this to show your knowledge of the client and their brief.

4 Where possible, use your analysis/results to justify decisions.

This learner looks at poster designs and how they relate to a brief. Some constraints are listed in the brief, but some you need to interpret.

Sample notes extract

I researched artists that have produced posters for petrol companies as well as posters for films made by Saul Bass and unofficial posters by Olly Moss. I collected these together into groups in order to compare and contrast each and inform my ideas development. I annotated each with critical reflection that summarised the research, and set targets for how these would inform the constraints of the task. The next phase began with active research by placing colours with textures and materials. I photographed or scanned these at clear stages of progress that enabled me to look back and identify which worked the best. Placing each text next to each other, I was able to analyse which suited the audience for the brief more and summarised this in annotation.

Organise and collate research into sections to help develop ideas and potentially an image for your presentation.

Research can be both analytical and practical as in a process of testing. Keep it methodical and balance action with recording to help you make informed decisions and keep the task organised.

The annotation of the task needs to be able to communicate your creative thoughts and decisions without you being there.

Recording techniques

Record your research using:

✓ drawing techniques – diagrams of processes or set-ups as well as visualisations of ideas

✓ photography showing the development of large-scale work or yourself at work

✓ screen grabs of practical working processes

✓ drafts – using digital or traditional mark making

✓ annotation – critically analysing work, noting ideas and planning future ideas

✓ scanning or photocopying 2D work, tests and experiments.

Now try this

Choose an exercise from this Guide and write a short annotation that covers:

- what you did
- why you were doing it
- what you learned
- what you would do differently next time
- how the learning will impact on the preparatory stage.

Ideas generation techniques

Once you have a full understanding of a brief and its constraints and requirements, you can use a variety of techniques to generate ideas in response to a client's brief.

How to generate ideas

Before starting to generate ideas, make sure that you have a clear definition in your own mind of the issues to be addressed. Use a variety of ideas generation techniques – find out which ones work best for you.

Visit exhibitions, galleries, museums and design shows to look at contemporary or historic examples.

Look at contextual sources – starting points for images might come from films and literature, products from sculpture, public art from performance.

Research related or existing solutions used by your client or other similar organisations.

Think how you could use the constraints of the brief creatively – e.g. using materials in a new or different way.

Ideas generation techniques

Describe the characteristics of what you think would make a successful response to the brief.

Use visual based techniques, e.g. collage and cut-and-paste techniques are useful for playing around with imagery and situations.

Use word association, quotes and straplines.

Produce mind maps.

Analysis of a similar or existing solution

☑ Is it currently fit for purpose?

☑ Does it answer your brief?

☑ How does it work? E.g. engaging visuals, recognisable and effective branding, innovative visual imagery.

☑ Does it fail your brief? Is it out of date, addressing the wrong target audience, not user friendly?

☑ Is the solution functional? Does it meet users' needs?

Evaluating your ideas

☑ Relate your ideas back to the purpose in the brief – themes or issues, client requirements and any constraints.

☑ Conduct contextual analysis of your ideas by considering them in relation to current practice in your specialism as well as purpose.

☑ Identify mistakes made by previous solutions – try not to repeat them.

☑ Reflect on your ideas as you develop them. Use annotation and critical language to justify how your ideas meet the client brief.

Think about its purpose or target audience as well.

Now try this

Take a piece of design such as: Frank Lloyd Wright – Fallingwater; Malevich – *Black Square*; Louise Bourgeois – *Maman*, and describe its characteristics, justifying how these make it successful.

Applying client and audience analysis to ideas

At this stage, you will have a lot of ideas. Now you need to refine and develop them using your understanding of the client and target audience to ensure your ideas respond to the brief.

Using your analysis

Use your analytical skills to reflect critically on your ideas. This will help to:

- support your decision-making as you develop certain ideas, or use specific materials, techniques and processes
- select and refine ideas to produce the most creative outcome
- justify why you have rejected one idea and selected another.

Meeting your client's needs

Understanding your client and their requirements will enable you to:

- select relevant information and material from the brief to inform ideas
- make links between the client's requirements and your ideas
- justify your ideas
- organise your presentation in a logical way.

Analysing audience requirements

Contextual analysis will inform your work and help you to **select** which ideas to develop. Be aware of what other practitioners in your specialism are doing currently, as well as those in the wider fields of literature, film and so on. How do your ideas link to their work? How does this relate to the needs of the target audience?

Materials

☐ Bright 5%
☐ Synthetic 10%
☐ Pastel 10%
☐ Natural 75%

Details from test firings for ceramic tiles. These were made in response to target audience analysis showing a preference for natural looking materials as opposed to synthetic, pastel or bright. A questionnaire was used to obtain this feedback, which is shown in the pie chart.

Target audience analysis of test firings of ceramic tiles.

Now try this

List three different aspects of audience demographic that may have an impact on your designs.

Creativity and purpose

As you develop and refine your ideas, you will need to continually assess how well they meet the criteria of the brief. Your response and presentation should also demonstrate your creative skills and your choice of formal elements and materials, techniques and processes.

What is the purpose?

👍 Materials. Are they functional, safe and ethical? Are they exciting and interesting, perhaps even challenging?

👍 Scale. Is your design appropriate for human scale? Does a public artwork or sculpture reference its surroundings?

👍 Functionality. Does the design solution need to be ergonomic or user friendly?

👍 Communicating an idea. Does your solution need to communicate an idea? How well does it achieve this?

Remember

Be adventurous! Try out imaginative ideas. If your ideas don't work, can you explain why not?

Being creative

- Select relevant information and material from the brief to inform ideas.
- Communicate your ideas.
- Make links between the client's requirements and your ideas.
- Explain how your ideas meet the brief.
- Justify your ideas.
- Organise your presentation in a logical and professional way that covers all areas of the task and meets the requirements of the client brief.

🔗 **Links** For more on how to plan a presentation, see page 114.

Sample notes extract

Client information: A soft drinks manufacturer plans to promote its latest product – a juice drink – to younger audiences. It is keen to stress that the drink is packed with natural exotic fruits, is exciting and full of flavour.

Client brief: Design 2D and moving imagery for advertisements for the new product.

I have used scale as a way of making the image stand out more. I wanted to incorporate some of the ideas I had seen in many adverts that employ surrealist techniques which vary scales and use juxtaposition in their work – this acts as a visual device to 'shock' the viewer by presenting something that shouldn't really exist. I think this juxtaposition would appeal to the target audience more than just facts, and would make viewers sit up and take more notice of the visuals, which is ideal when trying to attract attention to a product in a busy environment, alongside other similar products. This could work well as still imagery and a moving sequence.

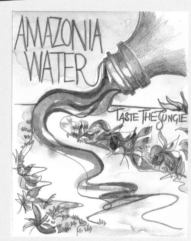

In this extract from ideas development, the learner has recorded their thoughts about the target audience and demographic age range and tried to use techniques that would stimulate them, such as juxtaposition.

The learner has concluded that the target audience is continuously saturated by media stimulus and has tried to use an approach they feel will stand out from the wealth of daily input.

The learner has considered the audience and tried to develop a unique selling point (USP) within their visual language that differentiates this brand from other similar products. This approach is often used within the design sector to draw attention.

Now try this

How would you define 'purpose' in a client brief? Write down a maximum of three sentences that explain your definition.

Think of the experience you want the audience to have or the way you want them to respond.

Choosing ideas

Your development and refinement of ideas will result in several initial drafts in response to the brief. Some may be more suitable than others and you will need to select which ones to take forward to the next stage of development.

Which idea?

The idea you choose to take forward is the one you think best meets the needs, purpose and requirements of the brief. It should be relevant to the needs of the audience, as well as demonstrating your creativity.

Think about the ideas in your mind maps and select one to take forward.

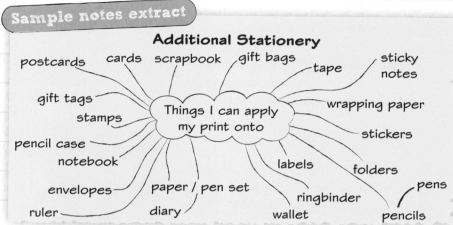

Sample notes extract

Additional Stationery

Things I can apply my print onto

postcards · cards · scrapbook · gift bags · tape · sticky notes · gift tags · stamps · wrapping paper · stickers · pencil case · notebook · labels · folders · envelopes · paper / pen set · ringbinder · pens · ruler · diary · wallet · pencils

Why this idea?

When you select one idea to take forward, you need to show *why* you selected this particular idea.

- What does it have that makes it better suited to the purpose of the brief than the others?
- How is it the most creative solution?

 Links There is more on justifying your ideas on page 110.

 Links There is more on selecting images that show your ideas on page 112.

Making good selections

To test and find out which of your choices are the best ones, you could include the following ways:

- Set up a display of your work and compare examples that you have selected with peers.
- Use focus groups that feature the same demographic audience as the client brief targets.
- Use a blog to get feedback from other learners and users, if appropriate.

When working in an assessment context, you may need to work independently with your own critical review. Check the Pearson website for the most up-to-date **Sample Assessment Material** to find out what is required of you.

Explain your selection

Why did you select certain ideas for development, and discard others? In your preparatory work, use your annotations from generating ideas to:

- select ideas for development
- explain how they need to be refined
- justify your selection.

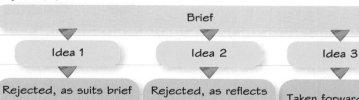

Brief

Idea 1 — Rejected, as suits brief and audience well, but repeats current market trends too much

Idea 2 — Rejected, as reflects audience well, but misses some details from the brief

Idea 3 — Taken forward as reflects brief and audience needs well

Developing work

After selecting the idea you are going to take forward, you will need to develop your work in more detail.

👍 You should plan for time to reflect, select and develop certain ideas, even if you don't know what they are going to be at the start.

👍 You don't have to have a fully finished outcome.

👎 Avoid having an idea at the start but not testing it early on.

👎 Avoid having a wide range of research and experimenting that doesn't connect to the idea you take forward.

Now try this

Your local college is redesigning its careers and employability centre. Using your current careers centre as an example, identify two ways of improving it and explain why.

 Try to create an informative and aesthetic layout.

Justifying and refining ideas

As you develop your ideas, add notes and comments to your work. Annotations help to record your progress, justify your decisions and act as a critical tool to help you refine your ideas and evaluate the relevance of your response to the client brief.

Using annotations

- Continually refer back to the brief and its purpose – the issue or theme you are developing.
- Keep in mind the audience and client, and what they require.
- Show how you are refining your ideas and why.

Sample notes extract

On the bottom right is a photo showing what the original paper looked like. I thought this might be an interesting surface to print on to – it might give the image depth, though I would lose some of the detail in the print. This would give it a hand-made feel. I think the contrast between the very black ink and white/brown mixed paper works well, and is more effective than when printed on to a plain surface.

Good critique

Your judgements should go beyond mere like and dislike. You need to evaluate your work objectively.

- ✓ How well do your ideas and visual images function together?
- ✓ Do they meet the brief's purpose, technical requirements and constraints?
- ✓ Will your ideas reach the target audience?
- ✓ How creative have you been?

Annotation will help you to refine your creative ideas. Remember to use critical language and correct terminology.

Making judgements

Refining your ideas will direct you towards a more concise and effective response.

Sample notes extract

In this print, again on hand-made paper, I think the negative print effect – where the background elements are darker than the objects – creates a visually interesting effect. This way of working stresses the importance of negative space in design work. I think the detail in the print works well, creating a very delicate effect. I could explore the potential in working with materials like lace and peacock feathers further. For instance, I could print text on the paper before working with the objects, and once complete the lighter spaces would show text as well as shape.

Assessing your work as it progresses is important as the ideas are being developed.

Now try this

Choose a page of imagery in your sketchbook and annotate it, reaching a judgement about the strongest image on the page, and justifying why you think this.

Selecting and refining ideas

You need to carefully select and refine your ideas and must be able to justify your selections. You will begin this process during the research and development stage prior to your supervised assessment.

When recording and reviewing research, this learner has:

- placed their work together in order to compare and contrast the ideas to take forward
- selected a preferred visual idea that is still in draft form and applied it to the product they are creating in order to have a better understanding of how their selection will perform on their actual product.

You can use systems like this to help ensure your selections are the ones that most effectively respond to the brief.

Sample notes extract

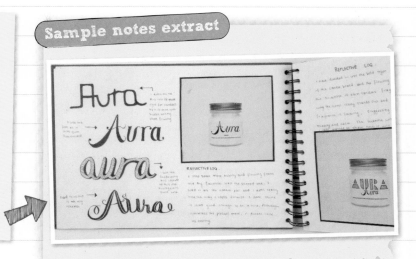

Refining ideas

This involves reviewing your concepts and modifying the use of materials, techniques and processes. Visual imagery can be used to show your thinking about potential solutions to the brief and how they function.

Sample notes extract

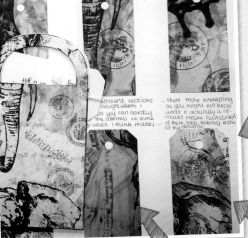

Contextual analysis can be included – covering client and audience needs, and the purpose of the brief.

🔗 **Links** For more on materials, techniques and processes, see Unit 7, page 135.

The way you lay out images and annotations on a page influences how easy it is to read. Display your ideas as clearly as possible.

Compare different design approaches. In this example, some of the design approaches have been slightly amended. This has then been used as a platform to work up some annotation.

Compare and contrast – a single page can contain a lot of information simply by including variations on a theme or idea.

Page layout is a part of visual language and can communicate order as well as balance. Look at the spaces around the images (gift tags) and consider how they allow the design ideas to breathe.

Now try this

Think of two ideas for a poster that promotes awareness of dyslexia. Write a short sentence that explains why one is more suitable than the other.

Selecting images

When selecting images, choose ones that are interesting and show your creativity. You can use these both to record your research and development work, and in your presentation. Keep a record of how the images work for you. You will then be able to use your annotations if you need to write speaker notes for your presentation.

Sample notes extract

Wall study

I was researching examples of formal elements that I could use for starting points, and really wanted to focus on pattern. I used the camera as a sketchbook tool – for recording thoughts, not a polished product. The formal elements I looked at were shape and colour, leading into visual language about pattern.

The wall gave me a set of unique shapes as it wasn't regular. I thought this was useful as it showed I was looking beyond the obvious regular, neat brickwork in lines. The shapes and textures also seemed to communicate something about age – they looked really old and had been repaired. This gave me the idea that I could use pattern to reference age and time (which I hadn't thought about before).

If you are using the camera, aim to take images that are clear, focused, well-lit and readable.

You can crop and edit the imagery to clear up any defects.

When looking at a surface or pattern, take time to make sure you record it effectively. The images and annotations/explanations you produce during the research and development stage can all go towards the work you present to your client.

You are conducting visual analysis when you make notes on your ideas and art and design developmental work.

Sample notes extract

Natural pattern

I thought I could use natural form as it was an area I felt the company had some sort of link with through their products. Natural form would allow me to develop an interesting background to use for overlaying text (like a layer in software). This image has a limited range of colours. This range works as it is harmonious and has enough variation in the shapes to make it interesting. I enjoyed using the camera as a sketchbook in these examples as this allowed me the freedom to record instantly and with a lot of detail. I used drawing alongside this work to pull out and exaggerate the main shapes.

Use images to show your thinking. Your visual analysis can help you to make decisions as you develop your work.

 Links For more on formal elements, see Unit 7, page 152.

Describe the formal elements in what you are recording.

Work out how you can use a variety of different recording techniques to develop your ideas.

Now try this

Take your camera and record a formal element clearly and effectively.

 Use the camera as a sketchbook to record the real world: isolate details, reduce the object to formal elements (colour, shape, texture) and look at the components of pattern.

Presenting a response to a client brief

Presenting your response to a client brief takes time and planning. Presentation skills are an important aspect of the role of an art and design practitioner.

A presentation

As part of Unit 6, you will plan and structure a presentation in response to the brief, covering all aspects within time constraints. You will need to make effective use of visual prompts and organise the presentation material. In a commercial environment, a presentation will often be a pitch to a client to try to persuade them to commission an idea or a product. It may be produced in response to the client's brief and is one way in which many art and design practitioners find work.

Remember

✓ You will gather a lot of information during the research and development stage of your enquiry, but you won't be able to include everything in a presentation. Try to select materials that clearly communicate your ideas and how they link to the brief.

✓ Explore different ways of presenting your ideas to find the methods and formats that work best for you. Practise methods that you are less familiar with to build your confidence.

Presentation format

To find out what format you should use for the presentation in your assessment, check the Pearson website for the most up-to-date **Sample Assessment Material**.

How your ideas address the target audience

How your ideas are appropriate to the brief

The art and design issue you're responding to

How you selected and used information from the client information to inform your ideas

Presentation of response to include:

The justification for how your ideas meet the brief

How you developed your ideas from the initial stages through to your final idea

Formal elements, materials, techniques and processes you have chosen

Your final idea, including visual representations

🔗 **Links** For more on formal elements, materials, techniques and processes, see Unit 7, pages 152–154 and 160–162.

Now try this

Put the above list in an order that you would use for your actual presentation.

Professional presentations

Your presentation should look professional. Make sure your ideas are put across clearly to the client and are well supported with high-quality images.

Getting it right

Effective presentations have usually been tested out on an audience and modified where necessary. This enables the presenter to get a sense of how the display or slides work and how much information the audience receives.

✓ *Explore your presentations by trying them out on peers or invited audiences.

✓ Ask yourself 'what makes a presentation effective?' and think about those examples you research – are they effective? And if so, how?

*For the purposes of your assessment, you may have to work independently. Check the guidelines on the Pearson website by accessing the most up-to-date **Sample Assessment Material**. However, you can try out and improve the presentation yourself. When you are not in an assessment context, testing out your presentations with peers is a great idea.

Use quality images

Professional presentations rely on accurate, clear examples and images of work. If the work is of a high standard, it can be compromised by poor presentation and images. Use appropriate recording techniques such as photography, video and scanning to capture your work. If you're unfamiliar with a technique, you must practise all the tasks and stages involved in the process before recording any images.

 Links More details on photographing work is dealt with on pages 180–181, in Unit 7.

 Links For more information on effective presentations, see page 118.

Mount physical artwork

Art and design pieces should be presented using a sympathetically selected mounting material such as card or a frame. You could use non-traditional materials such as coloured plastics, wood boards or textured card as long as the results keep the main focus of attention on the artwork. Plinths and stands are used to present small-scale 3D work that can then be photographed. Make sure to include an object to give a real sense of scale.

Displaying digital presentations

A digital presentation can be uploaded and viewed anywhere. To facilitate this you need a workable balance between image quality and file compression. Always try to have the maximum file size to ensure visuals are of the best quality for viewing. JPEGs are a good-quality image format, but make sure the file size is a minimum of 300ppi. Where this is not possible, don't go below 72ppi.

Large-scale and 3D pieces

You may not have the option of mounting work if you have worked on large-scale projects in 3D, moving designs, installations or larger-scale pieces. Where models and maquettes are used, they can be photographed using controlled lighting.

Links There is more about photographing 3D work on pages 180–181, in Unit 7.

Physical artwork can be part of any presentation so long as it's recorded in a way that shows it to its full potential.

Now try this

Scan two sketchbook pages that work effectively in showing your art and design development on a project and prepare a single slide based on the two scans.

Presentation methods and formats

There are different ways of delivering a presentation – your client might request a specific format, or you can establish what works best for you.

Different ways of presenting

A presentation can consist of a single method and format, or a combination of the techniques below.

> ### Presentation format
> To find out what format you should use for the presentation in your assessment, check the Pearson website for the most up-to-date Sample Assessment Material.

Physical display – work can be mounted (as in an exhibition) or hand held (informal). Benefits are: the audience can see the tactile and surface qualities in the work; for some briefs (e.g. sculpture or 3D modelling) it is important to actually see or engage with the work.

Digital-based presentations – the work is scanned or photographed, compiled in software and put into sequence. Benefits are: portability (can be shown anywhere there is a screen) and can be professional.

Web-based presentations – work is presented via a blog or vlog, so it will have to be recorded digitally, then uploaded. Benefits are: allows comments and responses, possible in real time. There are many online presentation tools that are used as an alternative to PowerPoint. The benefits include being able to have different features and sometimes less linear presentations.

Presentation methods

Videos – the presenter may use a video to explain a product or service and then leave time for questions and answers at the end or they may combine short pieces of video along with verbal presentation. The benefit is that it combines audio and visuals in an exciting way.

Verbal presentations – the presenter explains individual ideas and images. Benefits are: more detailed explanations of the main points and processes; an opportunity to respond to queries.

Practical matters – your presentation

Consider the following when creating your presentation:

- ✓ Digital formats – what is required by your software? Will it work on all platforms?
- ✓ Do your images tell the complete story? Do they have impact? Avoid overcrowding individual pages and your overall display.
- ✓ How can your presentation notes contribute to the images?
- ✓ Do the images need any text displayed alongside them to clarify their content?

Now try this

Organise information for a slide, showing how you tested a process or material in a project.

Selecting for a presentation

Selecting the right visual imagery will improve the effectiveness of a presentation.

Selection criteria

The selection process is key to the success of your presentation. You should aim to show the viewer how you have met the brief and addressed the client's requirements and audience needs. Try to set some criteria for your images and slides. These could be statements you can use to help decide which images to include, for example:

- key stages of the creative process
- major issues you had to deal with
- major creative decisions.

What to include

Try to select from your whole body of work. You could include:

- annotated visual recording
- visual representations of your ideas, and the one that you take forward
- your selected formal elements and visual language
- tests, samples, models, prototypes, maquettes, studies.

Slide show

If you are using presentation software, plan out each slide – think about what it should show and say. Each slide should have a very clear purpose.

👍 A slide can use imagery from different pages.

👍 You can collage images together on one overall slide to explain or highlight points. Practise using basic image-editing software.

👍 Make sure every slide is readable – keep it clear and straightforward.

Remember

✓ Check the Pearson website and the latest version of the Sample Assessment Material to find out what kind of presentation is required. If you are required to present digitally, you can find out how many slides you should use.

✓ Avoid repeating information. When you explain how you have approached the brief, just explain your interpretation of the needs and purpose.

✓ Avoid overfilling slides if you're using presentation software.

Speaker notes

Spend some time thinking about the sequence of imagery. How will it best explain your work on the brief? If you are using presentation software, you need to think about the speaker notes and select the most relevant imagery.

There will be a sequence of activities you have worked through in the brief. You can use the selected visuals alongside the notes to explain how your response to the brief developed, as well as justify your decision making, and demonstrate your ability to critically reflect on your progress.

Think about how you could show the developmental work and the key aspects of your journey through the brief.

Checklist

You could create a checklist from your selection criteria, which can be used to refine the presentation as you are compiling it. Check that the different stages in the brief are all addressed by the slides.

Purpose	
Client needs	✓
Users' needs	✓

Now try this

Take the ideas generation stage of an existing project and select imagery for two slides that best show the ideas you developed.

Structuring a presentation

To be effective, your presentation should be well structured, include relevant information and reflect the brief. If you are using presentation software, the speaker notes can contain supporting information.

The structure

A good presentation follows a clear and ordered structure.

> The introduction, title and name

| Your target audience and the theme or issue | The brief – purpose and creative approach | Your ideas – how you developed them, what informed them | The stages in your development – testing, experimentation |

> Effective visual representation of your ideas and progress

| The final idea – why you chose this | Outline your points logically and in sequence. | Detail your response – how did you use formal elements, materials, techniques and processes? Identify the vital aspects you tried to address – refer to your brief to make sure you have included everything. | Make small summaries or sign-posts as you progress – did you meet the needs of the audience for the brief or the client's needs? |

> The conclusion – how you met the brief

| Use your introduction outline to summarise your main points. | Make sure you justify your conclusion using appropriate language and terminology. | Summary |

Relevant information

Only include information that is informative, and keep it snappy. You need to show what you decided were the key areas to research and develop, and what you found out.

- Relate your points to your visual content.
- Minimise the amount of text on your slides if you are using presentation software.

Speaker notes

If you are using speaker notes, they should contain the important details and explanations of your presentation.

- They can be structured in different ways. Use bullet points to highlight the main points you want to get across.
- They should contain all the important things you need to say.
- Remember that your speaker notes may be used to assess your presentation.

 Links For more information on speaker notes, see page 126.

 Now try this

Using presentation software, create a grid on a page that you could use as a template to present all pages.

If you are using presentation software:
- before the presentation, practise producing your presentation, managing the time, and, if presenting on a computer, using your hardware and software
- during the presentation, ensure your explanations (which may be formatted as speaker notes) sound informative and clear.

Presenting your information clearly

Your presentation should communicate information clearly and support your response.

Getting the information across

Think about how you want to use text in your visual presentation, which may use presentation software and slides. The structure (of slides, as well as your presentation) should tell the story of your enquiry and support your approach to meeting the brief.

Making good use of text and visuals

- Avoid reproducing the detailed text of your speaker notes. Use text for the title of each slide and to focus the viewer's attention on particular aspects of the slide.
- Use the key points from the client brief as headers for some of the slides.
- Make a montage of different images taken from different pages or slides. Don't feel you have to make simple records of each page – collect them together to express your ideas.

Considering your options

You can use different techniques to present your work, depending on how much you have and what you select. These might be:

- photographing examples of pages and work under controlled light in a studio
- scanning flat artwork from sketchbooks (you may be limited by the size of scanner available)
- photographing using cameras with built-in flash, or if permitted, a smartphone.

Photographing an example of work in a studio

Photographing your work

If you are photographing samples, tests, larger pieces or models/maquettes, think about using a proper set-up. The difference a well-shot image will make to the professionalism of your presentation is measurable.

 Links To learn more about set-ups see page 120.

Before the presentation

If you are using presentation software, practise your computer skills.

☑ Use image manipulation software to drop images together.

☑ Work through basic editing tasks to clean up and correct any image faults like over-exposure.

☑ Set up slides – especially complex ones where you may be collaging imagery from different pages together.

☑ Time yourself when you set up slides, and adapt and modify your plan for the presentation accordingly.

Now try this

Take photos or scan two different sketchbook pages, and try cropping and combining the strongest drawings onto one page, timing yourself.

Producing and finalising visuals

You should work closely with your imagery and text when you are producing and finalising the visual parts of your presentation. In the example below, the learner has used software to create their presentation.

Sample response extract

Ideas and imagery for single head idea based on research for 'antique'

Image 1 – original idea

The two smaller drawings are an important part of the design development process. They are smaller in scale so they don't detract from the central purpose of the slide, which is to show the main image at this stage and provide some background information.

Image 2 – amended idea, using software

Think carefully about the purpose of each slide so that you get the right layout.

Image 3 – reworked head combined with different surfaces in software.

Make the important imagery stand out. Here the largest image is the most important on the slide. It is large enough to show the viewer the relevant detail and to allow the explanation to be meaningful.

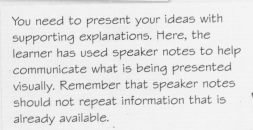

You need to present your ideas with supporting explanations. Here, the learner has used speaker notes to help communicate what is being presented visually. Remember that speaker notes should not repeat information that is already available.

This image was preferred as it:
- stands out as the most effective visually
- shows the research theme in the most dynamic way
- is most suited to the original intention in the brief.

Development:
- The background marks stood out too much, so these needed to be re-layered in software.

Now try this

Practise laying out slides using existing imagery. Include some description and evaluative comments.

Using visuals, language and terminology

Use visuals, language and terminology that the client can relate to in your presentation. If appropriate for the requirements of the brief, you could include the use of set-ups to help the client visualise your response.

Language and terminology

The language you use with clients should be fit for purpose. They will want to know how you think your ideas will meet their brief before delving deeper into your processes and influences. Use terminology that makes sense to them.

Commercial examples

Think about how visuals and text are used commercially to present work in:

- ✓ catalogues
- ✓ brochures
- ✓ websites
- ✓ online galleries.

Using visuals to demonstrate the theme

For the set-up opposite, you could discuss colour and layered imagery as themes. You could explain what the image shows, and discuss the colour range being applied across a suite of products. Your presentation would then explain how the products would all have an identity linked by the marks, printed imagery and colour.

In this set-up, the brief required a motif that could be used across furnishings and have a surface pattern. The entire set-up is unified by the motif and the way it is printed. It is an excellent example of how to present a cohesive product idea.

Set-ups

A set-up is a useful way of demonstrating a response to a brief, where appropriate for the requirements of the client. It shows the viewer and clients how you visualise the ideas you have produced as actual products. Different types of product can lead to creative set-ups to showcase the product:

- in use
- on location
- mocked up
- with a sense of scale
- in a studio commercial setting
- in a pack shot.

Now try this

Select a product or image from a physical or an online catalogue. Use bullets to jot down how the visuals and language are used to appeal to an audience.

Organising information

The strength of a presentation will depend on how well the information is organised.

Structure

Organise information to clearly communicate your intentions and justify what you did.

1 Work through your selection criteria. ▶ **2** Identify the stages in the brief. ▶ **3** If you are using presentation software, decide how many slides you will need for each stage. Some stages may require more slides than others – somewhere between 1 and 3.

🔗 **Links** See page 116 for more on selecting visual imagery for a presentation.

▼

4 Start selecting and organising your information using this initial structure. Identify the key parts in your response. Make your headings and layout clear.

What are the stages?

You can classify the stages and group together the images for each stage in an order like this:

1 Research and information gathering

2 Ideas generation

3 Design development and testing

4 Selection of final idea

5 Production of final piece(s)

6 Justification of ideas to show how the brief was met

7 Selection of work for presentation

Text and visuals

It is important that:

☑ information is organised so that it supports or explains the process

☑ both visual and textual information is used – in this way the main points in the response to the task can be both viewed and explained

☑ you provide supporting explanations for your ideas (this can be via speaker notes if you are using presentation software)

☑ you include evaluative statements

☑ if you are using presentation software, your slides are legible – you may need to reduce the number of words you use.

🔗 **Links** For an example of an effective slide, see page 122.

Explaining

Think about the things you want the audience to know about, for example ideas, purpose, approach, methods and strengths. The final work will show the creative side of your response but you can expand on this with your explanations.

Speaker notes

If you are using presentation software, these give you the opportunity to support each slide. Your speaker notes might be submitted as part of the outcome for your assessment – if that's the case, there's no need to include huge amounts of text on the slides.

Now try this

Organise information for a slide showing how you tested a process or material in a project.

Meeting intentions with your presentation 1

Use your presentation to show the viewer how you engaged with the client brief. You need to demonstrate clearly what you intend. The example slide and speaker notes below are taken from a learner's presentation. They are responding to a brief to design a new logo for a pre-school.

Sample response extract

This slide from a presentation contains a lot of information. The learner has demonstrated a purposeful engagement with the brief – to design a logo for a preschool.

The slide uses a range of imagery. It includes examples where the art and design work is applied to different scenarios (e.g. the exterior of a building). There are also close ups of the design showing how it would look as an image in its own right. The work in your presentation should show the viewer how you met the creative challenge in the brief – imagery will help you to get this and any other relevant points across.

Due to the cost of printing in colour, it is also useful to show the client how a design works in black and white. These are real-life concerns for companies and clients.

 Links Explore putting ideas and imagery together as you work through the selection process. There is more about this on page 124.

This design pays attention to some of the technical design aspects, such as colour and mark making.

In the design I have addressed the key constraints within the brief. These were: to produce a recognisable logo and ID that reflect the nature of the organisation, that are recognisable to the users and that show the client's areas of business; and that can be applied across different situations. My design shows how simple mark making and colour can be combined to create a clear and visible identity, which any audience can relate to.

In this extract from a presentation with speaker notes, the learner has summarised their intention in clear and concise statements, which show they have met the brief in a positive way and addressed the main needs of the client and audience.

Now try this

Take a client-led brief you have worked through and summarise how you met the brief in no more than two paragraphs.

Meeting intentions with your presentation 2

In your presentation, use images to explain your thinking and highlight your intention as well as the processes you have used.

DEVELOPMENTAL PRACTICAL WORK – initial shots and test shoot, fading light

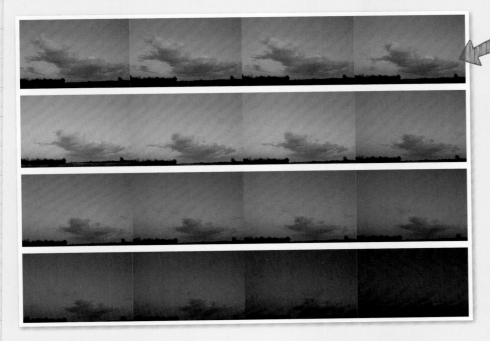

The slide shows:
- the theme, and approach to it (the environment and fading light)
- exploration and testing
- progression of imagery.

Row 1: Initial shots of bright clouds, the brighter colour of the pinks against the blue interesting but too vivid – was not about fading light, more about the cloud shapes. I'm aiming to develop awareness of fading light itself, so needs to be subtler.

Rows 2 and 3: A sequence of images that better shows the idea of light fading (expresses ideas about time and the way light fades at the end of the day). This imagery shows subtleties that allow viewer to be emotionally affected by the dropping in of the darkness. I also believe the deep blue of the later shots captures the essence of the environment that is made (seen or not seen) by the light. Sequence also has a good progression of tonal values.

In this extract from a presentation, speaker notes to accompany a slide are used to reinforce the points. They show:
- the idea behind the images
- how the images are related to the theme
- critical reflection on how the imagery addresses the intention
- some visual analysis.

Select a sequence of images – at least four – that are related. They could be drawings, photographs, prints, etc. Arrange them and write a basic outline for speaker notes to accompany them.

Presenting ideas with explanations

When responding to the client brief, you will need to use images for effect to present your ideas. You should explain how your imagery reflects your ideas and meets the brief.

Sample response extract

This image is the final design for a poster, commissioned by organisers of a film festival. The brief asked that the poster reflect the historical themes in the films selected. During the presentation of the poster, the practitioner explained their ideas both verbally and by using labels.

Introducing the concept

The background text includes an old-style projector with the name of the location. This represents the historical nature of the festival.

The truck uses the symbol of the Bedford Swan, which is a recognisable symbol of the area. In this design the swan shape is made using folded film stock to emphasise the nature of 16 mm film used in the films being shown.

Highlighting explanations

Use lines, arrows and circles, like those shown here, to highlight specific details on your images. Where an image is complex you can use a series of explanations to get your design ideas across.

Explain the depth of ideas

In the poster, the use of this style of truck, and the fonts used on the truck and for 'Film Festival', also represent an historical feel. The colour range is muted and the haziness at the poster's edge makes it look like an early projected film. Do you think this successfully meets the request that the viewers get a sense of the past when they look at the poster?

Supporting statements

Use language that describes the ideas as clearly as you can. It is vital to reference any visual language.

Supporting statements help you when you present back verbally and should be recorded as speaker notes in a digital presentation.

Now try this

Take a final image you have produced for a client brief and break down the ideas to show how you met the brief. You can use diagrams and arrows to identify specific parts of the work.

Summarising, justifying and concluding

A good ending is key to a successful presentation, and includes summaries, justifications and a conclusion.

① Summarising

A summary contains the main points you need to address in your work and presentation. A good summary will:

- use acronyms and abbreviations (avoid lots of abbreviations). Write out uncommon acronyms in full the first time you use them, with the acronym in brackets
- avoid repetition
- be succinct – try to keep sentences to 20 words maximum
- use appropriate terminology and language – practise writing descriptions and justifications.

Summarising	
Research	✓
Ideas generation	✓
Constraints	✓
Testing/sampling	✓
Refinements	✓
Final idea	✓

② Justifying

This shows how your ideas and work met the brief. Good justification involves the following:

- Express your personal opinions.
  What do you like and why do you like it?
  Remember to include the key factors you have to cover: how you met the brief, how it meets audience needs, etc.
- Avoid phrases and terms that don't add new information.

- Use supporting statements. For example, if you make a claim ('it met the needs of the client because...'), back it up ('the supporting evidence is...').
- If you have it, refer to feedback from focus groups on the initial design, modifications that were tested by a set of users, and statistics measured about function or appeal.

Statements and bullet points

Consider using bullet points to make clear any key points and punctuate your explanations. Blend these with prose to develop your ideas and discuss your points in more detail.

③ Bring it to a conclusion

This part is the standout moment of your pitch or presentation and should:

- be short
- be memorable
- address the most important issues
- promote your product
- leave the viewers feeling positive.

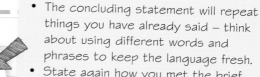

- The concluding statement will repeat things you have already said – think about using different words and phrases to keep the language fresh.
- State again how you met the brief, how it is a creative response and how it meets the client's and audience's needs. Conclude the presentation with a positive statement.

Now try this

Take a response to a client-led or live project you have worked on. Write a conclusion that explains your response to meeting the brief, using a blend of bullet points and longer explanations.

Writing supporting notes

Whatever format you have to use for your presentation, you may also need to prepare some supporting notes.

Structure the information logically.

Introduce new information in a staggered way.

Discuss key changes in the development process.

See how information can be condensed.

Supporting notes

Check grammar and spelling.

Use accessible language and avoid slang or inappropriate jargon.

Make sure information supports the image.

If you are using presentation software, use your speaker notes to support each slide in your presentation.

Writing supporting notes

You can write notes in different ways.

👍 Write in note form, not continuous prose.

👍 Use titles, headings and bullet points.

👍 Explain and provide information on the contents of each page or slide.

👍 Highlight any key points or aspects of your work the page or slide shows.

👍 Make it very clear how you have refined your work, and the reasoning behind this.

It's one idea ...

Your presentation will show how you worked up and selected one idea to meet the brief. Showing some of your rejected ideas is also important if you can use them to explain why they didn't meet the brief or why they didn't express your intentions as well as the one you have chosen.

Check the Pearson website

Ask your tutor or check the Pearson website for the most up-to-date **Sample Assessment Material** and Mark Scheme to get an indication of the format for your presentation. The details of the actual assessed task may change so always make sure you are up to date.

Sample response extract

Using titles makes it clear to the audience what you are trying to discuss. You may want to put the title on the the actual slide too.

You can talk about how this relates to the previous sections of the presentation and explain the results.

Supporting notes

Title: Colour decisions

Earlier colours were synthetic.

Final colour decisions come from nature.

Could have used any picture of nature, but elected to reflect the communication intentions of product.

Overall results were supported by test audiences.

Now try this

Take three products created by a commercial company and include these in a page or slide. Write three bullet points about what makes them stand out from the rest of the market in no more than 50 words.

Justifying and concluding

Whatever format you use for your presentation, at the end of it justify your approach and output to the brief. If you are using presentation software, make this the final slide.

What to cover?

Double check the points you need to consider when concluding – use the client brief for guidelines. Points should include:

- how your ideas addressed the target audience. This will depend on whether you have been given a choice of audience or a specific one.
- how your ideas got across the selected intention of your client. This is the theme or the issue in the brief.

Practise your presentation skills to gain confidence in your work.

Explain how it works

Imagine you are talking to another person about your task, explaining how the design idea works and justifying why you think so. This will help you to get across your ideas persuasively. Practise writing persuasive language.

Using terminology

The way you write the end of your presentation is important. It is your opportunity to express your views and it needs to support all the work you've done. The level of sophistication in your work can be mirrored in the way you use terminology on the page, or on a slide, and in your supporting/speaker notes. This shows the viewer that you understand the visual and technical points you are making and should make your reasoned arguments stronger.

Back up your ideas

Try to base your conclusion on facts as well as your critical reflection. If you believe you have designed some packaging aimed at children that is both attractive and represents the brand, are there any facts that support you?

Use information from focus groups and questionnaires to help. If certain package colours are mentioned by the focus groups, you can justify your use of them by referring to these comments.

 Links Refer to other units to make sure you are using terminology and language as effectively as possible. Unit 2 might be useful!

How to conclude

Put together a couple of concluding sentences that explain exactly why you feel your selected idea meets the brief and the needs of the audience.

The final slide or page is ...

☑ similar to an end-of-assignment critical evaluation you may have worked on for other projects or units.

☑ likely to be written more as prose (not bullet points) than the other slides or pages, as you will be putting across a reasoned argument.

Now try this

Write a paragraph that concludes a project you have worked on, justifying your ideas.

Your Unit 7 set task

Unit 7 will be assessed through a task, which will be set by Pearson. In this assessed task you will need to research, develop and create a set piece, which has a clear purpose, in response to a given theme.

Revising your skills

Your assessed task could cover any of the essential content in the unit. You can revise the unit content in this Revision Guide. This skills section is designed to revise skills that might be needed in your assessed task. The section uses selected content and outcomes to provide examples of ways of applying your skills.

Plan and carry out research.
See pages 132 and 137.

Understand contexts which influence the work of art and design practitioners.
See pages 158–159.

Respond to stimulus material and generate ideas.
See page 138.

Explore and select materials, techniques and processes.

Set task skills

Write a commentary and critique of your work.
See pages 168–169.

Create a finished piece which is fit for purpose.

Create a portfolio which highlights the development process.
See pages 186–187.

Document and record your work.
See pages 139, 165 and 172.

Workflow

The process of creating your own art and design piece in response to a given theme might follow these steps:

✓ Investigate possible ideas using a variety of sources and stimuli, keeping an annotated log of your research and developing ideas.

✓ Write a proposal which outlines and justifies your planned response to the theme.

✓ Create your piece, experimenting as you develop your ideas, and recording the stages.

✓ Compile a portfolio (digital or paper-based) to show the process you have gone through to create your piece in response to the project and the theme.

✓ Write a commentary to accompany your portfolio, explaining how you have achieved your final outcome and how it responds to the theme.

✓ Evaluate the development process you have gone through and your final piece of work.

Check the Pearson website

The activities and sample response extracts in this section are provided to help you to revise content and skills. Ask your tutor or check the Pearson website for the most up-to-date **Sample Assessment Material** and **Mark Scheme** to get an indication of the structure of your actual assessed task and what this requires of you. The details of the actual assessed task may change so always make sure you are up to date.

This Revision Guide

… will support you in understanding:

✓ the key areas of research and development

✓ the skills you will need to apply to the stages in your development work and outcomes.

Now try this

Visit the Pearson website and find the page containing the course materials for BTEC National Art and Design. Look at the latest Unit 7 Sample Assessment Material for an indication of:

- the structure of your set task, and whether it is divided into parts
- how much time you are allowed for the task, or different parts of the task
- what briefing or stimulus material might be provided to you

- any notes you might have to make and whether you are allowed to take selected notes into your supervised assessment
- the activities you are required to complete and how to format your responses.

Planning a response

When you are given a brief and theme for an art and design piece, you need to understand what is required of you and generate ideas. Here are some potential starting points.

Theme and purpose

The task might ask you, for example, to:

- produce a piece of art and design work in response to a given theme (e.g. 'Transformation', 'Conflict' – the theme will be different each time)

- use a discipline of your choice for the piece with a clear purpose (e.g. artwork for an exhibition, advertising/promotional material, interactive product, commercial design/product, functional object, fashion garment or accessory).

Ideas from previous work

You can explore and develop ideas from previous projects. You might have developmental work that didn't end up in final pieces – some of these can trigger initial ideas.

The theme you are given may well be broad, so you might find you have done something similar before – use this for initial inspiration.

Direct recording and the work of others

You can always generate some initial ideas by using direct recording from primary subjects, just to get you going.

You can also consider how others have approached and communicated ideas about the same theme in their work.

Planning a response

Ideas in previous work – look through your portfolio and sketchbook

Direct recording of subjects – use a camera and sketchbook

Look at the work of other practitioners – visit galleries, museums, exhibitions, shopping centres, historic places

Visit urban/rural settings

Starting points for a theme

Reflect on previous feedback for ideas

Use exploratory work from other projects, such as models and maquettes

Reflect on what you think industry or a university will want to see in a portfolio

Consider skills you would like to learn and personal challenges you would like to take on

Things to consider

☑ How best to record the subjects you choose using primary sources and secondary sources.

☑ The potential for a personal, creative response.

☑ How you can find out about contemporary practice in your discipline.

☑ How realistic your ideas are when you think about the resources and time available.

Now try this

Look at one project you have worked on during your course, and see if there are any suitable areas of developmental work that you didn't pursue that could be used for further development.

Taking creative approaches

When generating ideas in response to a theme for an art and design piece, think creatively, be prepared to take risks and avoid the obvious.

Opportunity

Whatever theme you are expected to work with, make it a really personal project. See it as a vehicle for your own creative expression. You might be able to bring things together that you have worked on before, but on which you were limited by the timescales or other factors.

Links You can use skills learned in other units, such as Unit 2, to support and justify your creative development.

Avoiding the obvious

When you work with a theme, there are things that will initially spring to mind. These are fine to think of as potential starting points, but do they offer you the right amount of creative challenge? Reject the obvious! Instead of a 'safe' commercial that simply stated the spec, comfort and performance of its vehicles, Honda's 'Keep Up' advertising campaign jolted the viewer out of their passive consumption of TV adverts by inviting them to speed-read, one word at a time, the car manufacturer's philosophy – that by pushing ourselves we can surpass our own limits.

Taking risks

You can take risks in your developmental work. Work out what might appear an obvious solution to the brief, then come up with a set of ideas and options that consider experimenting and creative alternatives. You can experiment with the way you think about materials, techniques and processes – it's almost a 'what if?' approach. How can materials be used in a new, different way?

You can challenge the viewer of your work to see things in a different way.

Creativity – defining it

You should have an idea what this means for your work. Think about the characteristics of creativity – innovation, doing things differently, making visuals exciting and engaging, and so on. Try to think as creatively as possible about how to approach the theme.

You can also critically reflect on past peer and tutor feedback to help you come up with ideas.

Your creative challenge

Define this in your terms, by asking:
- ☑ How am I going to avoid obvious solutions?
- ☑ How can I use the task for personal expression?
- ☑ How can I explore new ways of working?
- ☑ How can I use the task to explore the skills and creativity I have learned?

Now try this

Take the theme 'Interior' – what would be an obvious response to this theme and what alternatives might you consider, when experimenting for a personal, creative response?

Exploring primary sources

Primary sources will provide different possible directions or initial ideas. Select primary sources that are accessible – you need to be able to record from them.

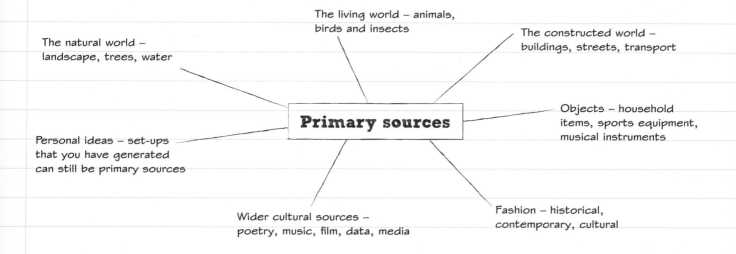

The living world – animals, birds and insects

The natural world – landscape, trees, water

The constructed world – buildings, streets, transport

Primary sources

Objects – household items, sports equipment, musical instruments

Personal ideas – set-ups that you have generated can still be primary sources

Wider cultural sources – poetry, music, film, data, media

Fashion – historical, contemporary, cultural

Choosing primary sources

You should select a range of primary sources to record from. You can then compare your primary sources and decide which relate best to your intentions and which provide useful images and inspiration. Having multiple primary sources will also demonstrate your breadth of research.

Remember

You have to work with sources that will give you the most:

- ✓ scope for creative development
- ✓ information to record from
- ✓ potential to generate ideas that will lead into practical work
- ✓ visually interesting and exciting starting points.

Recording

Practitioners always have recording materials with them since inspiration and ideas can be taken from almost anywhere. Look out for opportunities for recording. It is also important to record the same experience or object from multiple perspectives. Looking at things from different angles – touching, tasting or experiencing the source – can be more useful than simply taking a quick snapshot.

Recording techniques

To record your primary sources, you could use:

- drawings
- photography
- mood boards
- video or film
- written notes
- sound recording
- rubbings
- collecting objects
- annotation
- interviews.

Now try this

Go through one of your sketchbooks and list what kinds of primary sources you have used.

Recording your work

Keep an annotated log of your research and development of your ideas. This will help you to record your progress. You can select from your records when producing a proposal, final piece of art and design, presentation showing development of ideas, and accompanying written commentary.

What should be recorded?

The different tasks you have to carry out provide evidence of what is covered and learned in the unit.

It's important that these stages are recorded accurately in an annotated log as part of the working process.

The log should include samples and mock-ups of your work, evidence of your research into trends, contextual factors, and artists and/or designers who inspire you. You must also keep written notes on your decisions and your refinements throughout the process.

Links There is more on recording on pages 132 and 146.

Describe and reflect

Use recording to show the development of individual pieces. As you do this, add a commentary to the images, reflecting on how the image is changing – bullet points are fine here. When the piece is finished, run the different stages of the recording together – read them like a diary. This will show you how you have approached the work.

Check the Pearson website for the most up-to-date **Sample Assessment Material** and **Mark Scheme** to get an indication of the structure of your actual assessed task and what this requires of you. The details of the actual assessed task may change so always make sure you are up to date.

Your recording can still be visually interesting. Here photography has been used to show the different stages of a paper-making process, with supporting written information. This practice will give a lot of visual information if carried out as a regular part of the working methods in a task.

Having a good range of images to choose from is important. The more you have to choose from the better. You will need to select visuals when you produce a presentation portfolio that shows the development of your ideas and your final piece.

Remember

You can use an annotated log to record:

- ☑ different stages in projects
- ☑ processes
- ☑ the development of ideas, materials, individual pieces and series.
- ☑ Photography can provide visually interesting materials, as well as solving the problem of describing in-depth processes in words alone – how many instruction manuals don't have any pictures?

Sample response extract

A record of progress

MAKING PAPER FOR FINAL DESIGNS!

This process used parcel paper and pink financial pages newspaper. I thought these papers would complement the grey ink I planned to use. The paper was soaked in warm water to break up the fibres, and then blended into a pulp. This was placed in a tray, and filled with double the volume of water to pulp. I then used the frame or deckle to create the paper sheet. I sieved the pulp as I wanted the components I had added – herbs and other materials – to be spread out and not fall in clumps.

Now try this

Take a process you have used and plan out how you could best record and present it.

Recording from primary sources

You can combine different techniques to record from primary sources.

🔗 **Links** Find out about primary sources on page 131.

Sample response extract

Studies for an animatic
Theme: 'Human'

I am producing an animatic for an animated short on the theme 'Human', which will explore a very simple idea – the robot looks human, and when it stands in front of a mirror it sees a version of an actual human face that resembles its own robotic face. I am studying different ways to capture and record imagery that I can interpret into the robot face, and used mannequins as primary source materials.

I used drawings and photography, along with trying to get a feel for the objects, their material, form, colours and textures, which I recorded through annotation and close-up photography and creating colour swatches. I will support these with references to Ridley Scott's 'Blade Runner', Asimov's 'I Robot' and the closing sequence of John Carpenter's 'Prince of Darkness'.

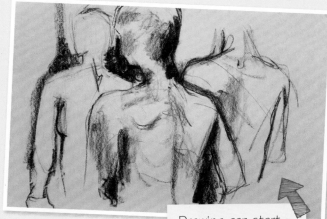

Drawing can start to suggest mood.

This extract records from primary sources, including visuals and explanations of development work. Record from as many sources you can, as well as you can. This will give you more quality materials to select from when creating your final piece, and then presenting and explaining the development process.

While the learner has taken pictures, some of the annotation may actually be more useful. You can record yourself interacting with the subject if necessary. The learner has also been imaginative and resourceful when considering sources to record from. Since they may not have had access to real robots, they have gone for the next closest thing.

Use the camera as an analytical tool – the more observation and information your photos contain the better. You can use these techniques to record early research and generate initial ideas and planning. Using the analysis and visuals will also support the early stages of creating your final piece.

Now try this

Practise recording techniques from a primary source, and produce a single page of studies.

Generating ideas

Ideas generation techniques can yield exciting results. Mind maps and mood boards will help you come up with ideas.

Developing the theme

You can use **mind-map techniques** to help you think about all the potential options that may be available to develop. The breadth of your mind map will feed directly into the next stages of your work, so it's important to get as many links down as you can. Mind maps can include materials and objects as well as images.

'Growth' is the theme in this mind map, which also combines some of the aspects of mood boards.

Materials and images can be used to stimulate visual responses.

Be thorough

Be creative and thorough when you develop mind maps. Think of all the different ways you could interpret the theme provided for your art and design piece. Words can have lots of different meanings, and you should try to use all of these – you can always discard the ones you decide not to pursue.

You can also generate ideas by shifting your approach – try thinking in reverse, or rewording what you need to respond to.

Now try this

Create a mind map in response to the theme of 'Fuel'.

Consider wider ideas such as consumption, lethargy, power, digestion.

Experimenting with materials, techniques and processes

During the ideas generation stage, you will need to experiment with a range of materials, techniques and processes. Remember to keep notes of how materials, techniques and processes could be used so you can justify any changes that you make.

Planning your materials

At this stage, you should be exploring all possible approaches that can become part of your proposal – it doesn't matter if you formulate plans or approaches that change due to your subsequent practical experimentation.

Constraints

There may be constraints associated with each material and associated techniques that you need to take into account. You can use prior knowledge to help you plan your materials, but you should also experiment with the materials to try out new ways of working.

Ideas in the notes

The notes opposite include ideas about:

- the type of paint that could be used
- different techniques
- links to contextual sources (Richter) – referring to other examples or other practitioners' work can help you clarify what you might do
- combinations of techniques
- the imagery and how it could be treated differently to communicate an idea.

Your initial ideas can contain detail on scale as well as materials. The size of the outcome for the project will directly influence the selection and application of materials, techniques and processes.

Sample notes extract

Potential materials

Theme: 'Interior' – Discipline: fine art

- Could be painted imagery – showing items in series located in their respective interiors, where they belong – using photography and handmade marks.

- Could explore collage and acrylic paint – on large scale – possible diptych-type image – plus use mixed media which I've used in previous projects and would like to explore in more detail (digital and physical).

- Could link to people and the interiors they 'use' or 'occupy', i.e. travel, work, living – documentary idea, would link to photography, and idea of image breaking down, becoming corrupted.

- Like the idea of dragging surfaces to allow paint to grow – like Richter paintings I saw on a recent gallery visit.

- Like the idea of combining photo and digital paint – again influence of Richter in photo and paint – see my image on right.

Interior of a train carriage, Berlin.

Now try this

You have been asked to develop a response to the theme of 'Growth'. What materials, techniques and processes could you use?

Exploring contextual influences

Art and design practitioners are often inspired by a wide range of historical, contemporary, social and cultural sources as well as artists and designers.

What are contextual influences?

Influences can take many forms – in the choice of subject, use of materials, techniques and processes, in how media is used and in the way work is presented.

Show how your work has been influenced by looking at the work of others – from your field of study and other broader areas. They may have influenced your ideas, the way you work, the materials you use and so on.

The need for contextual influences

• Contextual influences are an important part of your understanding of how your own work fits into contemporary practice.

• They are also important in helping you locate your work and ideas within a contemporary context.

• You should show how you use contextual influences creatively to:

  ○ support ideas

  ○ gain understanding of how themes are approached

  ○ understand how materials, techniques and processes can be used.

Tom Phillips RA used pages from Mallock's novel 'The Human Document', published in Victorian times, as the basis for his work 'The Humument', a project started in 1966 in which each page has been transformed through painting, collage and cut-out. He left areas of original text visible over some of the page, which were then joined with bubble shapes – these then 'told' a new-found story – the original meaning is changed. Every page can be seen on Tom Phillips' website http://www.tomphillips.co.uk. I found this approach to altering existing ideas about communication really interesting.

Tom Phillips

* I like Phillip's work the most out of all those I have researched.

* His approach to using words and meaning in some form really interests me. I find the way he takes a page from a book and creates new sentences and meanings by blocking out sections to be a really creative approach.

* He chooses words that seem to carry a greater importance or weight when they are separated out from the sentences they were originally embedded within.

* I'm going to explore some ideas of my own that relate to using words and meaning.

Recording contextual influences

When recording contextual influences, you should include some background information about the practitioner and also show how these influences are applied to your practical ideas. In this example, the practitioner explains how Tom Phillips' use of text and image might inspire them to pursue the same theme and ways of working. They also consider the visual characteristics of isolated sections of text on physical pages.

Making it personal

This unit is all about the development and realisation of your creative ideas.

✓ To support your contextual knowledge you should have an awareness of contemporary trends and ideas in your discipline, and in others where relevant.

✓ Keep up to date with contextual information in journals and exhibitions – you can always use this in your work.

Contextual research should include personal responses.

 Links Turn to page 158 to find out more about Tom Phillips.

Now try this

Think of a practitioner whose work has influenced you, and explain how.

Planning contextual research

An art and design piece may be influenced by current trends and contextual factors. You must carefully plan your research into both aspects.

Research sources

Investigate both primary and contextual research sources during your research.

The business and commercial world offers interesting starting points for contextual research, e.g. retail chains and independent retailers in your local high street, shopping mall or local markets

Magazines and journals provide up-to-the-minute information on contemporary practice in art and design

Trade fairs and contemporary exhibitions may point to new directions

Sources of research

Experience – putting yourself in specific places to experience things first hand such as the outdoors

Web-based research – an important source of ideas and information, both contemporary and historical

Media, film, music, literature – examples in these areas can impact very closely on art and design

Remember

☑ Combine different research methods – you can visit galleries/museums and collections as well as browse the web.

☑ Plan research so it gives you what you need.

☑ Make sure you check the sources you research – blogs are personal opinions and may not include factual information.

☑ It may be useful to keep a record of your research plan to feel confident you have researched all the sources you intended to.

🔗 **Links** There is more on this in Unit 2, page 41.

Now try this

Make a research plan to find out contemporary trends in your chosen specialism.

Developing ideas

The techniques and recording you use to generate, research and develop initial ideas will be included in your annotated log. The selection of visuals and explanations will contribute to your proposal, final piece of work, portfolio and accompanying commentary.

Links For more information on how to generate ideas, see page 134.

This is a good start, as it presents a logical method of generating ideas. Both visual and theoretical sources are being used to inform the ideas generating process. You can try taking segments of language, writing, or filmic ideas as starting points. Look for inspiration from popular culture, dance, music, film, drama, science, philosophy and entertainment.

By logging and annotating your ideas as they have evolved, you can keep a record of the narrative.

Sample response extract

The theme is 'Human', which appeared to be a straightforward concept to start with, but through early investigation, it was clear that the theme posed many questions. Looking at the dictionary definition seemed like a good idea to start with, but it almost opened more questions than provided answers.

Human

Adjective

1. relating to humankind
   'the human mind'
   Synonyms: animal, anthropoid

Noun

1. a human being
   Synonyms: person, mortal

Sample response extract

sadness

happiness

surprise

anger

fear

disgust

Introducing images can help provide visual stimuli for your early ideas.

I am looking into the different ways that the human face and features can convey what being human is. I looked at art sources and then moved towards psychology and less well known references. My main ideas for a real product are:

- a book for people with disabilities to help them understand people's emotions
- a series of posters that reflect how emotions are expressed by different cultures.

Investigating art and design and wider cultural sources (such as this psychology image) is best practice. This will develop your understanding and should provide the audience with something less well known.

This is a clear explanation of ideas and also starts to compare ideas to help focus future direction. Notes like these are useful in a log recording the development of ideas.

The focus of ideas generation keeps the task at the centre and ensures that the idea is for an art and design product that has a clear purpose and is functional.

Now try this

You have been asked to develop a response to the theme of 'Reconstruction'. Generate one page of ideas that includes at least one art source and one science source. Consider the purpose and function of your ideas.

Making experimentation effective

As you plan your experimentation you will need to reflect on how effective it will be. This will feed directly into your log, proposal, final piece of work, portfolio and accompanying commentary.

During the experimentation process, it is easy to get bogged down or side-tracked. Experimentation will only provide useful development and improvement if you reflect on it and see it as a logical and structured process. In this extract from a log, a structured approach has been used to review the progress of experimentation and develop a plan of how to improve through experimentation. Get used to carrying out a critical and reflective review as you go along, rather than merely diary-like recording.

Sample notes extract

Reflective log on theme of 'Reconstruction'

I wanted to see how the audience would react to the idea of using quite shocking images of before and after surgical treatment – especially plastic surgery that had gone wrong, operation scars and disfigurements. I was really inspired when others in the critique suggested I look at the work from the end of the First World War by Henry Tonks, as well as recent work by Orlan, who used her body as the art form. I am going to start by responding to traditional figurative techniques and see if I can carry these out through a series of experimental studies for the images.

I am going to explore drawing and painting techniques to see if I can control these well enough to make convincing images that communicate to the audience, which I have focused on as young professional females. To get valuable feedback on the experimentation process, I will try to get a focus group made up of the audience. I hope they will provide feedback on the validity of my experiments and ensure they are communicating the right messages.

I thought about the scale of the images of the faces and parts of bodies I am going to use. I really like large-scale painting like Jenny Saville so want to work as large as possible as I think this will have more of a shock factor for the audience and communicate the dangers of transforming their own bodies. My original intention was to highlight the dangers so I will try different scales with different images to compare and contrast how well the work meets the original intentions.

The learner is aware that the audience won't necessarily react or feel the same way as they do. Practitioners try to develop a sense of empathy with the audience through testing and feedback. Is it targeted at the correct demographic and is it communicating the right message or enabling the right experience?

The emphasis on debate and discussion of the experimentation process using critique is seen as best practice in the industry.

Working independently

While it's good practice to seek feedback, you may have to work independently for your assessed task. Ask your tutor or check the Pearson website for details of your actual assessment. These may change, so always make sure you are up to date.

The emphasis on questioning the validity of the experiments means the learner is aware they are not producing art and design for themselves, but to generate a a final piece with a clear purpose for an audience.

The learner is aware that their experimentation should be aligned to their original creative intentions.

Now try this

Explain three formal approaches you will use to review experimentation.

Planning a proposal

The **proposal** is an important milestone in the development of your work. A proposal explains your planned response to the theme you have been given. Your research log should give you the information you need to write the proposal. Use headings to construct the proposal – making sure these match the requirements of the brief, and that you address each heading. The areas you need to cover are outlined below.

The proposal

1 Initial ideas for focus of art and design piece

This is where you discuss your ideas. You will need to refer to the context you are going to work in – this might be:

- a piece of artwork for an exhibition
- advertising or promotional material
- interactive product
- commercial design/product
- functional object
- fashion garment or accessory.

You will need to research the field you are planning to focus your piece of work in, ensuring the work has a clear purpose. Explain your ideas in relation to the theme.

2 Reasons for choice of art and design piece

This is where you signpost just what it is you are trying to communicate – you define its clear purpose, and what it is you want to say.

3 Research plan into contextual sources and trends

This is where you will locate your work, through the research you have carried out so far, and the evidence in your log. You should have defined the creative potential in what you plan to do, and how what you are planning relates to contemporary trends. You also need to show the selection of contextual sources you are going to look at, and why. Remember the differences between primary and secondary research sources for your contextual research, and how it's best practice to blend these.

6 Equipment/ technical expertise

Identify any equipment you might need, and any specialist resources and technical assistance you could require.

A student planning a proposal.

4 Choice of materials, techniques and processes

Explain here your initial ideas on the materials, techniques and processes you want to use. Why you have chosen these? Has any experimentation led you to this choice? Will you need any specialist help?

5 Time plan

Identify the scope of the work within timescales. How do you plan to complete the work within the time? Make this realistic and achievable.

 See page 160 for more on access to resources.

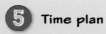

Make an initial plan for a proposal, using headings to structure what you need to cover.

Planning your time

Managing your time is an important part of any project. You will need to work out how long different aspects of your work will take and plan these into a schedule. The planning stages must show how time could be used to structure the work you need to complete.

🔗 **Links**   See also managing production on page 170.

Use time effectively

Any plan requires a lot of thought to make it effective, and planning to complete the work required here within the time is no exception. You are going to be working to tight timescales so the more structure you can provide the better. You can set the structure up by week, and set interim deadlines for achieving set stages. This is particularly important where you may be using resources that require specialist help and construction methods. Meeting deadlines is also important in the creative industries.

Plan week by week

Use a calendar to plan out the activities needed to complete the work within time. Arrange your time plan by week to get an overview:

Week no.	Task
1	Complete all planning by Friday
2	Develop initial visual ideas
3	Make visits to ...

Make individual week plans that show more detail. You can also use a Gantt chart or calendar apps for planning and recording progress.

Getting the plan right

Your plan should show you what you have to do, for example:

1. Plan the response.
2. Generate and log ideas, visual recording and linking contextual sources.
3. Experiment with potential materials, techniques and processes.
4. Write the proposal.
5. Apply research into contextual sources and trends.
6. Select, experiment and apply materials, techniques and processes.
7. Explore development of work through the production process, e.g. mocking up, sampling and modelling.
8. Ongoing recording of work in progress.
9. Ongoing critical reflection.
10. Review and refine ideas.
11. Produce the final piece of art and design.
12. Produce a portfolio and write an accompanying commentary.

Be realistic

The plan should contain realistic targets – you can use your SMART target-setting skills to achieve this.

Realistic targets are achievable. You should have built up experience and an understanding of how you work – use this.

🔗 **Links**   Look at page 41 for more information on SMART targets.

SMART

Your targets should be:

- Specific
- Measurable
- Achievable
- Realistic
- Time-related.

Remember

✓ It's also important to have a plan B in mind just in case you don't achieve the deadlines in your main plan.

✓ Try to stretch yourself by being ambitious.

✓ Think about the key areas of creativity, innovative ideas and aesthetics.

Now try this

Produce an outline plan for six weeks, giving each week a single title for the activity you would undertake for a task on the theme of 'Face'.

Producing a proposal

When producing a proposal you need to explain how you intend to respond to a brief and theme. The proposal could include:

- initial ideas and focus
- reasons for your choice of piece
- research plan into contextual sources and trends
- your initial ideas on the materials, techniques and processes
- your plans to complete the work within the time
- identification of the equipment and specialist expertise you may require.

Sample response extract

These extracts from an outline of initial thoughts for the proposal show attention to key elements required.

Proposal with clear purpose: A garment, based on my interpretation of the theme 'Animal'.

You can make the proposal wide-reaching if appropriate.

Initial ideas and focus: My initial ideas come from reading 'The Jungle Book' by Rudyard Kipling, which suggests how alike humans and animals can be and seems ideal for a fashion interpretation of the theme.

I will explore dyeing techniques to create prints along with freehand and machine stitching. I will use a mixture of my own photography, drawing and colour-based work to explore animal patterns and shapes. The choice of colours will need to reflect vibrance in nature. I will use silkscreen printing to generate and produce pattern in textiles to be used in the garment production.

In this extract, the learner has provided a logical reason for direction that combines the theme with the intended product well.

Reasons: Our desire to anthropomorphise animals is an aspect I would like to pursue. I think the potential to combine interesting visual prints with designed garments that reference their heritage or source could be interesting.

Research plan: I will look at designers and fabric manufacturers that have participated in the animal prints trends within their work and products, such as Alexander Henry Fabrics, Dolce & Gabbana, and Versace. With an interest in an Indian cultural link, I will look at Maria Grachvogel, Tarun Tahiliani and Ritu Kumar to see if there is a potential to mix these processes. From there on, I expect much of the research to be active and I will use the testing of fabric manipulation to help understand how pattern and shape can work together. I will go to the V & A Museum in London to collect primary research into fashion designers who use print.

In this extract, it is clear that plans for research are informed by critical sources, as the learner names practitioners and places for primary research. The learner mentions initial ideas on materials, techniques and processes, which will be separately developed for a focus on these ideas.

Equipment and expertise: Access to the sewing and print room, A1 screens and mannequins. I will need technical help and support with screen exposures. I will also need to use a variety of recording equipment – cameras, drawing and painting.

Time plan:

Research	Textiles and surface pattern
Ideas generation and proposal prep	Garment production
Testing	Presentation, recording, external assessment

In this extract, key stages of the creative process have been broken down. The stages will need to be allocated to the number of weeks allowed, in a realistic way. Ask your tutor or check the Pearson website for the time allowed in your actual assessment. Details of the assessment may change, so always make sure you are up to date.

Now try this

Scope out an outline proposal for a project of your choice. Use the above list as a guide.

Researching contextual factors

When taking forward research into contextual factors that influence practitioners' work, you need to consider a range of historical, contemporary, cultural, social, political, environmental or technological factors. Understanding how these factors work can help you develop your own creative work.

Contextual factors influencing practitioners' work

Cultural, social, economic and political

Many practitioners reference aspects of their own cultural identities and social backgrounds in their work. There are examples of art and design work that reference political ideas. Some practitioners take imagery used in political campaigns or reportage and redirect them back out to a new audience in a different way – they change the meaning of the original image, or make the audience think about the way images are used to communicate ideas. Sometimes practitioners reference their own cultures and politics through our associations with the images they use.

Technological

Technology can drive creative developments. It has been used by practitioners to communicate, or as a subject in its own right.

Social interaction

Social interaction is also considered by artists and designers, and can be found as a theme in many examples of work. When you are researching practitioners, find out about these factors and consider if they have any resonance with what you are developing.

An artist at work in a studio.

Historical and/or contemporary practice

You can learn about creative problem solving by seeing how practitioners have developed responses to themes and subjects in their work. You can use their examples to help you think about which materials, techniques and processes you can use, and how these could work. You can also consider how specific contextual factors have influenced practitioners.

The audience

Understanding their audience is a key aspect of practitioners' working methods. Audience needs may be complex – think about the appeal of an animated film, and the age ranges it can reach. This may go beyond one target group depending on the different levels of sophistication, storyline, narrative and themes. Some artists use the audience reaction as part of their work.

The environment

The environment can influence practitioners in different ways, e.g. geography, fragility of natural places under threat, inhospitable or damaged environments. Some artists question our involvement and exploitation of the environment – others celebrate our social complexities.

Now try this

List three contextual factors that are an influence on you today.

Researching creative practitioners

Your contextual research should include the work of creative practitioners. Identifying and exploring themes and ideas in their work will help you to clarify your own work and practice.

Themes and ideas

You can get ideas for your own work by seeing how another practitioner has approached theirs. This should be related to the theme you are working with. In the example on this page, the theme was 'Human'. The notes identify the scope of the project as being about the human condition, and how faces and body language can tell a story or narrative.

Making connections

Your research must clearly illustrate how it relates to the theme and how it supports the development of your work. Ideally, you would use it to justify the direction that you have taken to gain a greater insight into your own interpretation of the theme. You can do this by including images or research material, and annotating them with your analysis.

Photograph (2017) by George Ourfalian of a woman washing dishes after government forces reconnected the water supply during conflict in Syria.

Remember

☑ Research should state why an image has been included by making direct reference to it.

☑ Personal readings of the image are important – this explains what it is that you have gained from the work and how you might use it.

☑ Direct quotes and information can be used in research, as long as they are referenced clearly in any notes.

Links Pages 45–47 in Unit 2 give guidance on how to reference any sources you use in your research.

Sample response extract

Understanding the theme

When looking at the theme of 'Human', I researched examples that were deceptively obvious, yet had another layer of meaning. When I looked more closely I was struck by the apparent simplicity of these images and how they could represent the theme effectively. This image captures the subject within their own environment, and at first glance looks like any other domestic situation – washing dishes. The female subject is concentrating on the task, and this takes on a new meaning when the background to the image is uncovered: this is an image of conflict, but not an obvious one – the subject is returning to a domestic chore, the everyday, after having the water supply restored. It's an image about the basics in life, in this case water. The subject seems to become very open, even vulnerable. In this way the photographer could be placing us as voyeurs into someone's private environment.

The image is honestly portrayed as there doesn't appear to be any image manipulation. At first glance there wasn't an obvious narrative behind the image – so I found myself trying to read something into it.

The colour range is mainly pale, apart from the woman and the brighter everyday objects that you could see in any kitchen. I think this image works well as it has a sense of intrigue that makes the viewer want to find out what it is about – and then it has a deeper meaning. I am going to try and use this in my own photography.

Now try this

Think about a practitioner you admire. Choose one image of their work, and define clearly what their ideas are about through looking at the image.

Researching current trends

Contextual research into current trends provides an understanding of the ways that trends influence and shape how practitioners work. Art and design practitioners understand their contexts – they know about the backgrounds in which they are producing and presenting work. You should apply your understanding of current trends to your own work and practice.

Current trends

As a practitioner, you should have a genuine interest in and enthusiasm for the field.

- You must understand just how the work you create relates to current directions and themes.

- It is likely that some current themes reflect your own ideas and concerns – so you can feed them directly into the design development process for your work.

- You can get information from sources such as International Society of Typographic Designers (ISTD), Society of British and International Interior Design (SBID), Royal Institute of British Architects (RIBA), British Institute of Professional Photography (BIPP), British Fashion Council, Chartered Society of Designers (CSD) and Pantone.

Journals such as *Design Week* are up-to-the-minute sources of current trends; their editorials can provide a useful overview.

Where to research trends

There is a variety of ways of keeping in touch with current trends.

- Galleries and exhibitions can be a source of information on current trends, especially if they are showing the work of emerging practitioners.

- Practitioners' websites can also be a useful source of current ideas.

- Blogs can inform through their debate, but remember they are personal views.

Look more widely if you need to

Explore current trends in areas alongside the creative industries – think about current trends in music, and how these will often have a direct relationship with fashion. Ideas in literature may be translated into visual imagery through illustration and animation.

Remember

✓ You should be able to locate what you do in this unit within the context of contemporary practice.

✓ This understanding will help you and can feed directly into your ideas development.

✓ Your capacity to engage with subjects and critical ideas will be supported and informed through regular interaction with current trends and ideas.

Now try this

Look at the current issues of an art and design journal and identify the main themes and trends covered.

Recording contextual research

You need to document your contextual research, explaining how it has influenced you.

Recording thoughts and reflections

Explore contextual sources that relate to the theme and pick out examples to support and inspire the development of your work. Influences may be varied – don't disregard any of them without first thinking about how you might use them.

Using techniques

You can use a blend of written analysis and diagrams, notes, drawings, colour studies, photographs and video recordings. When recording from secondary sources you can use the same techniques, as well as photocopying/scanning. Avoid using only copied examples as these will generally all be secondary source materials, and you'll be missing out on the benefits and richness of using primary sources.

Research pages

You can use a range of different techniques, such as imagery and text, to record the contextual influences you research. Photography combined with drawing can be an effective way of recording imagery and adding this to your research. Working visually can help you to understand how the artists and designers have used formal elements and visual language in the examples you have chosen.

Documenting research

In this example, the practitioner has used their own photography and drawing to record the dynamic patterns and potential offered in the work of others, and has linked this to their own primary research carried out at Kew Gardens. 'Thinking visually' can feed directly into the design development process – it can act as a bridge between research and practical work.

Elena Boils

I have used my own drawing in the style of Elena Boils. I also used the photo I took as a guide. I like this style of drawing and the image could be printed using different screens for each colour. I like the fact that the outline doesn't match the exact colour. This technique reminds me of pattern-based work from the 1950s up to the present day – there is a strong relationship between outline and shape. If I was screen printing it I could explore different ways of using outline and colour.

Research pages can combine a range of techniques.

Now try this

Choose a practitioner whose work you like and identify their main influences.

Applying visual research

Visual research can be analytical or applied and is used to engage with the work of others and primary sources. Both involve considered and relevant selection, observation and recording of visual resources.

Applying analytical visual research

This involves analysing visual materials from primary and secondary sources that are relevant to your project. These should be organised and annotated to show how you understand the themes and how they are communicated through materials, techniques and processes. You will need to cover:

- the most important practitioners working in this area
- similar themed work in other disciplines
- critical data and historical information or examples
- primary and secondary evidence.

Applying active visual research

The word 'active' here means there is an element of doing, such as copying or trying to emulate a piece of work, for example by making studies and transcriptions from it. It doesn't have to be exactly the same as the original. This approach is used most often to develop an increased awareness of the activities a practitioner has undertaken to create a piece of work. It is also used when you are trying to develop your own skills in order to be able to do something similar.

Active research

Active research can also mean that the process of collecting or making observations actually results in the production of artwork itself. For example, Susan Hiller collects objects from around the world and displays these in interesting ways in her artwork.

Active visual analysis

In the example of active visual analysis below, the learner has tried to analyse examples of a practitioner's work by reproducing some of the techniques. By making a version that explores some of the techniques and motifs used by the designer, the learner has opened up their understanding of the work. They have gained ideas and insights into how they might use these techniques in developmental work. Remember you will be using visual research to record from contextual sources as well as primary sources.

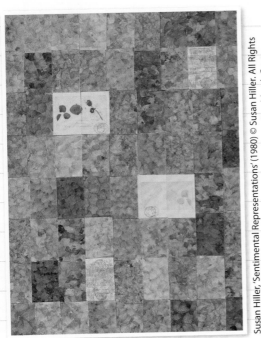

Susan Hiller's *Sentimental Representations*, 1980.

Active visual analysis.

Now try this

Take a practitioner whose work you admire and apply some visual research techniques.

Applying action research

Action research can help you to develop an understanding of how other practitioners use materials, techniques and processes – and you can use it to explore your own ideas.

Action research

This involves practical-based research, where you work with materials, techniques and processes when looking at the work of others. This also crosses over into your own design development work, and can be applied to generating ideas as well as practical experimentation with techniques and processes.

Sometimes there is a need to try out materials in the early stages of a project – this can feed back into further academic or contextual research.

 Links See page 149 for more on academic research.

Working with materials and heat transfer techniques in design. Drawing, photography and transfer printing processes are shown on a single sketchbook page.

Example

In the example opposite, the practitioner has explored:

- colour – the colour work is also applied to the garment design
- line – this is based on the illustrators being researched, so it is contextual information as well
- heat transfer techniques that use specific processes
- initial ideas for fashion design.

What has been gained here?

Think about the information shown in the example above:

- basic ideas about colour ranges
- how line-based work might be applied later in the project
- useful visual information for a research log
- how new techniques, equipment and processes work through practical experimentation.

 Links Find out more about experimenting on page 162.

Developmental work

Your action research will overlap with your developmental work – it's unavoidable, so don't be put off if it's difficult to see where action research on a practitioner ends and where your own practical research begins.

Now try this

Take an existing project and try out action research using one material on a single page.

Applying academic research

Academic research involves gathering information about practitioners and their working practices. This can support the early stages of your project by providing a basis of reliable and authoritative information.

Academic research

- Academic research relies on published writings, commentaries, essays and professionally researched articles as a source of information.
- The views contained in these sources are generally accepted as being a reliable source of discussion and ideas.
- Academic sources provide examples of critiques of a specific body or phase of a practitioner's work.
- Reliable recognised sources often provide access to contextual information and influences.

Books and journals

Books and journals can provide a wealth of information for academic research. This might be in the form of biographies, exhibition catalogues, essays on individual or group practitioners, or books that cover a theme, period or location. Sources can be historical and contemporary.

You can also explore resources from wider fields to match the theme if there is a connection, such as science books or websites (for example, if the theme is 'Technology'), or medical books and sources (for example, if the theme is 'Growth').

Blending research and practical work

It's good practice to get the different stages in research to build directly into practical work – this allows your ideas to flow, and you shouldn't get 'stuck' on a theme or lose impetus.

Explore the library facilities in your centre to get an idea of the types of books, journals and articles available.

Combining research methods

The research stage in a project should combine different types of research – visual, action and academic. You will need to record the results of your research in all of these methods.

Links See pages 147 and 148 for information on visual and action research.

Links For guidance on the correct way to reference your sources, see pages 45–47 in Unit 2.

Remember

✓ You can take the points you read in academic works as accepted fact.

✓ Use quotes from the sources to help you understand practitioners, their ideas and themes.

✓ Reference your sources clearly in your developmental work, your log and any formal writing you do.

✓ Take your time to find the right source. Some academic writing can be hard to understand – don't be put off by this.

Develop your research skills by practising reading and extracting information.

Now try this

Explain how using academic research has helped you to understand a practitioner's work and whether it informed any of your own work and practice.

Making research work

Make the research that you carry out work for you, as you apply it to your own work and practice. The records of your research in your annotated log will reflect the research you planned in your proposal, and will contribute to your final piece of art and design. You can also select from your records to demonstrate the development and realisation process in your portfolio and accompanying commentary.

'Make' studies

🔗 **Links** For the different types of research, see pages 147–149.

Record how you have made your analysis and application of research work for you. In this extract, the learner has balanced active, academic and visual analysis to help form a holistic understanding.

Link what you are researching to your own set task at all stages. This will keep you on track.

Bring in your own ideas about possible materials.

Try to demonstrate where you have informed your knowledge of the work you are analysing by making reference to literature.

Try to use technical terms such as 'formal elements' when discussing artwork.

Try making a version of the work you have researched. By remaking a version you can sometimes get a fuller understanding of its components: composition, shapes, colour, and relationships between elements.

Sample response extract

In this study I have used Cézanne's ideas about painting and the way colours work together with line, in an un-blended way, to show the form of something. This is because the theme is about transformation and I think colour can do this really well. Alongside the idea of patches of colour, I was also interested in composition. I have read about Cézanne's ideas in his letters to the painter Émile Bernard, where he discussed the notions of form and how he could represent volume and shape. I am trying to get inspiration from Cézanne's use of colour on fruit for a printmaking project that uses fruit and organic shapes as its motif. I want to try and do something that uses vibrant colours. I used collage and paint in this study. I learned from my research into his letters and my practical activities that he arranges the shapes using positive and negative space carefully. He also uses a blue line around parts of his objects to make the edges show – otherwise they would be made up of colours that run into each other.

Record your research

You can record images and thoughts as part of action research. It's important that these are all recorded in your log and in subsequent development work.

Remember

Working with visuals and materials can act as a bridge between your research and your developing practical work.

Now try this

Conduct a short piece of materials-based action research into a chosen practitioner.

Research in action

Research in action allows you to explore alternative approaches, a key part of art and design practice – things can happen as a result of unseen or intuitive approaches. Research can be developed using materials and media exploration. You could show how you have used this to develop your response in your annotated log and production of your final piece, selecting records for your portfolio and accompanying commentary.

Sample response extract

This sketchbook page showing printmaking records the learner's research.

A more successful print: the monoprinting technique works better on the plainer cartridge paper as this provides more contrast. This was made using an acetate plate that had some of the ink removed by hand. This provides the objects with much clearer details, and would act as an ideal background image. I want to explore the potential for more texture-based imagery.

The image here is too dark, as I haven't been able to control the weight of ink. It's one of my first attempts so I am still experimenting with the ideas as well as the process. On other examples, I will try using less ink, or rolling it out to make the film much finer.

As you develop your project you should push your experimental approach to try out different ideas. It is important that your practical research is just that – you are using materials and techniques to see what will happen, and if these can give you any interesting ideas and directions to take forward.

Sample response extract

Keep annotating as you work through the set task – it's a way of recording your thoughts and critical reflection on specific processes, i.e. what works and what doesn't. Use the correct language and terminology when you evaluate work in progress, and describe clearly where you feel a piece has yielded something you can use.

Examples of the handwritten font I have chosen to develop for use on a photo screen. I have sourced the font and explored my own way of working with it: it uses a scrolled technique and suggests a historical and almost intimate expression. I am incorporating the text in my designs, as I want to create a visual piece that encourages the viewer to read more into it. In this case, it's really about looking in more detail to read the words – and the words will help me narrate an idea and the story. I want my designs to work on different levels.

In this example, the learner has incorporated text to see if it can become an integral part of their design idea and developmental work.

The ideas you research may not always be the ones you use – but keeping a record of them is important. You might be selecting from these to show the journey of your work in your portfolio.

Now try this

Take an idea that you haven't fully developed and think about how you could explore it through conducting research in action, using one or two materials, techniques or processes.

Analysing formal elements

You need to analyse and deconstruct the work of art and design practitioners and communicate why they are an influence through their use of formal elements. Analysing their use of formal elements is one way to gain insight into practitioners' work: this type of analysis can be conducted visually as well as academically.

Analysing formal elements

The first elements you encounter within an object or image are the formal elements:

- Tonal values
- Colour
- Texture
- Pattern
- Form or shape
- Line
- Scale.

You experience these and they are a valuable way of engaging with art. You don't need to discuss all of them when looking at work, as some will be used more consistently within the work or will stand out more.

Formal elements in work

When looking at practitioners' work, you will notice that they may gravitate towards or use certain formal elements to communicate more than others. In order to distinguish these, you can:

- copy the most important elements
- turn an image into a black and white copy
- trace details
- create a colour pallet from the work
- make notes about what strikes you the most.

Analysing formal elements in Paul Cézanne's 'Still Life with Plaster Cupid', oil on canvas, 1894

In this image, Cézanne has used line and shape to create a composition where shapes are echoed. The sense of perspective in the whole painting is tipped forward, and the lines exaggerate this. He uses lines around the edge of forms in the cast such as the leg to try to delineate where one object ends and another begins. His use of line is broken, reinforcing his view that edges were difficult to see and define. He seems to sometimes blur the edges of the cupid, as if he isn't sure of where the edges are. His use of line to 'hold in' the form is partly developed to do just that – and sometimes he uses more than one line, at different points – as if it's been re-drawn over the top, and the original lines left behind.

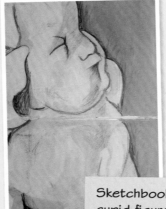

Sketchbook study, cupid figure.

Study of the cupid's leg.

This section of the painting primarily uses a range of blues and off-whites, which work together to give it an overall harmony.

My studies show use of colour and line, and how the rhythmic qualities in the composition are achieved by the edges of the plaster cast and reinforced in the overall compositional arrangements in the painting.

Drapery study.

I've used drawing and painting to try and visualise this effect.

Now try this

Conduct an analysis of formal elements in an image using one drawing or painting method.

Analysing process

Researching and deconstructing the production methods and techniques – the process – used by practitioners will help you to understand how they work and communicate why they are an influence.

Choosing a process

For some practitioners, the process of making is central to their work; for example, they may want you to be able to see that a work is handmade. In other cases, the process of making may be deliberately hidden, such as in examples of product design. You must be able to identify which is the case and ask which you would prefer to research in relation to your own work. You should also try to assess the process of making in order to learn similar techniques and understand the work more.

Remember

✓ You will have to conduct research into specific practitioners and their ways of working to analyse and communicate why they are an influence through their use of materials, techniques and processes.

✓ You can conduct visual analysis using techniques that allow you to develop practical work – you can combine this with academic and action research.

✓ You can focus on the way a practitioner uses materials generally – it doesn't matter if they are not working on the same theme as you are.

Using visual-based analysis

In the sketchbook page on fashion below, the practitioner has considered the use of formal elements – colour and shapes as well as the transparency of the patterns and fabrics, and is finding out about the process. You can use this type of visual-based analysis to tie into your own practical work as it develops – bridging research and developmental work.

General research: Maria Grachvogel is a British fashion designer born 1969. She was interested in fashion from a young age and started a career in this field, being mentored by Isabella Blow. She developed work that gained her recognition in London Fashion Week 2000 – she also designed a dress made from 2000 hand-sewn diamonds. Her clients have included Emma Thompson, Scarlett Johansson and Angelina Jolie. Grachvogel is known for her precision cutting techniques, slim fit garments, and experiments with digital and printed textiles.

Her prints are very textural and remind me of inks that have bled and run together, although this seems to be very controlled, as in the symmetrical colours in the dress on the far left – a mixture of experimentation with technique, yet at the same time managed and controlled. The shapes and forms within these designs really complement the 'floaty' kinds of fabrics she uses to make these beautiful garments.

Practical experimentation:

I decided to experiment with splattering and flicking inks onto fabrics. I made these wet first to provide a surface on which the splattered, dripped ink would bleed and stain softly. As this fabric is translucent and synthetic I wasn't sure how it would work, but it did in fact behave in a predicable way – producing some results that I can evaluate as part of my development process in the project. At first reading, these prints might make interesting backgrounds – I could imagine using them either as designs in their own right (possibly with stronger colours) or as background imagery to be worked over.

This learner has explored different ways of interpreting the treatment of fabric they are researching – as shown in the images of garments and subsequent interpretations of their textures and patterns.

Now try this

Research how a practitioner uses a specific technique and processes in their work.

Materials and media analysis

Analysing and deconstructing the use of media and materials by artists and designers will help you to communicate why they are an influence, and inform your own making process.

Media and materials

Sometimes assessing materials and media is straightforward. The practitioner will clearly be using certain materials in an overt way to draw attention to an issue or debate surrounding that media. However, sometimes the material is hidden or transformed to appear like something else, in some product design for example. When analysing media and materials, you can apply a blend of visual, action and academic research. Recording from work in your own way will often give a deeper insight into how materials are used.

Media and material potential

When you look at work, it may be difficult to separate the media or material and the techniques that have been applied. In many cases there are traditional materials that correlate to traditional techniques that have been tried and tested. In other circumstances, the media or material being used has been taken out of its usual context and used with an unorthodox process. You should discuss both scenarios when analysing and ask which is more pertinent to the practitioner's work.

Links Refer to the information on media and material analysis in Unit 2 on page 69 to help you.

The collaged imagery and research in this sketchbook analyses media and techniques.

Sample response extract

Edwin Parker 'Cy' Twombly was an American painter born in 1928. His work consisted of freely made, sometimes scribbled graffiti-like calligraphic marks, made on a large scale. He worked on solid fields of colour, mostly tan, off-white and grey. Later in his career he made paintings that I think symbolise romance – this is seen in his use of pinks and reds, and, in the example here, the word 'love' can be read. I've used materials to make my own transcription version of his work. His work requires the viewer to interpret the marks and colours, and is evocative rather than being representative in a visual sense. He uses various mark-making techniques to apply the paint and work into it. There are examples of smudges, scribbles, dragged marks and scratched words. I am interested in how words can be used to present an idea alongside visuals in work, and find his painting gives me ideas as it relies on interpretation.

Cy Twombly, 'Wilder Shores of Love' (detail) (1985) © Cy Twombly Foundation

---

Now try this

Conduct media and materials analysis into a piece of art and design work, outlining the main points you find.

Subject and imagery analysis

The subject matter of a work is often linked to the **imagery** that is used. Analysing this relationship will help you deconstruct and understand this in the work of practitioners, communicate their influence and develop your own communication methods.

Subject and image

Initially, it may seem that subject and image are always connected in an obvious way but in many cases, the subject isn't literally the image. Think, for example, about Carl Andre's *Equivalent* series of works that consist of 120 bricks. While they are just bricks, they suggest all sorts of other topics, issues and debates, such as order, strength and permanence. Sometimes images are deliberately made out of unexpected materials to provoke discussions about subjects that would not otherwise be connected.

Analysis approach

The subject matter of the artwork above is made up of a combination of subjects and components:

- People are placed in an unusual context.
- Objects are disproportionate.
- Perspective appears forced between the images in the collage.
- Colour is used to suggest tabloid and popular culture.

Note how the subject is multi-layered.

The learner's analysis opposite shows how the initial description and subsequent reading of the imagery and subject matter move on to analytical statements.

You can bring together research methods such as academic and visual research to help understand subject matter.

Example of image and subject analysis

Richard Hamilton, 'Just what is it that makes today's homes so different, so appealing?' (1956) © R. Hamilton. All Rights Reserved, DACS/Artimage 2018. Photo: Richard Hamilton Archive

Sample response extract

The image above is of 'Just what is it that makes today's homes so different, so appealing?', a pop art piece by Richard Hamilton. It creates a sense of consumerism – this would have been considered modern in the 1950s – through its use of colour, composition, shape, pattern and text. It shows an interior space that is filled with objects and items that would have been part of the emerging popular consumer culture. The arrangement of the images is carefully set out to be balanced. The objects are arranged so they are all readable – they are meant to be seen by the viewer, and interpreted – and are used as references or symbols to tell a story. The image would resonate with a younger audience of the time as it shows a modern environment, with examples or references to items from the world of pop culture, i.e. music, romantic novels and consumer products. All these things could be seen as being important to the new type of modern lifestyle. So in a sense it's a picture about lifestyle, about being part of the new consumer group or demographic. It represents what consumers at the time wanted, and could be said to be a comment on the materialism of the consumer culture of the day.

Remember

✓ There are different ways to access this type of analysis – initial descriptions can quickly lead into personal readings of the work.

✓ Use appropriate language in your analysis.

✓ Your view counts – it's not just about repeating what you might find in books. You should aim to develop your own analysis, which may be informed by others but is still your own.

✓ Analysing the relationship of image and subject is a way of really getting to know about imagery.

Now try this

Choose a piece of work by a practitioner you have researched. Write some bullet points that analyse how the imagery conveys the subject of the piece.

Analysing messages and meanings

When deconstructing and analysing practitioners' work, and communicating why they are an influence through their messages and meanings, you need to consider both explicit and implicit meanings.

Explicit meaning

This refers to a work that is quite easy to define and explain in terms of meaning. A lot of advertising, for example, doesn't need to have a hidden or subtle meaning – its message can be blatant and not require further knowledge or analysis. However, there are many examples of artwork that initially may appear to have a simple function or message but on deeper analysis contain subtle messages.

Subtle and ambiguous meaning

In some artworks, the meaning and message may involve decoding (especially if they are deliberately hidden), require interpretation or require you to have certain knowledge in order to appreciate what is being communicated. If the meaning isn't immediately obvious, you may need to read about what the practitioner intended to communicate and what critics and others have said about it. Your initial reactions may change the more you find out about it. Some work is deliberately ambiguous, so this will require careful analysis on your part.

> Jenny Holzer projects bold statements on to buildings with direct and clear statements that do not pretend to have anything more than an explicit meaning.

> Antony Gormley creates humanoid sculptures and sometimes places these within the environment. It isn't immediately clear what they are about, but they suggest a range of implicit meanings about being human, mortality and permanence.

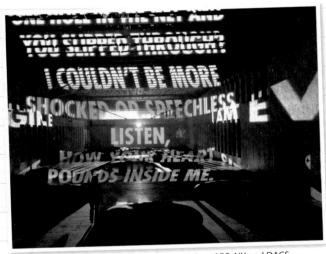

Jenny Holzer, 'Projections' (2008) © Jenny Holzer. ARS, NY and DACS, London 2018 Photo © Mark Wilson/Boston Globe/Getty Images

Anthony Gormley, 'Another Place' (2007) © Anthony Gormley

Match the theme

You will be developing an understanding of themes and ideas through this type of analysis. At this stage of analysis, it is really important that the work you are analysing is connected to your own creative intentions and what you are trying to communicate. Ideally, you should be aware of other contextual work that has similar messages and meanings. It is important to show how you will use the results to feed into your own work – what you have really gained from looking at the work. You will show this in your annotated log of research and development of ideas, and include research plans in your proposal. The research will help inform your own final piece of art and design and your portfolio with accompanying commentary that demonstrates your development and realisation process.

Now try this

Select any example of work and analyse the meanings and messages in the piece.

Analysing symbolism, mood and aesthetics

The overall impact of an artwork depends on your appraisal of the intentions of the practitioner and consideration of the aesthetics and symbolism used within the work. When analysing and deconstructing practitioners' use of symbolism, mood and aesthetics, and communicating why they are an influence, consider also the emotional impact.

Drawing conclusions about work

Any judgements you make about a work and the power of its impact will depend on your assessment and a balanced consideration of:

1 how well the artist or designer has achieved their intentions

2 the use of aesthetic principles

3 any explicit or implicit symbolism or connection to a culture in context.

 Links For more information on aesthetics, look at page 176.

Example of an annotation

Sample response extract

Grayson Perry's work 'Sex, Drugs and Earthenware' shows some of the themes that have occupied Perry in his ceramics and subsequent work. There is a strong visual impact through the juxtaposition of image and shape in the piece. He has made what is essentially a 'classical' pottery-shaped vessel that references ceramics from different periods in history and uses their symbolism. However, the decorative elements are taken from his own cultural interests and ideas – and are collaged on in a very rough and 'non-classical' way. There are images of Michael Jackson, Kurt Cobain, and Pepsi, the impact being to jar the viewer into recognising the contradiction – the shape says classical pottery, and the decoration says contemporary popular culture. Aesthetically it is a challenging piece as it cannot be read easily. I want to see it as a well-considered shape, but the contradiction of the shape and the decoration gives it an uneasy aesthetic. Reading about Perry, it is clear that his intentions aren't to make the audience think about one specific message, but to question identity in our cultural climate.

Symbolism

This refers to symbols and signs that are used within a culture. For example, the symbol for 'no entry' is widely recognised and accepted. Practitioners use symbols within their work to try to enable their intentions and add a specific type of impact.

The 'urn' created by Grayson Perry in his piece *Sex, Drugs and Earthenware* (1995) reflects the classical shape of ceramics such as these: Wedgwood blue and white stoneware (1774 onwards) and amphora, Greece (eighth century).

Remember

☑ Aesthetics are connected with notions of beauty and/or ugliness.

☑ This part of analysis is going to be formed at least in part by your own views and thoughts.

☑ When recording thoughts and conclusions about aesthetics and impact you need to have some control over the language you use – apply the correct terms and descriptions to make your points.

Now try this

Use the internet to find an image of Grayson Perry's *Sex, Drugs and Earthenware*. Read the sample response extract above and try to add one or two comments about the urn's aesthetic and visual impact.

Analysing practitioners' work

You will need to demonstrate how you apply contextual influences – such as your analysis of practitioners' work related to the theme – to your own work and practice. You will also need to communicate why they are an influence. You will do this through the records in your annotated log, your proposal explaining how you intend to respond to the theme, the production of your final piece, and your portfolio that demonstrates your development and realisation process along with a commentary. The extract below is a record of how a practitioner is influencing a learner's own work and practice.

Sample response extract

In this extract from deconstructing and analysing a practitioner's work and communicating why they are an influence on the learner's own work and practice, there is an assessment of the potential of the work and how it can contribute to the task as a whole. Deconstructing the imagery has helped to inform the learner's ideas.

Investigating Tom Phillips RA

My investigation into Tom Phillips has introduced me to the idea of layering text and imagery, using a range of different techniques and found materials. I really like the way he creates a hand-made feel with the types of resources and materials he uses. I like his use of inks as I find the way they bleed into the paper something that I am interested in – they become a part of the fabric of the surface rather than sitting on top of it. He uses imagery with association – images are taken out of context and made into something with a new meaning (his pictures of park benches and stripes). I really am inspired by the way he references his techniques visually – the making is part of the finished item – and this is something I am going to propose in my developmental work.

I have created my own piece in the style of Tom Phillips. I worked on a page from an old book, and explored the way he used words taken out of context and isolated to produce new sentences – the words have a different connection and take on another meaning. It also looks like a kind of code. There is a strong visual dynamic where the formal arrangements of words in a line is broken and remade. There is also the potential to explore the relationship between the words and colours/stains.

I really like and am inspired by Phillips' use of collage techniques to remake images. I like the picture on the right with its rough textures, colour wash and areas of white. This layering of colour and shapes gives the piece a real sense of depth, and adds to the mystery – is it a fragment of a bigger, older document? Is it damaged in some way, or is there a secret code that is being uncovered?

Phillips has used multiple layers and linear elements to isolate areas of text that the viewer then connects. This taps into our ability to read these words as well as an inherent way we try to make connected meanings out of half said or hinted words. The isolated text really does seem to float on the surface – referencing the idea that this page may have hidden meanings, or more depth than initially meets the eye.

Tom Phillips, taken from 'The Humument, page 18 (First Version)' (1973) © Tom Phillips RA
www.tomphillips.co.uk

The annotation reflects on the overall purpose of the work and recognises that the process of the production is integral to its meaning.

Practising artists and designers use vocabulary such as 'fabric' and 'surface', to demonstrate a deconstruction of the components.

 For more on Tom Phillips' work see page 136.

The images selected clearly relate to the task. The learner has worked out the processes involved in creating it and is able to break it apart into separate components that make a whole.

Deconstruction step-by-step

- What are you are trying to find out?
- What attracted you to the practitioner's work, and to this specific piece?
- What have you found out up to this point?

- How can you apply what you have learned to your own work?
- Are you going to look at other examples?

Now try this

Describe and review the imagery in one work by a practitioner you have studied.

Making analysis work

Analysis is a major aspect of the assessment of this unit and impacts on all of the activities.

Sketchbook annotations analysing own work.

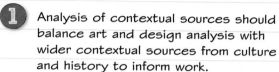 **Links** To revise analysis, see pages 152–158.

The photo immediately right shows my handmade paper, where I added torn pieces of gold and silver foils into the pulp as it was being formed. I experimented with layering pulp over the top of the foils to consolidate the surface but it covered the foils completely. This meant that the paper, once dried, was unstable – the foil pieces could be brushed away and came off the surface fairly easily. I had to mark this as an unsuccessful experiment.

The image below shows another example of working with the paper pulp idea – where items where sprinkled onto the drying pulp, and then covered with another layer of pulp that wasn't consolidated. Once dry these two surfaces could be pulled apart and the sprinkled items would remain – this was more successful, as some of the items had in fact become part of the paper.

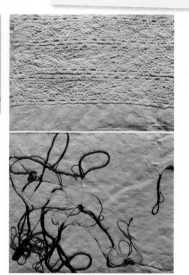

The image at the top shows a sample of the paper I made using woollen lace strips. Using this technique meant that the lace would actually stay within the paper. I sprinkled some pulp on top of the lace, and built the paper up around the lace. It provides a subtle and delicate surface that has creative possibilities.

The image immediately above is an experiment piece where I combined embroidery thread in with the paper pulp. I pulled some of the layers of paper apart so there would be some thin and some thicker areas, rather than it remaining the same thickness across the surface. However, I'm not sure if the thread isn't too dominant in this. Some parts have ended up with the thread sitting very much on top of the paper. I think the best sections are where the thread is part of the surface – the finer areas in the middle section. I could explore the potential for using thread as a drawing tool in some of these pieces

Analysis in practice

Analysis can work in two distinct ways.

① Analysis of contextual sources should balance art and design analysis with wider contextual sources from culture and history to inform work.

- Assess the materials, techniques and processes used by others.
- Determine how others have used formal elements to communicate.
- Relate your own practice to wider cultural narratives.

② Analysis of your own work should be critical and used to judge your progress, especially if you are refining work, or dealing with an aspect that isn't working.

- Assess the benefits of contextual factors that have influenced you.
- Use testing to improve the quality of outcomes.
- Quantify strengths and weaknesses against benchmarks you have set.

Sample response extract

Making paper – a summary

My ideas were based on including natural objects within the paper itself as part of its fabric, which is a tradition that dates back to the start of paper making. I wanted to use objects that would support the way I was approaching the theme of 'Growth'. I used papermaking pulping techniques to make the raw materials, and then moulds to produce the paper. The pieces do have a very natural feel and texture – they seem to say 'organic'. I think they are pale enough to use as a basis for overprinting imagery. Overall, after a comparison of the samples, I have decided to take the direction of using coloured thread, but ensuring it is more part of the surface. I have compared my samples with samples taken from high-street craft shops along with those collected on my travels in India and it is hard sometimes to tell the difference, so I feel like I am on the right track.

This extract demonstrates how analysis of contextual sources has influenced the learner's own work and practice. It also shows analysis of the development of their own work. You can summarise information as you go along in analytical annotation.

The analysis is framed within the theme of the assessment. The analysis also confirms how the learner is trying to approach the theme and supports this with analysis.

It's good practice to make an analytical comparison between the different experiments.

Commercial products have been used as a benchmark to help assess the quality of the experiments overall. Wider primary sources are used to set standards.

Now try this

Analyse a stage within your development process, concentrating on one technique you used.

Selecting materials, techniques and processes

You will have experimented with potential materials, techniques and processes when you generated ideas and carried out contextual research. Your proposal will have included initial choices. You need to develop this work as you experiment further, ensure you have access to resources, test out and document your ideas, and justify your choices.

Selecting materials, techniques and processes

The materials selected should be appropriate to the intentions and scope of the project, as well as providing opportunity for exploration and experimentation.

Selected techniques

These should be linked to the intended outcome – the example below explores techniques for a proposal on the theme of 'Face'.

Sample response extract

Theme: 'Face'

I'm exploring further the ideas included in my written proposal. I really want to reference examples of painting and lighting in my photography. I have used Rembrandt lighting in studio shoots but never really explored the potential for creating a menacing mood – I've always kept the lighting balanced – and I want to explore other ways of doing this now. I want to create an image where the face seems to appear out of the background darkness, so will be experimenting with different lighting techniques, accessories including softboxes and gels, and layering in software.

Contextual as well as visual information is included in this example.

Examples of lighting set-ups
Effects of each lighting pattern
Test shoots
Rembrandt lighting

Main light illuminates one side of the face.

Eye is illuminated with small triangle of light on the cheek.
Nose shadow connects with the cheek shadow to create the triangle of light on the upper cheek.

I am going to explore lighting on a face to create specific shadow effects and to create interest.

Butterfly paramount lighting

Note: light goes above and is directed down on the subject.

Butterfly lighting, also known as Paramount lighting, became a staple pattern for the Hollywood photographers of the 1930s. This lighting is characterised by the butterfly-shaped shadow that it casts below the nose. The butterfly pattern can be quite useful for a variety of faces, but is at its best on lean subjects with high and pronounced cheekbones. It is produced by placing the light source above the face (typically 25–70 degrees) and in line with the direction in which the face is pointing.

Availability of resources

The materials you choose should be readily available to you. When you are working up your final selection, make sure you have access to any specialist help you need to match your selection to the resources available.

Links You will find further guidance on how to get help and technical assistance on page 171.

Access to resources

☑ Fine art resources require sourcing and preparation.

☑ Lens-based resources may need to be booked in advance.

☑ Screen-based work may require preparation of stencils.

☑ Build an allowance for production and drying time into resource planning for work in ceramics and 3D.

☑ Plan how you will use digital resources, including when you will be able to access them.

Now try this

Based on the theme of 'Face', identify at least five sources and five materials that you might use to respond to the theme using bullet points.

Experimenting further with materials

You will need to experiment further with your ideas about materials for your art and design piece, testing them out and producing samples to evaluate how effective they are. This will help you make an appropriate selection. Make sure you document, annotate and justify choices made, to demonstrate the development process.

Why experiment?

In many art and design projects, across all disciplines, there is a phase where materials are tried out. Ideas can be developed further through using materials in tests and samples, studies and swatches, models, prototypes and maquettes. This will give a set of results from which decisions can be reached on what to develop, or if further experimentation is required.

Why are you experimenting?

Experimentation has to be focused – even if it seems practitioners are trying out random materials, they will be focused on a specific end. Clarify early on what you are trying to do. During this stage, you should keep a record – include physical examples, the work itself, photographs of versions and stages, all of your samples and models, studies and roughs.

Describe the ways you have used materials. Lay the imagery out carefully so you can use it in a portfolio if required.

I printed a second time onto thicker handmade paper. I really like the indentations and they way this leaves a raised surface detail behind. This works like an embossed effect, and is interesting in this example due to the accidental colour dye in the corner of the paper that fades out – from top right down. To develop this I'm going to explore using more dyed papers, with harmonious palettes; I will work with this style of collagraphy again – and I will also explore cutting deeper and cutting away more layers so the design stands out.

Tell the story

You need to explain what you are trying to achieve using appropriate terminology. Get the blend of visual and textual information working together.

 Links See also Unit 2, page 83 about how to summarise information.

Remember

☑ The materials you choose can give new and unexpected results.

☑ You can take risks with combinations, although not if this compromises health and safety.

☑ Exploring materials may take you in a different direction – don't worry about that. Document it and review the results.

Now try this

Look back at a project where you experimented with materials, and clarify what you learned from this.

Experimenting further with techniques and processes

Materials, techniques and processes will often interrelate. Experiment further and test out your ideas about techniques and processes to evaluate how effective they are, to help make an appropriate selection.

Techniques and processes

Techniques are the particular methods you use to make your work, such as using dry brush in painting or appliqué in textiles. There are traditional methods that are used with specific media, but you can also mix alternative materials with traditional techniques. The technique is the way the media is manipulated or applied. The process of making work may involve multiple techniques and stages from start to finish.

Which technique to try?

Just as with materials, you can experiment with techniques at this stage. Try out things that others have used that you have researched, methods from previous projects, and any that you feel might fit the theme for the project. Trying out means just that – exploring what the techniques can do, and recognising their limitations.

Example: using processes

The example shows 16 versions of the same piece, based on the theme of 'Flooding'. It was developed through the process of two practitioners sharing ideas and swapping their work in progress. The individual techniques used in this work included photography, digital manipulation, drawing and painting, printmaking and physical drawing. Both practitioners brought different ideas and changed the work, as part of the processes used to develop it.

Processes can allow you to explore alternative versions and various techniques.

Critical reflection

It is very important to record your critical reflection on your progress as you work through the stages of your set task. This will link your understanding of formal elements and visual language with your initial research.

Linking materials, techniques and processes

☑ Materials, techniques and processes are all linked – so they will overlap in your developmental work.

☑ They can be used to generate new ideas, as well as confirming existing ideas.

Now try this

Evaluate a process you have used on a project – did it work, and did it give you any new ideas?

Documenting and annotating

Documenting your work as it progresses will show your development process. Annotate your ideas and the choices you have made, to explain your thinking and to make judgements on successes and areas for development.

Documenting

It's good practice to:

- ✓ record with clear images
- ✓ use text and images as required
- ✓ document processes and ideas.

Photographs are an ideal way to document what you are doing, changes in your working practices, ideas development and different versions and directions. You can also use them to support records of materials, techniques and processes. If you are documenting 3D maquettes think about the background and lighting.

Images can show a great deal

Think about how you can use images – photography, drawing and screengrabs – to show both your practical work as it develops, and the range of your creative ideas. It makes sense to use visuals – ensure you use every opportunity to annotate the images, and explain how you are developing your work.

This means using photography and drawing in a different way from generating ideas and recording source materials. Make the images clear and arrange the items to be photographed in a good light.

Annotating

Annotate specific aspects of your work as it progresses – explain how you have used certain materials, for example.

Annotation should go beyond purely documenting and start to look critically at the way you are developing your work. Be critical about your work rather than self-congratulatory – when all is going well it's great, but are there ways you can stretch the work or process further to make it even better?

Using documentation and annotation

Use visuals and text – this will make for an interesting record, and provide a sound basis for documentation. Annotation can refer directly to specific visuals in your record and can be used to show critical thinking, refinements and decision-making.

Get the terminology right

As you document and annotate your work, make sure you use appropriate descriptive language and art and design terminology. Think about specific terms you need to use to describe an aspect of your work, for example, 'composition', 'colour', 'form', and so on.

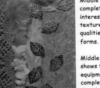

This is an entry from a log used to record work in progress.

Log entry:
Left top: This is my log record for how I made collographs. Firstly, I laid out double side tapes all over the piece of card – this would form a surface for my items to be stuck to – and make the plate

Right top: this image shows the placing of items over the card surface, and building up a range of textures.

Middle left: This shows the completed plate. I was interested in combining textures with abstract qualities, and recognizable forms.

Middle right: This image shows the materials, and equipment I needed to complete the inking up of the plate. I mixed the colours to achieve the earthy tone I was intending to use,

Bottom right: the colour was thinned with vegetable oil, and I used card spreaders to ink up the surface of the plate. The card allowed me to leave areas of the plate free from ink, so producing a negative shape or space when printed – and this could be an inherent part of the design.

Bottom Right: an example of the inked plate

Now try this

Take an example of visual recording – it can be a drawing and/or photographs. Annotate this, explaining how it could be used to develop a specific idea.

Making experimentation work

Your experimentation when you are carrying out initial research, and in the research and development process of creating your piece, will be more effective if you target it towards specific aims and objectives. You should set a target you want to achieve, and link this to the context for your set task, the needs of your audience and your creative intention. Documenting and recording your experimentation in an annotated log will help inform the production of your final piece and selection of records for your portfolio with accompanying commentary.

Sample response extract

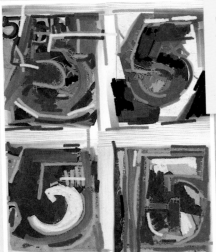

This learner has recorded some of their experimentation as part of their log. They may be able to use this when they compile their portfolio.

It's important to use experimentation as a way to develop and improve your work. This may sound obvious, but this means that experimentation needs to be strategic and considered, not rushed. Ideally, you will create a range of experiments that work as a group, with each test contributing something important to the outcome overall.

I am developing my response for an illustration on the theme of 'Combinations'. I have focused on the typographic qualities of different number systems, as this is what I have researched. I want to explore how different combinations of texture, surface and type can create interesting compositions through being combined – my plan is to create a background that I can then overlay with the word 'Systems' in much brighter text over the top. I will also explore if numbers can be used to suggest the word systems – as in COMBINATIONS = COM31N4710N5 (I can play around with different typefaces, or reverse the number 3, and so on).

Notice how the different operations and stages in a creative task don't always follow one another, but may provoke a return to an earlier stage such as research.

The experiments with the backgrounds have a very rough feel as a result of the textures and materials I have used. After this experimentation, I think it would be a good idea to look again at Kurt Schwitters' and Bauhaus' ideas, such as their visual language programme. I need to bring in a wider range of materials to give the pieces a more contemporary feel – such as card, and possibly some photographic elements.

Often, experimentation will yield an uneven range of results of different quality. That's the nature of experiments – you have to accept that some sort of failure is built into the process. At this point, you need to identify potential solutions to the creative problems that experimentation throws up.

I deliberately want to avoid so-called 'clean graphics' at this stage as I can easily scan some of the surfaces and clean them up using software.

Now try this

Select a set of materials you would use to experiment with for an idea you have for a project.

Recording work in progress

As you continue to experiment and develop your ideas, think carefully about ways of recording your work in progress. Consider how you will show your work developing, so you can demonstrate the processes you used to reach creative decisions.

🔗 **Links** See page 163 for more on documenting and annotating.

Weigh up the pros and cons

- Consider ways of using and presenting annotation and visuals in your log and documentation, to show work in progress and the processes you have experimented with. Make a decision about which ones you are going to use, and try them out. Once you have established your format, use it regularly.

- If you are working digitally, make a back-up of your images and information on an external hard drive.
- Make sure you record the key developments in your set task. You can use these to inform your final piece of work and select from them for your portfolio and accompanying commentary.

Work in progress and review – a page of compiled imagery and text

Sample response extract

Recording processes through a series of images

Sample response extract

Digital style recording, showing a contact sheet and thoughts on images, provides an opportunity to add a review to the page at a later date.

Try and avoid lengthy descriptions of a process – it's better to précis this and evaluate what you've learned from working on this process.

You can arrange a sequence of images to show a process.

You could use photographs of yourself engaging in activities.

Now try this

List the different ways you could record work in progress and creative processes. Evaluate them, and decide which ones you feel are most appropriate, explaining why.

Developing through the production process

You will need to review and refine your work throughout the creative process. When exploring the development of work through the production process, consider the following.

Design sheets or screengrabs

If you are using screen-based techniques and processes, use screengrabs of the key parts in your creative development. You can use them to show viewers how you developed your work, and any key refinements you made as you went along.

Short film, games or animation clips, and photographs

You can show how animation has developed through recording drawings and story boarding, concept drawings on paper and in software, and any animatic work. Photographers can record their work through contact sheets and rest prints, showing how they have selected and developed work.

Samples/drafts/working drawings

These allow you to develop your work through different stages of recording, experimentation and exploration, and see successes and further areas for development. In doing so, they help you manage production and direct your project to its conclusion.

> **Explore the development of work through the production process.**

Toiles

You can develop samples and design work through illustration into garments and sections of garments using basic materials, as a way of developing your ideas from concept through to outcome.

Models and maquettes

These can be used to show how you have developed ideas in three dimensions (3D). It is important to show the transition from any 2D drawing to 3D modelling and construction. It will also allow you to see what you are developing 'in the round' or in real space.

A designer working on a toile.

An artist working on a model in clay.

Now try this

How could you use different recording techniques to record the development of a project in your specialist pathway? List them and what they would record.

Reviewing and refining ideas

As you develop your work through the creative process, you will need to review and refine your ideas.

Reviewing the potential
and evolution of ideas

Reflecting on the
strengths and
weaknesses of ideas

**Ways of reviewing
and refining ideas**

Critically reviewing your work

Planning to adapt
or change things to
improve

Peer feedback
can give users'
perspectives
on work.

Sample notes extract

Response to reviewing my creative intentions
with my poster and development work on
'Living Healthy Lives' campaign, aimed at
teens and young adults

Reviewing my initial ideas against my
development work was really interesting –
and a bit disappointing in some ways, though
I've realised I need to pick up on the points
I noticed. I had thought that I had really got
the message across very clearly in my work,
as I had used a set of images that would
tell the story as well as provide information
about benefits of living healthier lives. I was
disappointed that the work looked a bit old-
fashioned and may not have the appeal for the
audience that I intended. I had in fact used
fairly standard images that were accepted
symbols for healthy living – crisp, clear images
of vegetables, exercise and positive faces –
however I may need to adapt the approach
to the images and will look again at my
research to evaluate ways that I can change
and improve.

Critical review

An important part of the review process is asking
key questions about how far the work you are
developing matches your creative intentions.

You can ask questions about:

- the strength of your ideas – do they meet the
  purpose of the brief? Are they communicating
  what you wanted to get across (your intention)?

- how your ideas have evolved – have you
  developed them fully? Is there a range of ideas
  to choose from, or have you stuck to the same
  idea? Could you develop others, to get a
  wider range of potential solutions?

- adapting and refining your ideas – how can
  you use critical review to do this? Could you
  review how you have planned to use materials,
  techniques and processes, and could this plan
  be improved?

Remember

✓ If you are reviewing and refining your ideas
in a context that is not formally assessed, it
can be very helpful to organise one-to-one,
peer and group reviews.

Now try this

Think of a project you have worked on. How did you review it and plan to adapt or change it?

Reviewing ideas critically

Reviewing your work is an important part of refining creative solutions. The quality of your review will inform any plans to adapt or change things in order to improve. This may affect the production of your final piece. Your recording of the review process can be used in your portfolio and accompanying commentary to help explain how you achieved your final piece and how it responds to the theme, and to help evaluate the development process and final piece of work.

Why review?

A review is based on more than simple sequential explanation – 'I did this then I did that'. It explores strengths and weaknesses, asks key questions about functionality, purpose or message, seeks conclusions and proposes solutions. Its primary function is to improve practice.

Reviewing a task

Sample notes extract

This extract reviews a design for a new homescreen for an information graphics system about the learner's centre.

Set the context for the review.

I reviewed the development of my work against my original intentions and research. I felt it had a number of positive points, as well as some inherent weaknesses.

Explain the positive points clearly and succinctly – this could be developed, i.e. which specific images were strong?

Positive points:

- The layout looked visually exciting.
- The colour range was uplifting, exciting and would be interesting to look at.
- There were some strong images used.

Summarise weaknesses. In this case they were all to do with user friendliness and functionality. There are some interesting points that immediately link to formal elements and visual language, such as colour and space.

Weaknesses:

- At a basic level, some of the type was lost against the brighter colours, so could be difficult to read.
- There were no neutral or restful areas – everything was busy and energetic. This might suit some of the target audience, but not all.

Functionality in this scenario is key – it's no good if it doesn't work.

- The links to the next pages were too small, and too far down the page – they should be clearer and at the top.

Plans to adapt or change things in order to improve:

It's useful to apply these headings. This is a summary after all – it needs to be viewed quickly.

- I need to resolve the colour and text issue. I can reduce the saturation of the background layer and/or the transparency channel.

There are some points about technical responses here, which show an ability to problem solve in a creative context.

- I need to explore different layouts for the buttons – there is no point having them if users need to ask where they are. The location needs to be much more obvious.
- I need to achieve these changes by the end of two days, and review how successful they have been.

Another point about functionality and the importance of making the buttons and links work.

It may seem obvious, but it's important that the response and actions have a timescale – and a way of being reassessed.

Now try this

Select a piece of work you have produced and critically review it.

Adapting and refining ideas

When you have reviewed the potential and evolution of ideas and reflected on strengths and weaknesses, you can make plans to adapt or change things in order to improve.

Why does work need to adapt?

Your work will adapt as you learn more about the theme, get more ideas and absorb influences, see how materials behave, react to experimenting and testing and clarify your own intention. This is perfectly natural and is in fact an opportunity to explore alternatives.

Sample notes extract

I reviewed my development work, in particular six sketchbook pages and one rough print.

Positives:

- Liked the reduced colour range.
- Saw the potential for making layered imagery that still had detail (by reducing depth of colour saturation).
- Thought the product could have a broad appeal – references to botanical drawings and older engraved images.
- Could be used on surface design and fabric equally – so had more potential.

Negatives:

- Wondered whether the reduced colour imagery would be lost on a large-scale design – like the wallpaper I was planning.
- Wondered if the fabric would have a contemporary mass market appeal if used as a covering for furnishings – felt it was maybe a bit old fashioned – or would be appealing, but very niche.

Plans to adapt or change things in order to improve:

- Investigate niche markets.
- Consider further research into textile fabric.
- Mock up large-scale use of design on PC.

This learner has reviewed their development work and planned to adapt in order to improve.

It can be useful to select key development work for review, so you can plan specific refinements to improve your work.

A balanced assessment that considers the positives and negatives.

Sample notes extract

This learner records how they have refined their work.

As a result of review, clear targets can be set for future refinement.

Refining work may only involve slight changes, often related to visual language. All the parts of the image may be there, it's just that the colours or composition may need changing. You don't always have to radically change an image or an object.

Now try this

Review one of your completed projects. Identify at least one point where you think the work clearly evolved.

Completing final piece to deadline

The success of completing your final piece of art and design to deadline will depend on how well you manage it. Planning is important.

Managing production

Managing the production phase is about working with the resources: materials, techniques and processes. These will have been planned in earlier, so it's likely that the first part of the production will involve testing out ideas practically, for instance:

- trials, samples, studies, swatches, working drawings
- test shoots, proof prints, animatics
- roughs, mock-ups, maquettes, prototypes, models.

Keep a space in your planning for reviewing the testing phase and the developed work.

As you review, you might need to refine your work or modify it slightly – this is all part of the production process.

Timing is key

Scheduling the production of your final piece is important. This can predict possible issues with timing, and show any shortfalls in the planning. You need to research the amount of time processes take. Some of this may be governed by the complexity and number of tasks – such as exposing an image to screen and getting it ready to print – or physical characteristics, such as drying times for wet materials. Remember you may also have to book time to use certain equipment or facilities. When you are waiting for things to be done or to dry, plan in other activities so your time is used effectively throughout the task.

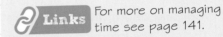 **Links** For more on managing time see page 141.

Be professional

Adopt a professional approach in all that you do as you work through your tasks. This might involve ordering resources, asking for technical support, responding positively to setbacks or working for longer at certain points to achieve a result. If the plan is well structured and addresses all the potential issues, it should progress smoothly.

Timetable

Break down the stages and allocate time to each one. For your actual assessment, ask your tutor or check the latest Sample Assessment Material on the Pearson website for the time allowed for production of the final piece.

Time	Activity
	Image processing – studio only open with software on Mon and Thurs
	Image refinement and manipulation
	Printing – leave at least half the time for proofing

Set targets

Use **SMART** target setting. You can develop smaller targets within each week to keep on track. Make sure these are realistic, and leave some time spare just in case something does go wrong. Plan in your resources – this might involve ordering in advance or making sure they are available in your centre and designated for you.

What if it goes wrong?

If you have:
- ☑ planned effectively
- ☑ researched your options
- ☑ considered effective methods
- ☑ conducted appropriate testing and sampling
- ☑ used review to refine ideas
- ☑ kept to your schedule
- ☑ worked safely
- ☑ used the right resources for the job

… then it's unlikely to go wrong.

Now try this

Consider managing production for a final piece of art or design in your chosen discipline. What would be needed?

Managing health and safety

Health and safety is vital to professional practice and is covered by specific legislation.

Working safely

Health and safety is everyone's responsibility to manage, including yours. Some art and design processes can cause injury.

Studios can be busy spaces, with practitioners working on individual projects – not everyone is working with the same equipment and processes at the same time.

What do you need to do?

- If you don't know how to use something, ask or find out before you start.
- Refer to and act upon the guidance you have been given in studio guidelines, such as risk assessments and regulations, e.g. Control of Substances Hazardous to Health (COSHH).
- Always use the required personal protective equipment (PPE), such as safety goggles, gloves, masks, aprons and gauntlets, when working with specific equipment and processes, following manufacturer guidelines.

Risk assessment

Risk assessments are important as they show you are aware of the nature of the materials and processes you are using.

Consider the example opposite, which is part of an initial risk assessment into 3D cardboard engineering techniques.

There are hazards associated with the activities, and control measures in place to minimise the risk. The hazards are still there, but following the control measures should keep the risk of injury or harm to a minimum. The risk assessment can make reference to previous guidance.

Hazard	Control	Notes
Using scalpels with card	Health and safety induction, tutor guidance, guards on large rules, cutting mats	Needs reminders, proper studio practice
Using glues to bond surfaces	Use low-impact, water-based adhesive	Use water-based PVA

🔗 **Links** For more on risk assessments, look at page 172.

Get help!

You should be able to ask for technical help when working with a resource. Technicians can show you how to use materials and equipment. Managing the technical aspects of any task requires forward planning – it's a balance of keeping options open to be creative, and making sure you work safely.

Your final piece

You may need to consider health and safety in relation to your final piece. Consider its functionality and intended use.

Remember

✓ Plan your work time effectively – avoid rushing.

✓ Follow all the health and safety guidelines.

✓ Don't bring any materials into the centre, unless these have been risk assessed and cleared.

✓ Record all aspects of health and safety in your log.

Now try this

Look critically at a studio in your centre. Identify what hazards are associated with the functions and processes that happen there and list the health and safety controls.

Recording your safe working

It's important to observe health and safety by identifying and managing any risks. You must work safely on your practical work when you are creating a finished piece, and also when you are producing a portfolio. You also need to show evidence of your safe working in your portfolio.

🔗 **Links** For more information on health and safety, see page 171.

Sample response extract

Risk assessment for using glazes in ceramics

Hazard	Control measure	Additional information	Risk level
Glazes may contain toxic compounds	• Use PPE, wash sources • Use approved tools to apply • Induction training • Technician support	• Mixed glazes can be bought, ready prepared • Avoid toxic-based glaze compounds if possible	Low
Ingestion of glazes	• No food or drink allowed in studio • Wash hands and surfaces thoroughly • Apply glazes using approved techniques		Low

PPE is often used as a control measure.

This risk assessment focuses on hazards and has identified control measures. Your own centre will have risk assessments for:
- the studio
- equipment and tools
- materials
- activities.

There may be risk assessments in place that will cover your work, or that you can adapt to your specific purposes.

Sample response extract

Working safely in paper-making

You can use photographs to record how you have managed health and safety in the studio, and then use them in your portfolio.

Before you work with a process make sure you are familiar with any associated risks. There are a number of activities in art and design that involve some risk, so it's important that you are aware of these so you can work safely.

Set your workspace up properly. Protect surfaces, make sure you have all the tools ready, and check if you require any PPE – in this example the learner is making paper using natural materials, and their risk assessment identified that PPE was not necessarily required.

Safety beyond the studio
Think about how you will work safely if you go out on location, or on a visit.

Now try this

Conduct a risk assessment for one process that you are going to use when you create your finished piece.

Developing the final piece

While you are developing your final piece, you can still review your techniques and processes. It's not too late to change your mind about any of them. You should also document the development of your work with a view to using it in a sketchbook or portfolio.

How can the work develop?

As you work up your ideas, you will be doing a number of practical things simultaneously, such as:

- selecting and using techniques to realise ideas
- exploring further materials, techniques and processes
- considering formal elements and visual language in terms of meeting creative intention
- critically reviewing and refining against expectations, using documentation and annotation
- recording review and progress.

Documenting development

Frequently, development comes from being increasingly ambitious with drafts or prototypes, and from combining learning from previous experiments and consistently trying to improve the outcomes.

You may not be able to record every single activity you undertake, but you should aim to evidence key stages of development together with reflection and review of progress towards initial intentions.

Sketchbook pages can be a place to develop ideas as well as a space to collect evidence from development that takes place outside of the sketchbook.

FINAL PIECE LOG

Exploring ink opacity in relation to design and screen image: the screen image was quite finely detailed as it contained some graphic marks, fine lines and some fine hatching. I was exploring how I needed to mix the proportions of binder with inks to achieve a workable system, using recording techniques to do this.

The techniques and equipment I used here were very much part of the print-making approach that I wanted my project to explore. I enjoyed working with different aspects of print – screen, mark making, engraving – and taking this into ideas for embroidery. The application of my own hand-made fabric into a further design piece was really exciting.

I used a wood-engraving tool to burn segments of my writing onto the cards, and explored the potential to layer image, background and words.

What does it show?

The production process can involve a higher level of technical requirements than design development. Don't completely shut off the notion of still allowing your work to evolve even as you are producing it. You should have a plan that you are working to, but if you see something that you want to change, it's not too late to do so.

Remember

✓ Use your smartphone to record your progress if you can – you may find it helpful to record your production as it happens.

✓ You can still amend and develop your work further in the production phase if you want to.

✓ If you do this, critically reflect on the reasons for doing it, what you wanted to change, and the effect the changes will have.

Now try this

Identify a personal project you have worked on. Was there a point when you changed something – a colour, detail, shape or process as it was being produced? Critically assess what effect the change had.

Realising the final piece

As you complete your final piece of art and design, consider the following factors.

Demonstrate what you can do

This is where you make key decisions about the work, based on your review and developmental work, any feedback and the progress of the practical work. The decisions you make here will dictate the quality of the final piece(s) – and will need explaining and justifying in your commentary.

Apply a high level of concentration to all of the different aspects in the task – this should ensure a consistency of approach across all of your research, trials, testing and samples, idea generation, development work, review and the final outcome.

Accuracy and fluent application

This is simply how well you have used materials, techniques and processes in the different stages of the task and in procuring the final piece:

- in a creative sense, to match your intention
- in an imaginative sense – maybe different or unexpected combinations
- in terms of dexterity and skill – how well you managed the different parts of the processes from start to finish.

Bring together skills that you have learned to inform what you are producing if appropriate.

Fullest interpretation

This is about pushing your developmental work to achieve its fullest potential. It's not about following every single idea that you had indiscriminately, nor is it about taking the first idea you come up with. It's about taking the right idea and developing it fully, justifying your choice, exploring materials and processes, and taking all of this, and any feedback, to end up with the strongest final outcome possible.

> Remember that, while feedback can be very helpful, you may need to work independently for your assessment. Always check the Pearson website for the latest details.

Modifying and quality

This involves review and decision making. It will occur where you have taken an idea relating to the theme, developed your work, reviewed it and then modified it. It can be in modifications to the ways you use techniques and processes, or in your selection of imagery, or use of visual language. Many of these decisions will relate to quality – and the revisions you make should be positive steps towards improving and achieving quality outcomes.

You may find tables or grids helpful when summarising the information you gather.

Fitness for purpose

Fitness for purpose is whether the creative work is effective in what it was meant to do – such as provide information or show ideas about the human figure. Your planned intention is what you wanted it to say creatively within that context. As you realise your final outcome, you need to reflect on what this purpose was, and use your own critical judgements and any feedback from focus groups and users to inform your conclusions.

Fitness for purpose can be reviewed at different stages in the task, not just at the end.

 Links There's more on fitness for purpose on page 177.

Intention

When you define fitness for purpose you will also be considering your own intention as the two things are closely interrelated. Here you have to gauge your work against your original creative intention.

Now try this

Explain how far a final piece of your own work takes account of the above factors, and any changes you would make.

Showing creative fluency

The creative fluency of your art and design piece should develop consistently.

What is fluency?

Creative work that lacks technical proficiency can seem clumsy and inarticulate. Technically proficient work that lacks creativity can seem purely about skill, lacking ideas or imagination. Fluency is a bringing together of both these elements. It's a way of using, applying, making and doing. It can be how materials, techniques and processes are used in a way that is a balanced blend of technical skills and creativity. To develop fluency takes time and practice.

You will need to do it your way

The fluency in your development process and outcome should be there to see. Sometimes it can be simply a sensitivity to the inherent qualities of materials, or a way of combining design elements that is fit for purpose. As you progress towards realising your final piece of work, regular review will enable you to maintain the fluency in your work.

Developing fluency in sketchbooks

Fluency can involve simplification of design elements. For example, in this design for surface pattern and textiles, colour, form and positive and negative space have all been used.

Develop ideas using techniques

Practise using materials and developing ideas – the more you try this, the better the potential to become fluent.

An idea, visual device or motif can be carried through the task – so experimentation can become fluent in exploring visual ideas across different media.

Review is still important

As your final piece of art or design reaches its conclusion you should still be applying ongoing review. This might involve recording thoughts about how fluent you have been in some of the stages of the task, and whether you could develop this fluency more.

Fluency

This can be a combination of:

☑ the way you approach the different stages of the task

☑ the level of skill and sensitivity to materials you show

☑ your creativity, imagination and the way you use materials.

Now try this

Select an aspect of your work that you believe is fluent, explaining why.

Showing quality

The quality of a piece of work can be determined by its aesthetic value – its feel, look, fitness for purpose, innovation, application of materials, techniques and processes, and how it affects the user or audience.

Aesthetics

Aesthetics is concerned with notions of beauty, harmony and balance – the style of the work. It can be the result of simplification and refinement, and/or choice and treatment of materials, and how formal elements and visual language are combined. It can be in the look of a piece, the innovation it displays (think of an iconic design item), the way it uses materials, how and what it communicates, and how the user or audience interacts with it. You should have an idea of the aesthetic value of your work as it progresses, and you can use feedback to gauge if others see it in the same way that you do.

Refining for quality

To get quality into a work it is often necessary to refine. This links to the cycle of experimentation, critical reflection and refinements, and developing work taking into account these factors. Aesthetics can be determined by aspects such as composition and colour balance and how these interrelate.

Quality of imagery

The quality of the imagery and the way it is produced are important.

In this printed sample, colour has been simplified to provide a harmonious aesthetic. The imagery has been produced using processes competently, ensuring that it has a quality feel.

Quantifying aesthetics

This can be established by comparing your work to examples of work by practitioners who have been inspirational, where the researched examples have a clear aesthetic value. You can be inspired by visual themes and motifs, and take visual leads from these examples. Sometimes it can be as basic as the way designs are laid out. Look at examples of layouts in design, where you can track the simplification of an image.

Remember

✓ You can learn about aesthetics through your research.

✓ To achieve a piece with an aesthetic value you may have to work through several revisions.

✓ Colour schemes and layouts can appear simple, but this may be the result of many changes and revisions/refinements.

✓ Take inspiration from this and try out the same process of refinement.

✓ Work can be deliberately un-aesthetic – if it can be justified.

✓ You may well reference aesthetics in your commentaries to accompany your portfolio.

Now try this

Select a piece of work you have produced that you believe has an aesthetic value, and explain why.

Showing fitness for purpose

When realising your final piece, you will need to show fitness for purpose. This might be demonstrated in relation to the brief for the piece of work.

What is the purpose?

'Fitness for purpose' is a term associated with creative briefs, but it applies across the range of disciplines – think of it as a question. Did the final piece achieve what it set out to do? Does it reflect my planned intention? Design briefs can offer the opportunity to ask potential users their views – these might be the clients or the intended users. In fine art and personal-themed projects in other areas, audience feedback is used to consider how well it worked. Asking questions alongside being creative takes concentrated effort – you almost have to do something, then stop and ask 'Is this going to work?'

What if the initial purpose changed?

Many projects are amended and changed as they progress. If the theme has been addressed, and the work has met the criteria, then it will be the justification made for the changes that will be important. This reinforces the importance of keeping an accurate and full log of your progress, which includes effective review. If you have been reviewing your work on a regular basis, you will have evidence of any changes of direction, or amendments to the purpose for your work, and can use these to explain and justify the changes.

Who is it aimed at?

Review techniques can be applied at the close of the project as well as its mid stages. Make sure you are asking the right questions in your review so that you don't simply make 'like it/don't like it' responses that aren't then developed – these responses are of limited use. Try questions like:

- Does it make sense?
- Is it simple and clear enough?
- Is it functional?

You need to adapt these to fit the context for your work.

Graphic design and interactive media projects benefit from reviewing and refining infographics, interactivity, user friendliness, communication, and so on.

How to gauge fitness for purpose

Think about fitness for purpose as you work through the project and experiment, test out, review and refine your work.

Refining practical outcomes

If your review indicates that the piece of art or design will not meet its purpose, it makes sense to adapt or change it, even at a late stage. This might involve some radical rethinking depending on the end result. As ever, if your refinements improve the work, then justify them.

Remember

✓ The portfolio structure and format will be determined largely by its purpose and audience needs.

✓ The portfolio should be a showcase of your skills, creative abilities, imaginative ideas and management skills.

✓ As you look at it, ask yourself 'does the portfolio show my abilities in the strongest possible light?' If not, refine and amend it until you feel it does.

✓ Use fitness for purpose as an area to consider when you are reviewing.

✓ If need be, you can adjust final outcomes as you work on the final piece, provided you can justify this.

✓ Define fitness for purpose clearly.

Now try this

Select one piece of work you have worked on. Clearly define its purpose, and reflect on the outcomes in terms of its fitness for purpose.

Compiling a professional portfolio

A portfolio should reflect its purpose and audience. Using professional practice when compiling your portfolio results in presentation of work that supports career progression, along with presenting how you have met the requirements of a brief.

Using it

The portfolio you create for this unit can be used to support your progression to higher-level study, employment in a company or studio, or setting up as a freelance. Researching examples of portfolios used for these purposes can inform the tailoring of your own portfolio, according to your aims. You can find guides on the web for portfolios and also contact employers and ask them what they normally expect to see in a portfolio.

Tailoring your portfolio

Portfolios for interview will vary according to purpose.

- Higher-level institutions may want to see examples of ideas generation and exploration, as well as finished work.
- Employers may want to see how well you know certain processes and your skill level – such as digital image editing. If this is the case, they will focus on these aspects at interview.
- Freelances may want to show the breadth of their finished work, rather than the process of realising the pieces.

Your portfolio and progression

The work you have produced can support your progression path as it shows:

- the level of creativity, skill and innovation in your work
- the manner in which you pursue a project
- your ability to plan effectively and consider all the aspects of a project.

A portfolio demonstrates the ability to...

- see a project through to a conclusion.
- think about art and design issues.
- generate ideas and work out creative solutions.
- use technical skills.
- manage resources, equipment, techniques and processes.
- liaise with others.
- use testing, review and refinement processes.
- manage time.

The pitch

You may use elements of your portfolio to pitch to clients – for example, to show your preliminary ideas in response to a design brief. Think about your portfolio for the assessment – you could use all or part of it to support an application for career progression.

When you are compiling your portfolio, remember that you may need to provide a written commentary to accompany each page.

Remember

☑ Think about the balance of visual work and information.

☑ Consider if you need a statement of intent or personal statement – many scenarios will ask for this directly.

☑ Your research will inform your selection, so make it purposeful.

☑ You may need to provide a written commentary to accompany each page.

Now try this

Research the requirements for a portfolio to support an application to higher-level study.

Selecting work for a portfolio

You can select work for your portfolio that shows key points in a project, as well as final outcomes. When you make your choices, consider the factors outlined below.

Selection criteria   Format   Constraints

Key points and project outcomes

Audience needs   Information

Selection criteria

Research into portfolios for your particular purpose will provide information on what to include, and this will dictate the selection criteria. These should then be applied rigorously to make the portfolio as succinct and detailed as possible. Repetition of work that has slight and limited variations is unlikely to make an engaging portfolio. The selection criteria are key, so spend time getting them right.

Format

Information gained from meaningful research will dictate the format. If it's a portfolio aimed at showing breadth of practice, there may be examples of 2D, 3D and 4D works that should be included. Digital-based work will need editing and formatting to ensure it will work properly. Try out a digital portfolio before you use it – it may need to be saved in a specific format, for example as a .pdf file. For an interview, take your own laptop.

Constraints

The main constraint is likely to be the number of images, pages or mounted pieces, or the digital file size. Think about budget, as well as time needed to produce everything. Taking well-lit and well-composed photographs is time-consuming if there is 3D work to record. There is also the cost of printing out large-scale images – for example in a photography folder – which can soon add up. Be realistic about the time you need and set an affordable budget to avoid running out of time or money.

Information

This is a key part of a portfolio. You might have to provide a specific number of words, or address set questions. Alternatively, it may be left up to the individual to come up with a personal statement. If the portfolio has to support a presentation or pitch, you may need to supply information about specific images. This can be presented visually alongside related imagery. If you are presenting text next to images, make it visually appealing – use layout and composition skills to arrange it so it doesn't look out of place.

Audience needs

Address these in any information provided beforehand. If it's a portfolio for a pitch, you can usually devise the information around what the audience wanted initially, and how you propose to resolve that creatively.

Remember

☑ The portfolio structure and format will be determined largely by its purpose and audience needs.

☑ The portfolio should be a showcase of your skills, creative abilities, imaginative ideas and management skills.

☑ As you look at it, ask yourself 'does it show my abilities in the strongest possible light?' If not, refine and amend it until you feel it does.

☑ Selection criteria are important – make sure they match the intention or purpose.

☑ Avoid repetition of examples, unless the differences make sense and/or are significant.

☑ Decide how best to present information.

Now try this

Identify the differences in a portfolio compiled for a job interview compared with one for a higher education interview.

Recording your work

Once the selection process is complete, you can record the work. Getting the set-up right is important to ensure you record your work effectively.

Getting the basics right

There are different ways of doing this:

- Photographing under controlled light in a studio
- Scanning flat artwork
- Photographing using available light – interior or exterior
- Using screenshots of moving image work
- Outputting compressed moving image files
- Using still images from final pieces and rough edits for moving image-based work
- Using flash photography to record (although it can flatten the contrast in an image).

Setting backgrounds

This will vary according to the objects that are being recorded.

- Regular-shaped objects can be cropped and used on a page or screen that way.
- Unusual shapes, or garments and 3D pieces where the space around or in-between the object will be visible, require a neutral background.

Think about alternative views of your work as well, to show specific details such as shape or texture.

A photo set-up.

Consider lighting

You can use simpler lighting set-ups if you have to – such as more general lighting – but you may have to edit the images more in software to get the right level of exposure, detail and colour. For exterior pieces, if you do have to use available light, think about the same things as you would in the studio – background, lighting level, glare, detail, shadow.

Getting equipment organised

High-end smartphones can be used to take photographs, provided they can be set up with a degree of control by the user. If not, it's better to use a digital camera.

Remember

☑ Allow sufficient time to record your work – you may carry out a shoot and then decide you want to redo some aspects.

☑ The images are important if they are all the audience will see.

☑ Take time to arrange your work to show it at its best – you will have spent a lot of time making the work, so allow some time to make effective images.

Now try this

Use your smartphone to practise taking an image of a piece of work, and try to get a neutral background.

Photographing your work

Managing your photo shoots effectively will help you to produce strong images.

Getting the shoot ready

You must organise the venue and accessories beforehand. Using the correct equipment is key. Try borrowing or hiring kit if you need to. For a self-managed shoot, it's useful to go through some of the many tutorials available online about shooting work. If you can't find a photographic studio, you can use daylight conditions. Try and shoot on an overcast but bright day.

Format and effects

- Think about formats – for screen-based work **JPEGs** are fine – but if you want to shoot without any compression you will need to shoot **RAW**.
- Different accessories, such as snoots, soft boxes and gels, provide different types of light – diffused and soft, or more directed/hard. Make sure you research the effects and use the most appropriate.

Using a digital camera

- Decide how you will shoot – manual, aperture or shutter priority. If you are in a studio there will be limited depth-of-field issues.
- Set the shutter to work with the synchronised flash if available – or if using standing lights (non-flash) use a tripod with lower shutter speed.
- Check your settings – white balance and ISO.
- Using a tripod will allow you to take the photos from a fixed position.

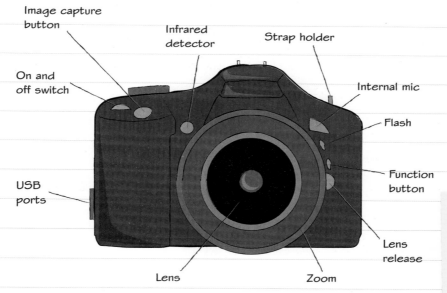

Familiarise yourself with the parts on a digital camera, and practise taking photographs.

Photographing larger objects

To focus attention on the object and to avoid unwanted backgrounds, you should try and use an infinity curve. If an infinity curve or backdrop roll is not available, for smaller objects you can use large paper or card taped into a curve.

Remember

Think about the whole shot not just the object – it's OK if you are going to crop it, but if it's a garment on a model or a larger 3D piece, the background will be seen.

Now try this

Take a series of images of a piece of work you have produced, noting the camera settings.

Scanning and copying

Some flat artwork can be recorded using techniques such as scanning and using a copy stand.

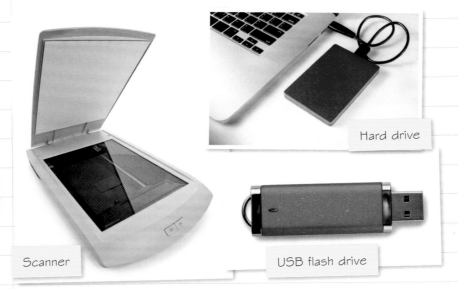

Hard drive

Scanner

USB flash drive

Why scan?

Flat artwork up to A3 size can normally be scanned – depending on the resources available in your centre. Anything that's moving into 3D, such as raised relief, paper engineering and small-scale models will not scan well. Scanning means that you don't have to set up a studio shoot, organise backdrops and use a camera, but the technique is limited by size.

Copy stands

Copy stands allow for recording of artwork that may not be completely flat – and make photographing work easy. Some sketchbook pages can literally bulge out of their bindings – scanning these can be difficult, and a copy stand allows a different approach. This is particularly the case when samples of fabrics and mixed media surfaces have been added to sketchbook pages.

> A copy stand is a device used to record images with a camera. Use masking tape to temporarily stick unruly pages down, or pin in other items to make a collaged page in a sketchbook.

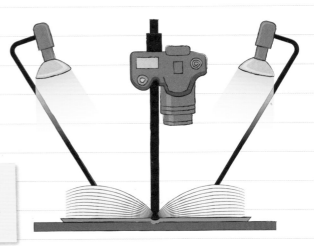

Record your techniques

If you use scanning and copy stand techniques and get good results, note how you achieved them – you can then replicate the process again and again. You can use screengrabs once you have loaded your image editing software to make notes of the settings and tools you used.

You may be able to use your own laptop to view your images straight away and make any necessary adjustments, or rescan/reshoot any images that haven't worked.

Remember

✅ Identify the equipment and resources you need and source these in advance.

✅ Recognise the limitations of the process – for example, you could scan an A2 image in two halves on an A3 scanner, and assemble it using digital editing software, but is this the best way to go about recording this kind of work? If you have other larger work to photograph, it might be easier to just include it in that shoot.

Now try this

Practise scanning some examples of flat 2D artwork. Experiment with the settings and note the results.

Managing image quality

Allow time to edit your images so you present them clearly and effectively.

Previewing images in the shoot

Review your images on screen as soon as you can – ideally at the shoot, so if you need to retake any shots, the set-up will still be available. Use the preview facility to view your images as you shoot them. This should give you a good idea of what is working and if you need to change anything.

Managing exposure

While you can adjust exposure in editing software, this all takes time and it's best practice to get correctly exposed shots through the camera, rather than relying on the software. You can also adjust other areas such as sharpness and colour balance – shown as hue, saturation, temperature and tint depending on your software.

Remember

✓ Planning is important.

✓ Make sure you have practised any techniques you should know about.

✓ Try to get the correct exposure through the lens rather than relying on post-capture editing.

✓ Think about the qualities in the work – and make sure your images reflect these.

In these three shots of the same image, the top image is overexposed, the middle underexposed, and the bottom correctly exposed. The way the image is recorded will influence the viewer's reading of it.

Ask your tutor or check the Pearson website for the most up-to-date **Sample Assessment Material** to find you how you should present images in your portfolio for this unit. The details of the actual assessed task may change so always make sure you are up to date.

Now try this

Practise shooting a portfolio piece and reviewing the images in terms of quality.

Managing digital work

If presenting a digital portfolio, you will need to use basic editing software and save files in digital format.

Saving files

Images can be captured from camera to computer in a variety of ways:

- directly from the card by removing this from the camera and plugging it into a computer slot
- via a card reader
- via a USB connection
- using wireless or bluetooth – however, as digital images are large files, you will need to check whether your WiFi can handle them.

Set up a dedicated folder to save your images, using a system that you know and understand.

Once your images are captured and saved, you may want to edit them using a commercial editing application.

Considering format

If you are loading a screen-based digital portfolio make sure it is saved correctly and, if necessary, compressed. Instructions may be provided, depending on its purpose and destination. If you are embedding video links or animated sequences, make sure all associated files are attached to the presentation and test them first. It's vital to test the portfolio for functionality – and if possible do this on a number of different machines and platforms.

Calibration

If you are producing a paper-based portfolio, you will need to output (print) some of the images so you can check they match the screen versions.

> Ask your tutor or check the Pearson website for the most up-to-date **Sample Assessment Material** to find you how you should present your portfolio for this unit. The details of the actual assessed task may change so always make sure you are up to date.

Digital editing

You should get to know how to use editing tools. Remember this is basic editing rather than full-blown image manipulation. The tools you are most likely to use are:

- crop, adjust orientation/rotation
- adjust exposure/contrast
- adjust colour – this might be tint, temperature or saturation
- adjust size, image size or file size
- adjust dpi – this may be when adjusting size
- keep the orientation or ratio of the image locked – so you don't end up stretching or squashing an image.

Avoid carrying out very large editing tasks – this may change the image beyond being a fair representation of the original.

Record editing settings

As in other parts of this unit, you can record the editing processes you use. In this way you can replicate tasks and edit other images to the same standard.

Recording can be made as screengrabs – these can be printed out and annotated in your sketchbook.

Check the file-saving requirements if you are exporting animation or moving image – these may require rendering.

Remember

☑ You may need a hard drive to store a large number of image files.

☑ Check the requirements for uploading – you can save images in different formats such as PDF, JPEG, TIFF, PNG and so on.

☑ Use file-naming protocols – add the date in digits or add v1, v2 to each filename when you save a different version. This will prevent overwriting and help you track iterations.

Now try this

Practise editing an image using a basic set of tools – crop, exposure and contrast.

Considering templates

Setting up a template will provide you with the basis for a consistent presentation and enable you to produce a professional digital portfolio.

Which format?

A digital portfolio can be produced in an easily accessible and free format, then exported as a PDF. If you are developing a response that uses digital technology (for example, an animation or moving image, a time-based piece or a record of performance), you should use PDFs that show the key points and aspects of the final piece that represent it fully. Make sure you check all the information – you can still produce the digital piece as your creative work but you will need to use PDFs to make the images.

Presentation requirements

Some briefs may require a presentation to be submitted in a particular format. Make sure that you provide what is requested. Ask your tutor or check the up-to-date **Sample Assessment Material** on the Pearson website to find out any requirements for presentation of your work for this unit. Assessment details may change so always make sure you are up to date.

Try out different templates

Programs such as PowerPoint™ have built-in templates that you can explore – you can change the file settings and amend formats to suit your needs.

Presentation software can be used to set up a digital portfolio.

Setting up

You will need to set up things like resolution and page size – if you do this and save it as a template you will be able to use the same settings each time. This will maintain consistency and help to make the presentation professional. You can use columns and grids to help you place images in an ordered manner – this will help the viewer engage with the work itself rather than being distracted by how it has been displayed.

The template design

Keep this simple – keep the attention focused on the images without adding any additional motifs or decorative elements. Create borders to link the pages and unify the design. Where you are placing larger, single images on one page, place them as close to the border as you can, filling the page effectively to show the work. If you plan on dropping more than one image onto a page, you can still use the borders to maintain a regular structure.

Colour settings

You should be able to alter the images once they are on the page – in a basic way – in areas such as contrast, temperature or tint. Try to show the work as a consistent whole rather than manipulating it in an exaggerated way, so just use these settings to make the colour and light on the pages look consistent.

Remember

✓ Try out different software templates – you can also practise setting up borders and grids, to help you drop a set of images together if you wish.

✓ You can make basic adjustments to images once they are on the page in order to make sure the pages all run together without any being suddenly darker or lighter.

Now try this

Set up a page with a border in a freely available digital picture software application.

Presenting your work

You should practise editing techniques when arranging images on pages. The image must show your work off to its best potential, as well as explain if you have edited the work as part of the creative process.

Establish the right settings for each page

- Set up the document sizes, including margins and orientation.
- When placing images, make sure you use picture editing and controls to arrange them in a way that is visually balanced.
- Techniques on presenting work can be found on page 184, where basic editing controls are identified.
- Save your work regularly when working with images in documents.

How much editing do I need to show?

- This depends on whether editing is part of the creative development – in interactive media, animation, graphics, moving image, photography and digital artwork, you should show it if it has been applied to develop the work.
- If you have printed or paper-based work, or 3D pieces, then the editing you do will be mostly targeted at making the images as professional as you can – this is not really a part of the creative process within the brief, rather something you are using at the close of the brief to present the work.

Sample response extract

Arrange images together to show a definite part of the set task – you can amplify this in the commentary that relates to the images, and you can use scale and layout to draw attention to critical elements. Note that 3D and larger work should be photographed, along with an indication of scale.

Consistency across images is also important as these should present a cohesive style. Here editing techniques have been used as part of the creative development – so recording them in screengrabs shows how they were applied.

Think about the colour of the background – is it neutral? How does the typography relate to the image? Look at examples of presentations that use digital text to make clear, concise pages that show the images really well.

Make sure images are of a sufficient size to show the quality of your work.

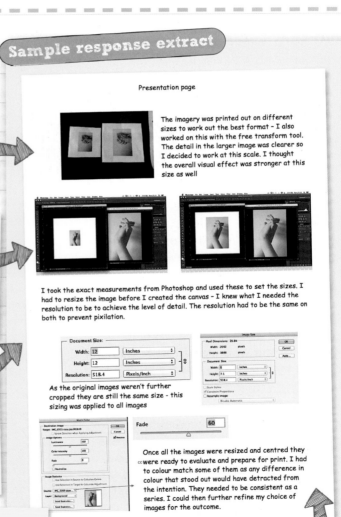

Presentation page

The imagery was printed out on different sizes to work out the best format – I also worked on this with the free transform tool. The detail in the larger image was clearer so I decided to work at this scale. I thought the overall visual effect was stronger at this size as well

I took the exact measurements from Photoshop and used these to set the sizes. I had to resize the image before I created the canvas – I knew what I needed the resolution to be to achieve the level of detail. The resolution had to be the same on both to prevent pixilation.

As the original images weren't further cropped they are still the same size - this sizing was applied to all images

Once all the images were resized and centred they were ready to evaluate and prepare for print. I had to colour match some of them as any difference in colour that stood out would have detracted from the intention. They needed to be consistent as a series. I could then further refine my choice of images for the outcome.

This example shows learner comments that can be used to create the commentary for a page showing the images and headings.

Now try this

Take a batch of work that includes text and imagery, and practise arranging it on a page.

Producing a portfolio

Your portfolio for this unit should include key pieces of your development and realisation work, images of your final art and design piece, and supporting written annotations explaining your development process.

Sample response extract

With a digital portfolio, you can compose pages so they show the maximum amount of information, but are also accessible and not overloaded. This page has visuals and bullet points about composition, visual language and communication. The points are developed in the accompanying commentary which includes information about visual impact.

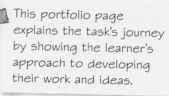

This portfolio page explains the task's journey by showing the learner's approach to developing their work and ideas.

The pages can be composites made up of different elements. You can include a combination of images, written work, notes, scans and materials.

 Links The written commentary that accompanies this page is on page 188.

You may want to draw attention to certain aspects of images through the use of lines, emphasis, highlighting or marking.

Qualities of your portfolio

Make sure that your portfolio shows:

- your creative response to the theme
- the use of contextual sources and influences in your work
- your exploration of materials, techniques and processes in your development work
- your ability to refine your work through review and evaluation
- your development and realisation processes
- a professional quality of portfolio presentation.

You will be able to select key visuals and annotation from the work that you have completed throughout the research, development and realisation process.

Remember

✓ Your images must show the quality of the work – balance this out when composing pages.

✓ The images should be of good quality.

✓ 3D work, installation and site-specific work should be photographed showing scale.

✓ When you are putting your portfolio together, consider the written commentary that will accompany each page.

Ask your tutor or check the up-to-date **Sample Assessment Material** on the Pearson website to find out details for your portfolio and whether a number of pages have been specified. Details of assessment may change so always make sure you are up to date.

Now try this

Take relevant images and information from a project and work them up into a digital page.

Producing a written commentary

If producing a written commentary of your development and realisation process to accompany each page of your portfolio, make sure that your explanations are clear.

Managing a commentary

An effective commentary needs to cover:

- explanations of your development processes
- explanations of how you achieved your final piece and how it responds to the theme
- an evaluation of the development process and the final piece of work.

Writing a commentary

Ask your tutor or check the up-to-date **Sample Assessment Material** on the Pearson website to find out details about your assessment and whether a written commentary is produced within a time limit. Details of assessment may change so always make sure you are up to date.

Qualities of a commentary

Throughout this unit, you will have made clear visual and written records of your work, and of any reviews and refinements. When producing a written commentary, it will support your portfolio through clear explanations and evaluation of the process that took place.

When you write a commentary, pay careful attention to:

- the quality and clarity of your explanation
- your use of spelling, grammar and subject-specific terminology.

Links The written commentary below accompanies the page from a portfolio on page 187.

Avoid bland descriptions of the work and what you did. Use critical analysis and an open approach when discussing your work.

You can practise writing commentaries and use the headings on the portfolio pages as points to build your commentary content around.

The commentary suggests at what stage in the process the material on the page has taken place. Framing it like this helps an understanding of the development.

There is a good discussion of how the technical stage of experimentation is contributing to the communication of the image, rather than just describing it.

This learner has used descriptive and emotive language to communicate intentions, rather than describe the page.

This learner has clarified any creative decisions they took at the time to aid an understanding of the development process.

Sample response extract

This page covers:

- <u>Composition ideas:</u> I wanted to explore the potential for compositional devices to work within the picture frame, so used the verticals of doorways and the frame of the window to reference aspects of the picture frame during an early period of experimentation.

- <u>Technical exploration:</u> the top image shows how my testing of aperture could have an impact on the viewer's reading of the image by forcing them to focus on a specific aspect.

- <u>Evaluation:</u> The images represent human involvement but require the viewer to read this and interpret it, as the human form is absent. The images also show aspects of an intimate interior – both everyday and personal, but somehow abandoned, empty, discarded. I feel the viewer will want to try and interpret the scenes, and ask what is happening here. There is also a tension between the inside and outside shown in the bottom series.

- <u>Plan:</u> I decided to develop the interior idea using the bottom set of images as there was more potential to develop multiple narratives – objects/interior; space/exterior.

Now try this

Practise writing a commentary for two pages of a portfolio. Try writing each page in around 10 minutes.